THE SEVEN EDWARDS OF ENGLAND

EDWARD I

FROM MS. COTTON, VITELLIUS A XIII

THE
SEVEN EDWARDS
OF ENGLAND

BY

K. A. PATMORE

WITH TWELVE ILLUSTRATIONS

KENNIKAT PRESS
Port Washington, N. Y./London

THE SEVEN EDWARDS OF ENGLAND

First published in 1911
Reissued in 1971 by Kennikat Press
Library of Congress Catalog Card No: 71-118493
ISBN 0-8046-1241-2

Manufactured by Taylor Publishing Company   Dallas, Texas

AUTHOR'S NOTE

THE Seven Edwards of England is designed to give, within certain prescribed limits, some account of the personal and family affairs of those sovereigns and of the minor, yet not insignificant, detail of their daily lives.

I am indebted to those, including Bodley's Librarian, who have permitted access to the collections under their control, and I desire to record the assistance I have received from those personally unknown workers, the compilers of Calendars of State Records, in dealing with some part of the immense material worked upon in the preparation of this book.

K. A. PATMORE

OXFORD

CONTENTS

EDWARD I

EDWARD II

EDWARD III

EDWARD IV

LIST OF ILLUSTRATIONS

THE SEVEN EDWARDS OF ENGLAND

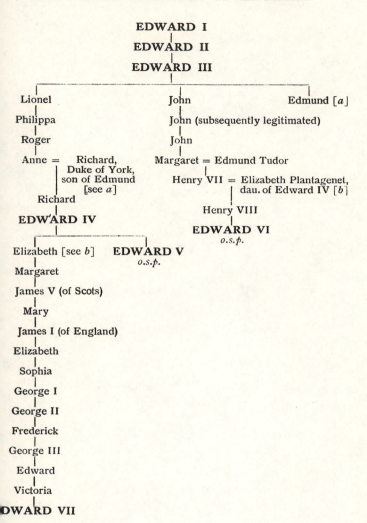

EDWARD I
|
EDWARD II
|
EDWARD III

Lionel   John   Edmund [a]
|
Philippa   John (subsequently legitimated)
|
Roger   John
|
Anne = Richard,   Margaret = Edmund Tudor
      Duke of York,
      son of Edmund   Henry VII = Elizabeth Plantagenet,
      [see a]   dau. of Edward IV [b]
Richard
|
EDWARD IV   Henry VIII
|
      EDWARD VI
      o.s.p.

Elizabeth [see b]   **EDWARD V**
| *o.s.p.*
Margaret
|
James V (of Scots)
|
Mary
|
James I (of England)
|
Elizabeth
|
Sophia
|
George I
|
George II
|
Frederick
|
George III
|
Edward
|
Victoria
|
EDWARD VII

EDWARD I

THE SEVEN EDWARDS
OF ENGLAND

CHAPTER I

ELEANOR

IF the first Edward of England could have looked
up the avenue of six centuries, it is quite probable
that the first sensation to stir within him would
have been a certain contempt for a people who should
have ceased to fight, in hearty fashion, face to face ;
displaying, rather, antic form in battle : ruled, indeed,
by one who never yet had led his liege-men into
battle—a sovereign travelling in peace like any bagman.

He would have beheld the havoc of a foe unseen,
and have heard the chill whine of the bullet, would
see in the waters Behemoth, and, against the sky,
winged creatures. Hawse-pipes yawning, grim-throated
slaughter bristling in the barbette : eyes and horns
of beasts of Daniel or Apocalypse : monsters all, not
animal, yet vital with the brains of men.

Yet even as the seeming impersonality of all these
things would move him to decry posterity as white-
livered, so, in another breath, would he pause in wonder
to behold how prerogative had yielded place to personal

prestige and to apprehend the hidden power of the King, dealing in that art of peace so infinitely less facile than is bloodshed.

And then the barons (had not he himself drawn his first breath amid their clamour ?)—had they not stood over John, his grandfather, on that river-mead, while he signed that parchment, so simple on the face of it, which confirmed rights born before the days of feudalism ?—that charter which has been a byword on the lips of thousands who could not cite from it a single clause. Had not he himself, to these same barons, in the days of his heirship, been a pawn for one long year ? For Simon, husband to "Alianor, myn aunte," had been a gadfly and a goad to Henry the King, and to his son for many a long year. And now these same barons—truly !—their apparition in the bioscope flash would leave our Edward much astonied.

This Edward, the first of our line of seven, the first Edward *post Conquestum*, the fourth since kings ruled in the seven kingdoms ;—some of those who were his namesakes were to succeed him out of course because of the death of elder brothers, as with his own son Edward of Carnarvon, or after an interloping house, as with Edward of York. Or again, as with the sixth Edward, because of a dissolution unprecedented of his father's previous marriages. And so onwards to the seventh Edward, in whom the threads of such wide ancestry were to be gathered up.

Nor should those Edwards be overlooked who never reigned, though in the ranks of heirship by descent or usurpation ; the Black Prince and his firstborn, the early-dying Edward ; or Edward son of the deposed Henry VI, and even that still remoter Edward, son of Richard

III, and again Edward, Duke of Kent, grandfather of King Edward VII, and Edward, Duke of Clarence, King Edward's firstborn son.

Let us now, in our turn, look back upon the first Edward, named from his saintly ancestor of the Heptarchy, for whom his father, Henry III, had special devotion, whose relics he had translated to a glorious shrine.

This Edward, long of limb, lean and athletic, whom the men of Scotland nicknamed "Longshanks." Bronze-toned in the flesh; with hair, lint-fair in childhood, tawny in his stripling days, and in manhood deepening to blackness. He is painted for us with the pen of ancient chroniclers, who tell us of the darkness of his eyes and of the fires which smouldered in them, blazing into redness with the call of anger. Wide-browed—deep-chested and slim-flanked he was, this king. From his father he inherited the drooping lid of his left eye. But from whom came his eager valour and his strenuous soul? Was it an atavism to earlier hero kings or an inheritance from the counts of Provence, his mother's kindred? In any case, he was the whelp of stirring times.

It was in 1239 that Edward Plantagenet was born. A year before, Simon de Montfort had married Eleanor, sister of Henry III, a marriage not accomplished without grave scandal in the eyes of Holy Church, for the new countess, previously married to the Earl of Pembroke, had, in her widowhood, consecrated herself by solemn vow to the religious life, and it is clear that only with difficulty was she dispensed from this pre-contract. Whether the turbulent earl really drew her by force of passion, or whether she yielded herself as fitting the common convenience of her brother and of her suitor, we cannot clearly tell. Within a year of the dangerous earl's alliance with the royal family, Edward was born to the King and Queen of England.

Tended by his nurses, Alice and Eleanor, the child grew up at Windsor and Westminster, for the Tower was rather the royal stronghold than a frequent place of sojourn. Tall and hardy, Edward in his early teens was already the subject of marriage projects. In the early fifties his father was making provision suitable for the heir-apparent, who might also be a bridegroom. The governorship of Ireland, the earldom of Chester, and other honours were bestowed on him, while, of the French possessions, Guienne was granted to the prince in 1252.

In 1254, Edward, with his parents, was on the Continent and went off by himself on a visit to the King of Castile, with whom, say some, an understanding already existed, relative to a matrimonial quest, while others allege that a device of political *entente* served to cover the real design of the visit. It was to gain sight of Eleanor, King Alphonso's sister, that the Plantagenet prince thus journeyed to the South. He saw and loved the Princess of Castile. At Burgos there were royal honours and festivities for the English heir ; Edward, son of Henry, was knighted by Alphonso on the feast of the royal patron, St. Edward the Confessor. Mr. Charles Marriott describes for us the chapel of the convent of Las Huelgas, the scene of the investiture :—

" Here are some very beautiful thirteenth and fourteenth century tombs, one with a sculptured canopy, a fine rose-window and other architectural details in a pure early Gothic.

"The whole building, indeed, is of a comparatively severe Northern character, in striking contrast to the rococo richness of Burgos Cathedral. The place has English associations in keeping with its appearance, for Edward I was knighted here in 1254 and Eleanor, daughter of Henry II, who, as wife of Alphonso VIII, was responsible for the foundation of the convent, lies buried in the chapel. . . . The abbess *por la gracia de Dios* came next to the Queen of Spain in dignity, with powers of life and death (*horca y cuchillo*—gallows and knife)." [1]

The marriage of Edward and Eleanor followed, in the Castillo, now—says Mr. Marriott—"a reddish dusty mound covered with crumbling fortifications of Moorish work. . . . Here, also, the Cid was married to Ximena in 1074."

Next year the princess arrived in London in October, and was received in state by the City fathers. What a separation marriage meant for these girl-brides of royal houses in those days of long ago, when etiquette and political exigency united with difficulty and distance to break the ties of girlhood !—to Eleanor indeed, it was, as to Ruth of the Hebrews, "thy people shall be my people." There was not, it is true, the great question of religious adjustment between the pair. Edward, though at times a somewhat unruly team in the hands of the Sovereign Pontiff, was yet in general a faithful adherent to Catholic and Apostolic dogma.

The marriage has remained as an idyll of wedded love. Edward's domestic integrity would seem to be unstained and the affection of the pair was punctuated by many children during the five-and-thirty years of their married life. Together they were doomed to mourn,

[1] *A Spanish Holiday.* Charles Marriott. (Methuen & Co.)

one with stern grief, the other with sad tears, the death of several of their children in infancy or early years. Three sons, indeed, came before Edward of Carnarvon, who succeeded to the throne.

There were many things, however, to engage Prince Edward, besides domestic joys and pains. Henry III and his barons were in ill relations. "The Lordes were murmuring against him," and Edward was occupied in his father's cause. There were difficulties, too, with Wales, which principality had been in 1251 deprived of her ancient charters, while again the French possessions were a cause of strife or international adjustment.

Altogether, as heir-apparent, Edward served his apprenticeship in warfare, and in the tactics of mediæval diplomacy, cruder in the England of that day than in the Latin countries. For we were younger then, and nearer to the natural man and to his methods. The long-limbed prince fought, with his knights around him, in hot blood, relying more on battle-cry than on *pourparlers*.

Then in the late 'sixties of the thirteenth century came a call to Edward to join in the Holy War. Ready enough he was to take the cross, but the royal coffers were drawn low from civil strife. However, Louis, afterwards the Saint, had turned an eye upon his nephew by marriage [1] and was desirous of engaging his ardour and his valour in the holy cause. He advanced a large sum to Edward, for which the prince pledged as security his appanage of Guienne, and gave his son, Henry, as hostage to the lender, who accepted the intention but did not retain the boy prince. Lewis

[1] Margaret, queen of Louis IX, was sister to Queen Eleanor, Edward's mother.

and his queen were already in Northern Africa when Edward and Eleanor started together on their long journey to the East in 1270. Louis was to die before the English prince arrived, but Edward remained to fight the infidel for some two years to come. Jerusalem, Nazareth, and Acre were visited in turn by the prince and his crusaders. Acre was the scene of the attempted assassination of Edward by a Saracen emissary of the Emir of Jaffa. Round this story is a good deal of confused report, and with it also is involved the beautiful myth or tradition, to which we cling so tenderly, concerning Eleanor's desperate effort to avert a fatal issue by sucking the venom from the wound of her beloved lord.

The assassin, we are told, had presented himself, on several occasions, as a confidential messenger of the Emir, and had secured, by various pretexts, private audiences with Prince Edward. Some tell the tale of his feigned yearning after Christianity as the basis of his reception by the royal crusader. Then one day, alone within the tent, he struck the English leader with a poisoned scimitar. Edward himself drew forth the weapon with such vigour that, in the rebound, he wounded himself a second time in the forehead. Then, in his turn, he fell upon the assassin and, pinning him to the earth, gave him a death-blow. We hear how his faithful knights rushed in, and how one of them, seizing the trestle or tripod which supported a table, dealt fearful blows at the prostrate Saracen, already in the coils of death, till Edward bade him cease from punishing the already slain.

Where the tale of Eleanor's intervention was first recorded it is hard to say. Many chroniclers there are, but on this point they hold a common silence. The monastic writers tell no tale, French stories of the crusades are mute. False scents have been pursued, to end in nothing, but Dr. W. Hunt has named one Ptolemy of Lucca, a prelate of the early fourteenth century, as originator of the episode. Ptolemy himself is, however, quite unassertive as to the genuineness of the event.

"Tradunt'," he writes (to him it was also an *on dit*), "they say that his Spanish wife, the sister of the King of Castile, displayed towards her husband her immense devotion, for that all day long, she with her tongue did lick the open wounds and did suck from them their humours, by means of which all the poisonous matter was drawn forth."

How and whence did this friar-preacher receive the tradition, ignored by monk and secular and lay-man chronicler of England? One can but offer the suggestion that the story was in the repository of the Dominican Order, entered upon the archives of the London house where, in 1290, the heart of Eleanor was laid to rest. Bishop Ptolemy had perhaps heard the tale from some of the Whitefriars from England. Let us treasure it, at all events, filmy though it be; a beautiful, if baseless, rumour out of the far-off wedded love of Eleanor and Edward.

Let us also hear the other stories. The wound grew black—they say—and many are the alleged authors of treatment for the deadly lesion. The Grand Master of the Templars proffers a remedy known only to the East. A friendly Arab medicine - man guarantees a cure. But a condition is attached. Has the prince faithful henchmen at his service? So let them take away the wife of the wounded man. And so, Eleanor, loving but powerless, is led away between two trusty knights, who strive to comfort her with their rough logic :—"For better far is it, O lady, that thy tears should overflow than that the whole realm of England should weep."

Edward triumphed in the direful hour and Eleanor could dry her tears and smile once more upon her husband. A year or so later some further trouble arose from the old wound, but after that we hear of no more drawbacks.

Surely, to her parents little Joan of Acre, who appeared about this time, must have been for ever a dear memorial of the valley of the shadow.

Meanwhile, at home in England, Henry III, stricken with his death illness, was nearing the close of his fifty-six years' reign. He sent urging his son to return to him, and Edward had already started when the King died. On his arrival at Capua the news met him.

It was long before King Edward reached his kingdom, for delays, due in part to the honours offered him upon the way, hindered his progress. Joy at the reunion with their young family, left behind during the crusade, was tempered with grief at the gap left in it by the death of John, their firstborn. Yet his father's death seems at the time to have moved the new king more deeply than the loss of the six-year-old heir-apparent.

Preparations were soon on foot for the coronation, an event which seems to have been postponed more than once. For it would appear that, at first, it had been announced for a date which would cause it to clash with the General Council of Lyons, fixed for the early summer of 1274, and Gregory X is found writing to Edward to express his surprise at this, and to remind him how important his presence would be at the Council, seeing that he had been in the Holy Land and could give valuable information, upon that subject, before it.

The Pope himself, then archdeacon of a Flemish see, had been in the Holy Land with Edward when the news came of his election to the Papal throne, and he had forthwith returned to Italy on this account. He now prayed Edward either to hasten or postpone his coronation in view of the more urgent consideration of the Council. At length a day in August, 1274, was fixed upon for the crowning of Edward and Eleanor.

Feasting on a regal scale was planned, and orders were issued to the sheriffs of the counties to provide great store of food-stuffs for the same.

Fat beeves and boars, pigs for fresh meat and pigs for bacon were requisitioned by the score in various counties.

It was an orgy of meat. Capons, in their thousands, gave a lighter touch.

Kilwarby, Archbishop of Canterbury, was the celebrant at the event, and among the royal relatives present round the throne was Alexander III, the King of Scotland, King Edward's brother-in-law.

The public celebrations were opulent and boisterous; " a fountain in Chepe ran with white wine and red for all to drink of," and a drove of great horses, five hundred say some, though others are contented with a fifth, were set loose that all might join in catch-who-catch-can.

But now there came a sterner note in the young days of sovereignty. For from the Parliament which Edward summoned after his coronation there was a notable absentee. Llewellyn, Prince of Wales, had stubbornly refused to come to Westminster, or even to a nearer meeting-place in the Welsh Marches, which Edward offered to give him a place for repentance.

David, brother to the Prince of Wales, did show for a time a more subservient spirit and received reward. " Edward preferred David to the marriage of a jollie widowe." This picturesque description of the bride is due to a sixteenth-century historian. There were other "merry widows" who failed to settle down so quietly at the King's command ; wards of Edward (for the sovereign was guardian of heirs during their minority) who chose husbands for themselves, incurring penalties for this *lèse-majesté*.

Llewellyn still remained recalcitrant. We can hear the King of England letting out a few good mediæval oaths. The Welsh prince was to be harassed, not only in the field, but in domestic and unexpected ways.

During the lifetime of Simon de Montfort there had been treaty for a marriage between his daughter, Eleanor, and the Welsh prince. When Earl Simon died, his widow, "a widow indeed" on this occasion, had gone to France and entered a convent of Dominican nuns, founded by a sister of her late husband. Here the Countess - dowager of Leicester and her daughter Eleanor remained till the death of the former, which took place about 1276. For the young Eleanor, now orphaned, a home across the seas with the Welsh prince seemed the rightful haven. With Amery, her brother, a Papal chaplain, she sailed for the Principality, then at war with the King of England. The voyage was one of disastrous adventure. For the King's good men of Bristol had wind of the voyagers, and before the craft could so much as sight the Welsh coast, they had sailed forth from the Bristol Channel and, falling in with her off the Scillies, had seized her as a prize for their sovereign. Amery was carried off a prisoner to the royal castle of Corfe, in Dorset, and his sister was placed under the care of Edward's queen.

Now Amery was, as we have said, a Papal chaplain, and his detention, quite apart from that of Eleanor, roused the Pope's displeasure. Much correspondence went on between Rome and England concerning the imprisoned cleric. Edward, inquiring into the matter, came to the conclusion that Eleanor was really on her way to a prospective husband, and he ordered her release, and next we find that, in an interlude of peace, the wedding took place in Westminster Abbey, where Edward and his queen were both present. Amery, however, still languished in prison, and there we find him four years later, when Nicholas III sent a nuncio to plead with the stiff-necked King of England on behalf of his captive.

The married life of Eleanor and Llewellyn was not a long one. Her husband and his brothers again re-volted against the English sovereign. In 1282, the Princess of Wales and " Lady of Snowdon " died, spared the terrible contemplation of her husband's end. For within the year, Llewellyn's bloody head, crowned mockingly with ivy, was fixed upon the grim walls of the Tower of London, with David's beside it ; while the younger prince's quartered corpse was distributed—an awful missive—among four English cities.

There were many other subjects of discussion between the Popes and Edward besides that of the captive of Corfe. In recognition of their services in the Holy

Land, Gregory X had granted to Edward and to his brother Edmund, Earl of Cornwall, the year's tithe exacted by the Holy See of all the English ecclesiastical benefices. Edward, not contented with his own share, laid hands as well upon his brother's portion and brought down upon himself a condemnatory correspondence from the Papal sovereign.

Again, in 1283, we find Pope Martin IV tackling him on the subject of a tithe which had been earmarked for the same pious object of crusading and on which Edward had laid hands. Quite a budget of letters arose out of this matter. Edward's replies, far from allaying Papal irritation, carried things to extremity. The Pope's replies became severe. He condemned Edward's "frivolous excuses" and pressed him to lose no time in handing over the money. Edward had a lusty grip and all the Papal adjuration failed to extort the Holy Land tithe from his fingers. So upon the Primate was entailed the unwelcome task of going to the King and admonishing him in person in order to extract the wrested tenth.

Traces of Edward's acquisitiveness are evident in many of his dealings. Jews and the regular clergy alike were made the victims of plunder. On occasion he would dig into the foundations of churches, in quest of buried treasure; indeed, his operations caused so much damage to the church of St. Martin-in-the-Fields, near the hamlet of Charing, that the King had to restore both walls and altar at his own expense.

We turn now to a gentler domestic page.

CHAPTER II

FAMILY AFFAIRS

WHEN Edward and Eleanor began their reign in 1272, they had already a good-sized family, to which they went on adding for many years to come. It is not easy to decide how many children they had nor in what order these were born. Some of the chroniclers place the birth of their eldest child in 1266, but this seems most unlikely to be correct. Perhaps the unimportance of daughters might cause those born before Prince [1] John in 1266 to be ignored. Again, they may have died in infancy and faded out of mind.

The marriage of Edward was not one of those infant contracts which were entered into before the nubile age. We have no ground for thinking that either Prince Edward or his bride was inapt for parentage at the time of their marriage in 1254.

Undoubtedly, eleven years of childlessness would have given rise to comment and concern. Edward's mother had remained without offspring for four or five years after her marriage to Henry III, and popular rumour

---

[1] The author has, for clearness, made use of the style *Prince*, though an anachronistic one, instead of the correct *Lord*, which obtained until recent centuries.

had accredited her with sterility. Yet we do not hear of any uneasiness such as would surely have arisen had there been for a period so much longer a dearth of offspring to the heir-apparent. It seems therefore reasonable to infer that some of the vague girl-children who left no mark, in their short span, upon the page of England, were born before the eldest son John.

Confusion arose too, we may note, from the circumstance that Henry's queen gave birth to children after her eldest son's marriage. Thus, by an erring monkish chronicler, one daughter at least is accredited to Eleanor the younger, instead of to her mother-in-law. So we may think that of these shadowy ones, Juliana, Alice, Beatrix, Blanche, some may have preceded John, who died before his father's accession. In the first year of their reign, Edward and Eleanor had, of living children, Henry and Alphonsus, and two daughters who were to grow to womanhood, Eleanor and Joan.

Matchmaking for their little family was on foot before the coronation. Here, in 1273, is an agreement between King Edward and the King of Navarre for a marriage between Henry, now the next in succession, and Joan of Navarre, and, since the death of John would have impressed upon the parents the necessity of providing against further sorrowful contingencies, the marriage convention provides additionally for a match between the next son, Alphonsus, and the said Joan "if anything should happen to Henry."

In the same year a contract of marriage was drawn up between Alphonso, son of Pedro, King of Aragon, and Eleanor, the "eldest" daughter of Edward I. The eldest surviving daughter we may at least consider her.

Next, in 1276, plans are afoot for the betrothal of

Joan, born at Acre four years before, and Hartmann de Hapsburg, son of the King of Germany, and, shortly after, we come upon the first of these projects which came to fulfilment, one of marriage between John, heir of the Duke of Lorraine and Brabant, and Margaret, Joan's younger sister, still in her babyhood.

All the other projects failed. Prince Hartmann died in 1282, by which time Prince Henry of England was also dead, and a fresh treaty had been made for Alphonsus Plantagenet with Margaret, daughter of Florence, Count of Holland.

Meanwhile, the affairs of young Eleanor and Alphonso of Aragon were running far from smoothly. In 1283, when the princess, now quite fourteen years of age, should have been looking forward to marriage, we find that Pope Martin IV had taken strong exception to the match. He writes a letter to the King of England in terms of surprise. He had already deposed Pedro from the throne of Aragon, and he goes on to remind Edward that, as he must himself be aware, Alphonso and Eleanor are within the prohibited degrees of kindred.

Papal dispensations were, of course, frequently sought and obtained for such cousin marriages. In many cases, indeed, the betrothed were related, more or less distantly. As at the present day, it was somewhat difficult for the royal houses of Europe to find non-related mates.

Edward, clearly, did not intend to abandon the plan without a struggle. Popes succeeded one another somewhat rapidly during the reign, and with each new Pontiff fresh negotiations had probably to be opened up. In 1287, Edward announces that he had already obtained a licence from Rome, and Alphonso now was reigning sovereign of Aragon, but, whether or not a licence had really been granted, it was clearly revoked or disallowed by Nicholas IV, who, in 1289, wrote to the King of France that he had no intention whatever of granting the dispensation. Eleanor, now twenty years of age, must, if she were allowed to hear anything of these contentions, have been a prey to impatience, mortification, or relief, according to her sentiments regarding her prospective bridegroom.

Once more the destroying angel had struck at the royal home. Alphonsus, now heir-apparent, just nearing the end of boyhood, was to die. We have indications, here and there, of his separate establishment. His nurse Felicia gives place to his master-of-the-household and his cook. He exercises the privilege of the blood-royal in claiming his father's pardon for one of the bodyguard convicted of some offence. In 1284 he was to die, in the same year which saw the birth of the only male survivor of Edward I, his fourth son, Edward of Carnarvon.

Before any of the marriages arranged for these children of tender years had been carried into effect, one of the princesses had entered the religious life. This was Mary, born in 1278 at Woodstock, who, when no more than eight years of age, entered the royal order of Fontévrault, taking the veil at its English house at Amesbury, in Wiltshire. Whether as the fulfilment of a vow made by her mother (for Edward himself was loath, they say, to let his little daughter take the veil) or from an early vocation to religion, we do not know.

Reconciled to the childish immolation, or desirous, at all events, of not appearing obstructive to her con-

secration, the King speaks, three years later, of having
" caused her to be veiled." A year after Mary's entrance
the Queen-dowager of England also became a nun at
the same convent.

The queen of Saxon Edgar had been the foundress
of Fontévrault, and other royal personages had
successively endowed it. A slim gold ring, set with a
sapphire, betokened the mystic marriage of the nuns
and was distinctive also as a memorial of the royal
foundation.

Henry III had promised to the Abbey his heart after
death—a common custom of royalty. It remained,
however, for nearly twenty years in Westminster Abbey,
and was then claimed by the Abbess of Fontévrault
when on a visit to England, and it seems that she carried
it back with her to the mother-house in Anjou.

Little Mary could hardly have practised any great
austerity in her cloister. At all events, provision for
comfort and good living was ample. Royal warrant
furnished her cell with fuel and wine. It is quite likely
that she had a little set of apartments for her own residence. One year, indeed, we find that twenty tuns of
wine were to be supplied for her use. The community
perhaps, or her own attendants, shared in the good
things.

The grandmother, Queen Eleanor, had received licence
from Rome to retain some of her temporalities for her
own enjoyment in the cloister ; in the first year of her
son's reign she had received his warrant to make her
will. Mary probably secured a similar privilege, for we
find that her father settled more than one estate upon
her during her cloistered life. She had a grant for a
weekly market in the town of Cosham. It is impossible

THE ABBEY OF FONTÉVRAULT

to resist the inference that the little nun had a way of curling herself round her father's heart. There are traces of his visits; the royal sign-manual dates in several cases from Amesbury, and, doubtless at her instance, charges due from the nuns on certain estates held of the King were remitted. Edward involved himself in a most unusual degree in the internal affairs of the community. They were not always days of cloistered calm at Amesbury. Far from it. Here in the early 'nineties of the thirteenth century is a perfect *émeute*. For here is Peter the prior ranged with the princess in battle-array on behalf of the abbess of the mother-house in Anjou, who claims her right to elect the prioress of the Amesbury convent, while, on the other side, the ruling prioress affirms that election rests with the nuns of the house at Amesbury.

Things came to such a pass that external arbitration was convoked; the Bishop of Durham acting on behalf of the Abbess of Fontévrault and the Bishop of Lincoln on behalf of the Prioress of Amesbury. The prelates were to be assisted in their counsels by a nun chosen by themselves, unless one was submitted previously as the proxy of the community.

All this litigiousness was a costly affair, for it is recorded that the revenues of the royal foundation suffered in consequence of the dispute. Edward, intervening in the tumult, appointed a secular custodian to take charge of the temporalities of the house and to administer them *pendente lite*.

It appears that Peter the prior and royal Mary got the better of the mutinous prioress and that King Edward then sent over to mother-abbess in Anjou to desire her to send him a suitable nun for the ruling of the house of Amesbury. Thereupon, mother-abbess by letters-patent appointed a Reverend Madame Joan de Genes to be prioress of Amesbury. There is quite a regal twang about these letters-patent of the sovereign abbess, a dignity more really impressive than the knife and hemp of that other reverend lady at Las Huelgas. Edward, accepting the nominee, ratified the choice by his own royal letters-patent and handed over to the new prioress the temporalities which had been taken out of the hands of the revolting predecessor. Madame Joan had carried out her office to Edward's satisfaction, and we may conclude that she was in the good graces of Mary, now a nun of ten years' standing. "As far as he could see," declares Edward, Madame Joan administered the revenues and estates in a satisfactory manner. He was indeed "pleased beyond measure," he goes on to say, at all he had seen of her conduct of affairs. Now the abbess in Anjou must have had a long and itching finger ; she desired to intrude it into the pie once more and to administer the English endowments herself. Edward clearly found the reverend lady a tiresome person—her advisers also, for there is indication of a power behind the abbatial choir-stall. His tone is quite restrained, the parchment of the royal records bears only the cooled-down, formal essence of the fierce wrangling of humanity. We have not the hot Edward of the Welsh Marches or the Scottish Border here : yet withal he is incisive. "The King, not unreasonably (*inmerito*), wonders "[1] at the abbess's interference, and he winds up with a request that she

---

[1] The English, here and in various other instances, is that of the Calendars of Public Records, from which, in rare instances only, has the author presumed to differ.

will in future abstain from any action of the kind
without his previous assent.

Rebel princes of Wales and insurgent Bruces were
simpler to tackle, we may well believe, than these holy
women of the royal monastery.

Leaving the little nun, let us come to the marriages
of her two sisters, which were accomplished in 1290.
Joan of Acre, after Prince Hartmann's death, had
been sought in marriage by Gilbert de Clare, Earl of
Gloucester. Now Gilbert had already been married
to Alice, who was a daughter of the Count de la Marche
and of Isabella, ex-queen, widow of King John. Alice
was consequently sister (uterine) to Henry III. From
her Gilbert had obtained a divorce, though on what
grounds the records do not state.

Rome, at the present day, annuls marriage on grounds
of physical ineptitude, of spiritual relationship, or of
pre-contract.

Divorce, as understood to-day in civil courts, with
option to re-marry, is, however, a different thing from
a declaration of nullity from the Holy See.

It is also difficult to assume misconduct of the usual
technical kind in the wife of Gilbert de Clare, though
the one instance in which scandal has attached itself to
the otherwise stainless domestic reputation of Edward I
was in connection with this Countess of Gloucester,
whose husband was, they say, jealous of his sovereign.
Yet a repudiation based on such a ground would have
made the subsequent negotiations all the more incredible
and unlikely of success. For, on account of her being
a kinswoman of Alice, his former wife, the Earl of
Gloucester had to seek a Papal dispensation for his
marriage with the Princess Joan. Alice was indeed,

upon her mother's side, a great-aunt to the bride whom the Earl of Gloucester now desired to wed. It is surely unthinkable that the Roman Pontiff would have sanctioned the marriage, had the horrible complication suggested as regards Edward I and the Countess Alice been existent.

The dispensation was obtained, at all events, and the marriage celebrated in festal style.

Eleanor remained unwed. She had to stand by and see her younger sisters enter wifehood while her nuptials with Alphonso of Aragon were still unfulfilled.

It was in this year of marriage feasting that the great domestic calamity of his life fell upon Edward in the death, after thirty-five years of marriage, of his queen, Eleanor. Cold research has claimed to hold her as not altogether the loving and selfless being of our dreams. The curt statement of one chronicler that " she was a Spaniard and had the gift of several manors," need not be wrested to her discredit nor set her down as a grasping or a mercenary being. " Not without dower " did she come a bride to Edward from her native land. In granting her estates and wardships and other perquisites of the Crown in feudal times, Edward was making no more than the usual provision, the " dower at the church door," which was customarily bestowed upon queen-consorts. When we hear of ecclesiastical censure passed upon her for grinding down some of her tenants, we are at liberty to question whether her agents were not rather the acting misdemeanants. The mother of fifteen children, travelling from one end of the kingdom to the other, crossing the Channel to visit the Crown territories of

England or her own countship of Ponthieu, Eleanor must have been a woman much occupied, even in days of simpler social conditions. There is a sufficient record of her goodness and of the love she won.

She and her husband were together, at any rate, almost throughout their wedded life ; together they had looked Death in the face when, sitting on their couch, the lightning entered the royal chamber in their rear and passed between them, in the sight of their attendants standing there, yet had touched them not at all.

Gentle tradition has it that they were a devoted pair, and let us not reject tradition, which oft-times has a nucleus of worth, wrapped though it may be in the *coma* of fantasy, or trailing its insubstantial incandescence across the centuries.

Edward was pressing on towards encounter with his rebel Scots when his queen was taken from him. Her death-place has been variously assigned, the county even differing in the chronicles. Hardeby, in Lincolnshire, and Grantham are the places most generally assigned, but scholars adduce others as their research suggests.

Now, for the time, Death had suspended the combat and thrust the sword into the scabbard. Then began that journey through many counties, when the King and his army bore the dead to her royal sepulture at Westminster. First the viscera, except the heart, were left at Lincoln Cathedral, where the saintly Hugh had ruled a century before, and where, in course of time, a marble tomb was raised above them.

Then on, along the Roman road, in a straight course, or curving in the by-ways, the funeral train pursued its way, guarding the fleshly tenement of Eleanor, vacant now and irresponsive to her lord—

"The only loveless look, the look with which you passed." [1]

The King, with face hard-set in grief, sharing the march ; sleeping at the halts, the difficult sleep of the bereaved ; half unconvinced, as yet, of the eternal silence. Caring for the dead, in the mid-transit of the soul, setting the voices of the cloisters on a heavenward flight in *Dirige* and *Requiem*, and so, at length, entering the City and pausing in West Cheap for the now shortening stages of the death progress.

Next, in four London churches did the bier rest for a night, in that of Holy Trinity, in the Franciscan church, in St. Paul's, and in the church of the Whitefriars. Then on the fifth day, passing along the Strand of Thames, the funeral train, swelled by the nobles, clergy, and royal personages, who had joined it in the capital, made its memorable halt at the little village in the river's bend, that Charing, where the Cross of to-day preserves the memory of the original monument which rose upon that spot to mark, as others do elsewhere, a halt upon the funeral way ; the final pausing of the dead before St. Peter's Abbey received her in the chapel of the kings to rest at the feet of Henry III, who there reposed in a stately tomb, adorned with jasper fetched from France.

There, with every ceremony of Catholic ritual fulfilled, with glaucous fume and mystic water—aspersion and incensing—with the slow-chanted stanzas of *Dies Iræ* rising to spread themselves in echo amidst the arches,

[1] Coventry Patmore.

with sacerdotal absolution and whispered commendation of the soul, did Eleanor rest in the soil of England, amid the company of the great dead and of the parish burial, through the centuries onwards, until now; there in her sepulchre of marble, under brazen effigy, rests the queen who stands in a fair tradition for royal wifely love. Two days later her heart was enshrined in the Dominican church, wherein its resting-place was afterwards made beautiful by the art of the painter and of the worker in iron.

The Eleanor crosses come to our mind whenever this queen's name is uttered. We think of them as the fairest tributes, the most lasting memorials that could have been devised by the bereaved husband. For some time after his queen's death, indeed, Edward was busy giving orders for them and also in granting lands to many monasteries and clergy for supporting perpetual oblations for the soul of Eleanor. Westminster and Peterborough, richly gifted, stand among a crowd of smaller beneficiaries. Upon her death anniversary special observances were decreed, and in her memory hundreds of poor persons were to receive a meal.

Whether the crosses, as the form of memorial, were due to Edward's sole initiative, we cannot say, but it would seem as though there had been, on Eleanor's part, some desire for a memorial, or possibly a bequest even, for the same. At any rate, it is by the executors of her will [1] that payments were made for the crosses both in London and the counties, as well as for the embellishment of the shrine where her heart rested at Whitefriars. The will itself either exists no longer or

[1] See *Manners of England in the Thirteenth Century*. From original records. Edited by Beriah Botfield. (Roxburgh Press.)

has, so far, remained undiscovered. Eleanor, in those last hours, may have spoken of her wishes as Edward sat by her death-bed. When, having received the last rites of the Church, she passed out into the great silence, the form of the memorial may have, as yet, been without definite shape. The crosses, as well as the many images which completed their adornment, were worked in portions and then transported to the sites, already destined, the resting-places of the dead queen.

Eleanor, queen-dowager, did not long survive her daughter-in-law. Within a year, she died in her convent at Amesbury and was there buried, her heart being brought to the Greyfriars Church in London.

In the midst of mourning shone a gleam of joy. Joan, Countess of Gloucester, bore her firstborn, Edward's eldest grandchild.

CHAPTER III

MARGARET AND THE HOME

FROM the first obsession of his grief, Edward was soon aroused, for the affairs of Scotland were urgent. His sister Margaret, her husband, Alexander III, and their sons were all dead, and dead also was Margaret, Queen of Norway, their daughter, to whom the succession to the Scottish crown had been assigned in the event of the extinction of male issue. As heiress to her mother's rights there remained another Margaret, a princess in her early teens.

Edward had already begun to entertain views regarding a marriage between his only surviving son, Edward, and the "Maid of Norway," and he sent to her northern home to summon the young princess.

The Norse relations, however, stipulated that a marriage between Edward and Margaret should not be considered as a *sine quâ non* of the ratification of the princess's title to the crown of Scotland. Then Margaret set out on the journey to unknown Britain. Whether she pined at leaving her northern home or suffered from the sea-journey is not definite, but at any rate the little princess seems to have fallen ill on shipboard, and the master put in at one of the islands off

the coast of Scotland to obtain "refreshment" for her
—rest from sea-sickness, medical attention—we may
infer either possibility, and here the little girl died. The
Maid of Norway never set foot on that shore of Scotland,
the land of her inheritance.

With her death, uprose a dozen claimants for the
crown, descendants of remoter Scottish kings. The
claims of some provide bewilderment by a surface
plausibility; others are provocative of scorn by the
sheer impudence of their pretension; even the bend-
sinister presumed to raise aspiring clamour. With the
ins and outs of their assertion we have no business.

Edward sought counsel of the archives; having
previously, no doubt, decided to be lord of the affair
in any case. In like manner did Napoleon, in the
nineteenth century, study Bourbon precedent for acts
performed under his own régime. By Edward, study
was made of Saxon custom; nearer home came confirmation from the late King Henry's attitude. Most
cogent of all, for Edward's suzerainty, was the fact that
Alexander III, after King Edward's coronation, at which
he had been present, had done homage to the English
sovereign for the crown of Scotland, or so said the
advisers of King Edward, while those of Alexander put
a different colour on the matter.

At length the crowd of candidates was reduced to two :
John Balliol, claiming *vice* his mother, Devorguil, who
had renounced her rights in his favour, and Robert
Bruce, who, though the offspring of cadet stock, pleaded
custom for the preference of male offspring over their
female senior collaterals. We may be allowed to roughly
illustrate the claim by saying, that it was as though
the late Duke of Cambridge should have alleged his

claim to the crown of England over the male offspring of Queen Victoria.

But Edward gave no sanction to the plea of custom and proclaimed Balliol as lawful king ; and the resultant of warfare between his party and the adherents of the Bruce stretched on into the coming reigns.

To come back to more domestic affairs, we find that, in 1293, Eleanor, the eldest living daughter of Edward and Eleanor of Castile, at last received a husband. Death, even more inflexible than Popes, had severed Alphonso from her, but upon that dire event a new betrothal had ensued between her and Henry, afterwards Count de Bar, and she was married to him in 1293, when there was a great raising of game and meat in some of the counties for the bridal feasting.

The King himself, by this time, was hankering for the companionship of woman. Edward I was not one to content himself with flimsy episodes, the "light-o'-love" found no corner at his court. Not his would be the protest of the Hanoverian king urged by his dying wife to take another consort :—" Non, non, j'aurai des maîtresses."

Edward looked for a wife, a queen to share his throne. There was young Margaret, now just leaving childhood for maturity, sister to the King of France. Edward entered into treaty for the girl-princess, but French marriage projects, like some Flemish ones, of which Edward had sore experience, were full of trickery. It was some years before the King of England carried his point and married a bride forty years his junior.

We do not know how the marriage was viewed by the young queen's stepchildren. Officially, during the part of her life which came into the reign of Edward II, she is described as the king's "mother," but this was merely by the custom of the age, which did not specify in-law relationship of any kind.

Edward of Carnarvon, who, at six, had lost his own mother, might have found cheerful company in the young queen of his own age had he not been wholly wrapped up in the baleful Gaveston.

Of grown-up princesses, there was indeed not one now left at home, for Elizabeth, born in Wales in 1282, was now married to the Count of Holland and Zeeland.

Queen Margaret was early a mother. Her children, like those of Eleanor, were born at various places, for she too kept the King company on his progresses through England. One son, Thomas, was born at Bretherton, another, Edmund, at Woodstock. A little daughter bore the still-loved name of Eleanor. She was to die in early childhood, yet not before her father had made provision for her marriage-dower and trousseau.

Margaret waited on the Border while her warrior-husband tackled the Scots once more. We find her there in 1303, when orders were issued by the King for the provisioning of her household.

It must have been a rude existence, thus wandering about the country in those days. The palfrey or a litter would bear the Queen and the ladies of her household; perhaps, occasionally, a clumsy chariot as comfortless as any hay-wagon. If life in general was simple, the royal home was more literally a castle then than in modern England. The palace, if a dwelling, was also a fortress. Windsor, less splendid than it afterwards became, was primarily a stronghold. When Edward had seized upon the contents of monastic

coffers or cleared the treasury of the New Temple, it
was well recognized that there was no redress when
he had got his prize safely behind the walls of "Wyn-
dlesore." Yet from conflagration his strongholds were
not exempt. At Windsor, fire destroyed a large part
of the domestic offices, while, in 1298, a "vehement
fire" burned down both the palace of Westminster and
the adjacent monastery. Queen Margaret spent some
months of her early married life in the Tower, perhaps
her only town residence at the time.

We can picture nothing luxurious nor even cosy at
royal Windsor. Tapestry would veil the lower courses
of the grim masonry; battle or Bible scenes worked
by the royal and court ladies. It may be accepted
that all were not patient at the needle. Matilda, the
Conqueror's wife, with her terrible achievement
of the Bayeux tapestry, must have made not a few
martyrs; impatient girlhood must sometimes have
fought its yawns over the eternal stitchery. To others,
the patient toil came as a soothing influence; again,
they had a pride in sharing the creation of some historic scene. The more skilled would deal with features
and design; the humbler needlers would plod upon
the background or the filling.

A certain rude grandeur there would be in the royal
dwellings—space and vaulted height, shafted light and
breadth of shadow. In the draught, the hangings on
the wall would oft-times billow outwards or ripple on
the stony background. Upwards, through chimneys
yawning open to the sky, would blaze great logs from
the King's forests of Windsor or of Dean; or blocks
of charcoal, throwing quivering flame-streaks on the
faces of those who sat around in the dusky hour.

A brazier, even, might be heating apparatus enough ; a hole in roof or wall, sole outlet for the smoke. The fumes of sea-coal were not here, nor welcomed even for commercial ends elsewhere. Indeed, smelters of Thames-side drew down on themselves most grievous penalties for substituting coal for the wood and charcoal fires of yore, "whereby an unendurable stench was diffused" throughout Southwark, Wapping, and East Smithfield.

Was it not Sir William Richmond who averred that the Smoke Abatement Society of the nineteenth century possessed an inspector "who knew all the wicked chimneys in London"? These early fourteenth-century iron-workers were made to tremble even more, "punished by grievous ransoms."

Food and feasting alike were concerned rather with repletion than refinement. There was plenty of beef and mutton ; of capon and milk-lamb ; of game-birds, such as the partridge, snipe, and woodcock. Kid and rabbits were provided for royal consumption. Preserved foods helped out the winter commissariat ; cured fish from the Eastern counties and from Cornwall ; salted carcasses of beeves ; fat bacon-pigs, always a requisition from the sheriffs, whether for the royal forces on the march or for the wedding-feast. The hunted buck and roe furnished roasts for the spit and filling for the pasty. The crane was sought in various parts of the kingdom. The kingly dish *par excellence* was the swan, the selling value of which in the open market was nine times that of goose or partridge. Even the peacock was less esteemed. The lamprey-pie, though at its door lay the death of an earlier Plantagenet, remained the portion of the *bon-vivant.*

Onions and garlic seasoned the dishes; pepper and other spices were purveyed by the apothecary with intent to their use in medicine even more than in cookery.

Lent and Advent made a large demand for fish, and the "stews" upon the royal estates were kept stocked for this end. The Queen's servants would be sometimes licensed to take fish for her use from the King's ponds or streams about the country.

From barley-malt, beer was brewed in cauldrons, without the tonic hop. At times, a woman did the brewing; at others, a man and wife are found receiving wages for their joint production of "home-brewed."

From the King's domain of Gascony came good store of wine. By royal warrant, Bordeaux wine was purchased; we read of St. Emilion, red and white. And in a certain year the King's tailor, being beyond seas on his majesty's business, is commissioned to bring one hundred cheeses of Brie for royal use. "Snips" (*cissor*), was he a judge of the ochre-coloured discs of Brie or was he merely the handy messenger of the moment?

Sometimes there was a dearth in royal camp or castle. Here are mutinous Cornishmen, for instance, failing to comply with demands for provisions or for wine made on their county and evoking stringent orders to sheriff or commissioner. The goods requisitioned were to be commandeered from whatever merchants might be found to have them in stock, and were to be shipped to the North at the King's expense, while mariners, or others, who remained obstinate were to see the inside of Launceston gaol.

During one year the import of wine from Gascony fell off very seriously in consequence of the Pope's visit to that country. Such was his retinue and its scale of living that it made a "corner" in the vintage of the season.

Foreign traders brought goods by sea to England for the use of Edward and his subjects, and not without travail and a rude welcome from the wreckers of Cornwall, or again of Dorset, on whose fierce shores adversity had cast their vessels.

Here at Corfe Castle was "Le Christofre," bound from Bordeaux to London, cast ashore, yet not a lawful prize as *jetsam* of the sea; for there had escaped from her several of her crew, besides two dogs, and these all coming to shore alive, preserved, as they might do to-day, her claim to be no wreck nor derelict. The men of Dorset, heedless of sea-law or logic, fell upon the hapless hulk and gear and cut them all asunder, next carrying off the cargo.

Spanish merchants were the plaintiffs in another case in which one of their vessels had been similarly dealt with on the coast of Cornwall.

Only to certain European ports was the royal trading licence given. Bruges was one; Bruges, then in the height of fame and wealth, with much of the trading of that day passing through her waterways; Bruges, which since then has slept—been, even, *Bruges la Morte*— to-day rising from her lethargy and opening to the world again by her new port of Zeebrugghe.

The Italian merchant guilds were powerful in this age; many had royal licence to trade in England. The Bardi, the Spini, the Perucci are among their names. From some we find Edward and Eleanor obtaining loans; they were the pioneers of banking and of Lombard Street.

From all parts of the English and French dominions

wax was brought for various purposes. The English monasteries had their keeper-of-the-bees, and they perhaps provided enough for their own use, but the King had needs much greater than the abbot. Candles for lighting and for use in the royal chapels would account for a good quantity. Tallow, used elsewhere, would not be admitted for ecclesiastical purposes. Then there were waxen images for the chapel or private oratory, while a great deal was needed yearly for sealing of the royal decrees.

England and Ireland had their cloths of homespun, baudekyn, and "scarlet"; cloth of silk and cloth of gold. It would not be easy to gratify the reader with a long account of Edward I's style of dress. The King must have lived too constantly in armour to be an interesting example of the tailor's art. With that part of his outfit which was not mail, the tailor had, however, to concern himself.

The dress of the queens displayed simplicity of form, combined, however, with richness of fabric; a robe fairly close-fitting of cloth from the looms of home or of the East, or of silk "purfled with pelure" at neck and wrists. The wimple hung behind and reached below the waist. Even when the crown, or golden circlet, was worn, the Queen retained her veil. Probably of other feminine wear there was a minimum. The smock or shift was quite possibly all that intervened between the person and the royal robes. On night attire we need not waste much speculation. If the home-spun flax of day-wear were discarded, it was probably in their native skins alone that royal ladies or the King himself lay in their simple bedding.

However, even in the most primitive wardrobes,

jewels have never failed. Adam the goldsmith goes to France to seek for ornaments for royal decoration, and in these we may, with confidence, look for the beauty of skilled workmanship.

It was in architecture and building that art and craft displayed their grandest scope. To the glory of God, arch and buttress, tower and pinnacle rose skywards. The strenuous restraint of the Norman, the less virile asceticism of the Perpendicular, were seen throughout the land. The Abbey of Westminster was already in a second edition. Still they rose, the greater and the less; from the void mass, the chisel called the leafage of the capital to crown the sterile column. Men gave the substance of their brain and of their coffers to house Shekinah. And, fearing not to laugh in stone, they set on high their gargoyles, which, with swelled cheek and impish mien, should spue the rainfall forth, without that clash of the sublime and the ridiculous which must have been had some angelic lips been set in the eternal incongruity of such a task.

And again, those unknown limners of the cloister who, by religious toil with reed and with hair-pencil, decked the Book of Hours or the great altar missal in tints that still lie warm and even as enamel-work before us; where gold still gleams from some process secret to our day, and the line, fine as spider web, clear as knife-edge, in black or white, enframes or decorates the larger space of scarlet or of blue; where miniatures display *dramatis personæ* so forceful in suggestiveness that anatomic errors pass us by. In the border here again, fancy bursts into

"Laughter, holding both her sides"—

where forest beasts or farm-yard fowl have been made to cut the capers of such living things as never entered into Noah's Ark. Was it by this garnish of distortion that these Cruickshanks of the cloister sought to lessen the unintentional grotesqueness of the main figures on their pages ?

Royal ladies gave orders for these manuscript works of art. Elsewhere, ornament concerned itself chiefly with the plate which made no lavish show upon the royal board. In furniture, simple strength would most prevail. Palace manners too were somewhat primitive ; the trencher and the hunch of bread were the " cover " of the feasters, the drinking horn or tankard might be tendered to the sovereign at state banquets by the Chief Butler of England, whose office still survives. The " salt " would display the fancy and the skill of the gold- or silversmith, and would mark the division of the royalties from any lesser princes or nobility who sat at the same board. Salt was always a large order in the royal commissariat, for much salted food was needed both during winter and for royal progresses, and especially " stockfish " when Church abstinence or fast entailed a consumption of fish beyond all fresh supply available inland.

In coffers of stout oak with wrought lock and hasp in iron would be contained royal finery. The Queen's garments too would hang upon cords stretched across the wardrobe. The wardrobe, an office as well as a set of rooms, gave orders for royal necessaries, received and stored royal property, movables and muniments, and was the bureau of accounts. Its functions stopped short of the requirements of sensitive modernity. Some vessels of copper and of glass were provided for the

King's sleeping-chamber,[1] but the finer attentions of the toilet were unthought of.

As to the art of healing, it was probably a confused affair of rule-of-thumb and superstition. Only the hardy could have had a chance of life. Of Henry III's nine children and Edward and Eleanor's eleven (or fifteen), a number died in infancy or early youth. The simple, sturdy life, the air which blew through the stone chambers of the fortress-dwelling—these were not what killed. It was no doubt the filth in which disease-germs flourished, the unclean moat, the septic conditions present in the medicaments themselves. The slaughter of these innocents came by the very hands of blinded love.

Amice and Felicia, the nurses, the Lady Eleanor de Gorges, the royal governess, could not avert their doom any more than Eleanor herself, their mother. Nor did the milk of the palace herd of goats atone for the evils of unsuitable feeding. Yet the percentage of deaths within the royal stronghold or the feudal castle was insignificant in comparison with that among the humbler people of the Middle Ages when the black death scoured the land, making so clean a sweep that often not a single kinsman was left alive to figure as the heir to estates which came into review at the inquest on the victims and their possessions.

The nostrums of the age, compounded scarcely less horribly than the broth, "thick and slab," of Macbeth's witches, could have done nothing to hinder the death progress. Italy and even France might have some glimmering of higher therapeutics. The dowager-queen, Eleanor, had her own physician, Le Provençal,

[1] *Liber garderobis,* 21 *Ed. I.*

and he accompanied her when she journeyed over-seas.

Edward himself did not, in general, trouble physicians much. The most serious illnesses of his life, apart from the wounding at Acre, were in early boyhood and in the last year of his life, and in both cases the patient was in a monastery. The monks were probably as skilled as anyone in the rude healing of the age. In the earlier case, the child Edward's sojourn with his mother among the monks of Beaulieu was by virtue of a special permit. For entrance to the religious houses was strictly barred, even to royalty. We find that dispensations were occasionally granted to members of the royal family to visit convents ; one lady being empowered to enter a certain nunnery, accompanied by "six virtuous matrons," but not to take a meal nor sleep beneath the roof. Princesses might claim *ne* lodging, *ne* refreshment, from the "brides of Christ."

Edward's observance of religious customs and beliefs combined a current orthodoxy with an individual common sense. We have seen him providing masses for the soul of Eleanor. He, doubtless, carried out the Maundy washing of poor men's feet. His queen, Margaret, at all events washed those of thirteen poor women and gave them alms. But when a fit of monastic hysteria ascribed to the dead Henry III miraculous cures at his tomb at Westminster, Edward poured cold water on his mother's excitement when, on a visit to her in the Amesbury convent, he heard the tale. "My father," said the downright King, "was too straight a man to lend himself to so vain trickery."

The minstrel and the story-teller helped to pass the long evening hours for the Queen and her ladies, for we cannot think that needlework would suffice for ever. In the castle hall or the Queen's closet, where the shadows struggled against the gleam of the log fires or the flickering flames of waxen tapers, the courtiers would watch and listen to the fingering of the strings and the voice and gestures of the performer. Guillot le Sautriour was the musician of the young Queen Margaret; no doubt he came from France with the girl-bride. Chivalry of old time, the miracle-play, and mist-enwrapped tradition would furnish themes for tale and song. The necessity of our complexity for amusement, which oft-times has no kindred with joy, did not grip this younger age. Some feminine soul may have revolted against existence even then, but woman's vocation was more clearly mapped than now. Marriage or the cloister—she was seldom a loose end.

The years are drawing on. Edward in the young years of the fourteenth century was a white-haired man, seared by warfare and fretted by sorrows of the hearth. His daughter Joan had incurred his anger by her second marriage with "a mere knight," one Ralph Montemery. His dissatisfaction was swallowed up by the greater tribulation of her death. Again *requiem* fills her father's mind, again he endows the monasteries on behalf of her eternal repose.

The Prince of Wales, as since 1301 the heir to the English throne had been styled, was causing his father grief and perplexity. The undesirable infatuation of the prince for Piers Gaveston had been brought to the King's notice by the trusted statesman and adviser, Walter de Langeton. The favourite was banished from the kingdom in the last year of the reign, and against Langton the resentment of the prince burned sullenly, fed with retrospect of *raptis Ganymedis.*

The story of Langton is beyond the scope of the present book. This Richelieu of the Plantagenets was a marked example of the great churchmen-prelates of the Middle Ages. His versatility found subject in his official career as Treasurer and his episcopal as Bishop of Coventry and Lichfield ; in many lesser ways as well. Out of his engineering faculty arose a *cause-célèbre* in the third Edward's reign.[1]

To his other splendours, he added that of a magnificent abstention from recrimination when the dark hours of Edward II had given opportunity.

There were not wanting others, less high-minded than Langton to pour into King Edward's ear the tale of fact or of suspicion against his son and Gaveston. Some did not hesitate even to breathe of treason as involved in the unhealthy obsession of the Prince of Wales.

And now, in 1307, Edward, like his Eleanor, was to die on an expedition towards Scotland. Recent illness and the harassment of warfare joined with the nearing seventieth year to snap the strong resistance of the Hammer of the Scots.

Again, a great royal train of mourning moved southward through the land.

[1] See " Walter de Langeton," *Antiquary*, July, 1906.

EDWARD II

CARNARVON CASTLE

CHAPTER IV

PRINCE AND PARASITE

OF Edward of Carnarvon, our earliest lispings of history have breathed the name. On a page of memory quite undisturbed by fact is that figment, fallacious yet picturesque, of the prince, not yet a day old, being presented to the Welsh burghers by the conqueror, to reconcile them to their bondage. This " Prince of Wales" was to blot out for them all retrospective yearning for old Llewellyn, or for young Llewellyn, whose head, so soon to be impaled upon the Tower, grew yet upon his shoulders.

"I will give you a prince, born in your own land, speaking no other language."

In sympathy with these ancient Britons, our childhood drew in its breath, with them its lip dropped at this offering of the progeny of Plantagenet. We felt the cheat, recognizing the strictly legal veracity of promise and fulfilment with the rasp which was evoked by such a "sell," such April-fooling. True, the new-born instrument of the fraud escaped our ill-feeling ; in its hairless innocence it was no more guilty than was the "purple jar" which brought such deep disillusion to poor "Rosamund" in our tales of a grandmother. The dissipation of attractive myths is always grievous. If more correct, it is far less interesting to know that Edward of Carnarvon was thirteen years of age before he was formally created Prince of Wales by the King his father.

Even Edward's anxiety that the daughter Elizabeth, born in 1282, and Edward, born in 1284, should see light in Welsh castles is none too certain, though the castles of Rhuddlan and Carnarvon were doubtless apposite places of residence for Queen Eleanor on the two occasions.

One of Prince Edward's nurses does seem to have been an inhabitant of Carnarvon, or to have settled down there at a later date. Her name was Mary Mansel.

It was on a stranger to his blood, however, that the boy Edward poured out affection, morbid in kind and in extent. To Edward I, one of his Gascon squires, De Gaveston, had rendered signal service. The King rewarded him by taking his two young sons into his household. One of these has left no mark on history; but the other, Peter, whom generally we call Piers, gained an ascendency over the young heir to the throne which was to involve both favourite and patron in disaster. From infancy they were together, the solitary boy and the sharp and self-seeking young foreigner. Edward's was a lonely childhood. Motherless at six, with sisters married or in the cloister, and a father rendered stern with the necessities of state and with grief for his dead queen, the boy had no natural outlet in his young life for the common family affections which should thrive even in palaces. In Gaveston he found a substitute for the ties of blood. His temperament, yielding, dreamy, and unpractical, impelled him to cling somewhere. Gaveston, ambitious, pleasure-seeking and crafty withal, responded with surface charm, if not with any true emotion, to his royal adorer's clinging and effeminate endearments. In his eye was the substantial profit of the infatuation. This youth, beautiful as a young god, was filled with sordid greed, with vicious inclinations. The atmosphere was for him, too, a baleful one. Like Cinq-Mars, in centuries to come, he was inflated with his own success, blinded in the glare of his own egoism. As they grew to manhood their relations should have changed. Edward should have thrown his ardour into the affairs of the kingdom and the cry of battle, should have transferred his sentimental necessities to the destined bride; for, after the failure of negotiations with the daughters of Flanders, a French princess had been found for him, Isabell, daughter of Philip le Hardi and niece of Margaret, Edward I's second queen. The betrothal was in 1303, when young Edward was nineteen and the princess still a child; the wedding was to take place as soon as Isabel reached marriageable age. Edward had already been created Prince of Wales, he enjoyed his inheritance of Ponthieu, and in 1306 his father granted him the duchy of Aquitaine, so that his appanage was a substantial one.

Young Edward had moved out into the light; he was in his father's company in the train of battle. Then disapproval grew into disgust—the finger of hostility was pointed at the nauseous infatuation of the Prince of Wales for the Gascon favourite. It was at the best inconsistent with the dignity of royal isolation; at the worst—there were not wanting tongues, dipped in unnecessary venom very possibly, to make their commentary. Then Bishop Langton, the Treasurer and

King Edward's right-hand man, spoke to his master of the evil that was being done. In an insolent outburst, young Edward and young Gaveston had broken into one of the bishop's parks, had caused much damage, and had injured the keepers who opposed their swashbuckling adventure. Like Junius Brutus, Edward spared not his own offspring. The Prince of Wales was imprisoned, while Gaveston received sentence of banishment. Bishop Langton's influence was very great, yet, judging by the light of after-circumstances in his life, we must exempt him from bringing pressure to bear on account of this merely personal, if weighty, wrong. It is clear that King Edward's eyes were opened suddenly to the undesirable entanglement of the heir-apparent and to the still more sinister rumour which hung about it. Treason—no less—some whispered. His son must be freed from this obsession, must find his feet, be braced for the future kingship. The fresh anxiety was a culminating one. Harassment and strain, the difficult journeys, the crude dietary, brought on dysentery. The King, seeing death upon the road, was urgent to press on to Scotland, to die upon the scene of his conquests. It was not to be. The Lord of Hosts had summoned him to lay down his arms. On his death-bed, he solemnly adjured his son never to recall Gaveston from his banishment. The dying voice had scarcely ceased to echo, a month alone had passed, when the new king, impelled by his wild infatuation, recalled Piers and poured out on him gifts from the royal estates all over the kingdom. The name of Gaveston stares from the early archives of the reign. The county of Cornwall with its stannaries is among the earliest gifts ; manors, here and there, in England ; titles and castles in Aquitaine and the viceroyalty of Ireland are among the honours; the list is richer than a royal bride's dowry—it befits a son of the blood-royal. Pope Clement is urged to annul the sentence of excommunication which had been passed against the Gascon squire for some deed of heresy, or blood, or debauchery. A little later, a royal alliance lifts the favourite into a family relationship. And Bishop Langton, through whose influence Gaveston had been disgraced—on him now falls revenge and every petty spite of the resentful Edward II. Taken a prisoner from his place amid the funeral train, the Treasurer is cast into the castle of Wallingford, anon into that of York, while his rich estates, forfeited to the sovereign, are added to the spoils of Gaveston.

Crowded were events in the opening of Edward's reign. For dynastic reasons, marriage was now imperative and was first arranged; his coronation was to follow. Lent would preclude the former for some weeks, and so the chief attention was given to its accomplishment. The widowed Queen Margaret travelled with the King, but Gaveston remained behind. As "best man" at the wedding his part would have been a secondary one; the reception at the French court of the upstart Gascon, with his reputation hardly washed by the heated flurry of the new king's lavished honours, might well have been a chilling one. He stays behind as regent, as keeper of the realm during King Edward's absence. The Great Seal, it is true, remains locked up in the custody of the Keeper of the Seal, but the "small part" of it is left with Gaveston to use during the period of his regency. The princes of the blood are made to stand aside for this outsider, this youth of glorious mien and evil mind. Might not great Edward, who had "gone the way of all flesh," stir in his regal sepulture at Westminster at such an outcome?

Great preparations were made on the Kentish coast in view of Edward's sojourn there before and after the visit to France. Forty leaden cauldrons were provided for the King's use in France. A great quantity of planking, too, was taken. The King's horses and the King's men needed food and shelter. A huge supply of logs and charcoal for fires was laid in to greet the new queen with a cheerful blaze, and two days before New Year Edward writes to his bride's father that he will reach Boulogne on the Eve of St. Vincent and that the wedding is to be on Wednesday, three days later (January 25th).

This journey of a king to the bride's country is a curiosity. To-day it would be unheard of when the heir-apparent even, of European sovereigns, awaits his bride on his own territory.

Edward II, however, went in person to marry Isabel, now in her earliest teens. In the first days of February he notifies his lords in England of his return. He will bring the new queen from Boulogne to Dover in his barge on a day soon after Candlemas (February 2nd). Certain of his kindred and of his nobles are summoned to meet him and his bride at Dover, his sister Elizabeth, Countess of Hereford, being among them.

The Chancellor cannot be in time to hand him the Great Seal upon that day, but on Friday he is to be received in audience at Dover Castle and deliver it to the King in person.

When Edward landed beneath the white chalk cliffs of Dover, it was not regal cares that filled his soul. Nor did the girl-wife absorb his thoughts and his emotions. No; it was on Piers Gaveston that he lavished caresses under the disgusted eyes of the nobles. What of the young Queen, who stood by while this was

going on ? The moon had not fulfilled her phases since
the wedding-day, and here was the bridegroom rejoicing
at the reunion with the Gascon youth as he had not
rejoiced in the most tender moments with the bride.
Into Isabel's heart, there, at the landing-place, there
entered in that drop of gall which, reacting on a temperament like hers, fiercely feminine and apt for
amorous emotion, poisoned her whole being and
evolved, in later life, the cruel and bitter darkness of
her maturity.

But little time remained before the coronation, which
was fixed for an early Sunday, and Isabel's resentment must have been blurred by a whirl of pageantry.
Already, wine had been brought from Gascony for the
feasting, and the Archbishop of Canterbury, who was
abroad, had deputed the Bishop of Winchester to be the
celebrant in his place.

The peers and peeresses were summoned to be present ;
among them the widowed Countess of Cornwall, whose
late earl, Edmund, had held those domains of the West
country which Earl Gaveston now enjoyed. Great
Norman names are on the list ; the princes of the
blood, who, later on, were to rise in rebellion against the
sovereign and his favourite, played their part. Yet here,
their rightful place, the rôle which precedence had
granted them, was trespassed on ; Gaveston was to oust
them from their offices.

The great gilt spurs came in an early place. Hum-
phrey, Earl of Hereford, Edward's brother-in-law,[1]
carried the sceptre with the cross in the King's procession up the nave ; Henry of Lancaster bore the regal

[1] Elizabeth, Countess of Holland, had been married to him after
her first husband's death.

wand surmounted with a dove, of which a counterpart is still among the regalia of England.

Then followed three sword-bearers, of whom one bore *Curtana*, the sword of mercy with the blunted edge. Behind them four great nobles, Lord Despenser, Roger Mortimer, and two others, bore the coronation robes on a "great chequer," which we may picture as a large square covered with cloth or costlier stuff and supported at each corner by one of the bearers.

Next came the Treasurer and the Chancellor of England, bearing St. Edward's vessels of the Mass.

Now, in the ultimate rank before the sovereign, comes, not one who should tread the path of honour thus on this great day. Piers Gaveston, newly Earl of Cornwall, it is who carries the crown of England before the King his patron. What a day of inflated pride and self-esteem! He recks not that, as "the cynosure of neighbouring eyes," he is the object of rancour, of mistrust, of dark suspicion. The glamour of his splendour is dazzling him still; he has no thought of reticence or deferential mien before the stern-faced barons: the gods are crazing him to lead him to his doom.

Then, last of all, is Edward himself, the hero of the day, bearing the golden ingot, a pound in weight, which he is to offer upon the high altar as his oblation to the King of kings.

Edward took the oath in French, and historians tell us that it is the first recorded form of oath of which we know in our own annals.

A busy year followed on these great functions. Edward was still at war with Scotland and had to give attention to those hostilities. A host of other matters called for settlement. The grievances against Langton had had to be postponed till after the coronation ; now they occupy a large share of the royal enactments.

To Isabel's dower, " wherewith he dowered her at the church door," Edward added, early in the year, the county of Ponthieu, appointing one " Peter, called ' le Cat ' " and two coadjutors to be King's proctors for all matters concerning it as regarded the King of France.

His subjects may have thought to celebrate the accession with tournaments, but a crop of enactments rose up forbidding these exciting assemblies and sports in various parts of England, and we find these renewed in later years. Sometimes the sheriff of a county receives the royal prohibition for all the towns in his jurisdiction, sometimes separate towns are interdicted. We find, indeed, among them Bungay ; who would believe that Bungay, that now quiet town, could once have lusted after tourneys ! To-day, it may burst forth in pageants.

As time went on, the strain became still greater, it grew to be intolerable. The favourite, now married to Margaret de Clare, the King's niece, was more presumptuous than before. The King still clung to him, leaving Isabel deserted. Her jealous plaint reaches her father, the King of France. But Edward was not warned.

Edward II was one of those unhappy beings placed by destiny in an inharmonious sphere. Harmlessly, if ineffectively, he might have passed through an ordinary career. Like the Bourbon Louis XIII, the Plantagenet Edward II had no vocation for kingship, he had no regal attributes, and acquired no kingly tenor, no calm-browed impassivity.

About him there was nothing of his strenuous father, save the height and fine physique. His mental and his

moral outfit harked back to Henry and John Lack-
land.

The day had come when the Earl of Cornwall was
overthrown.

The "son of the morning" had fallen headlong. In
the winter of 1311 there is an order issued by his
royal master, squirming under the pressure of the angry
peers, to search through four western counties for the
outlaw, who, it is believed, instead of leaving the
country as decreed, is wandering from place to place
and hiding here and there in Dorset or in Cornwall,
lately his rich estate. The proud favourite skulking in
the ditch or craving shelter in the barn—what a
picture of declension !

Then came one flare before the end. Gaveston was
recalled from across the seas, the King vouching for
him to the prelates and the nobles who had compelled his exile. But there was no mending of the
situation, and in 1312 Piers "lamentably" dies and at
first receives no honourable burial. Later, the King, a
craven suitor to the hostile peers, gains his desire to give
him a state funeral at King's Langley, where his corpse
had been removed from the Dominican chapel at Oxford.
Edward spent the Christmas Day of 1314 in making provision for splendid obsequies, and twenty-three casks of
wine were taken to Langley to flank the funeral bake-
meats.

Gaveston left one daughter, Joan, by Margaret de
Clare. His widow received a grant of her dead lord's
estates, which had returned to the King's hands. A few
years later she married Hugh de Audley, who, later, was
to lift his heel against the boneless King.

CHAPTER V

ROYAL RELATIVES AND SERVANTS

APART from the removal of the obsession of his favourite, Edward had now a happier object for his sentimentality. In 1312, was born his eldest son, Edward of Windsor.

John Lang, gentleman-in-waiting to Queen Isabel, brought to the King the news of the heir's birth, and received from the happy father a grant of £80 per annum for himself and his wife Joan, one of the young Queen's "damsels." This annuity was to be paid out of the revenues of the City of London, but it remained for long enough an insubstantial honour. Ten years later, we find that John and Joan had received no payment for the good tidings up till then, but a further grant gives hope that in the future they would enjoy this comfortable addition to their income. The previous years seem to have been neglected.

We may now ask something about the other royal relatives whom we saw in the last reign. Queen Margaret, still a young woman, continued to live in England, paying occasional visits to her native land. Her sons, Thomas and Edmund, the King's half-brothers, were objects of his favour as they grew to manhood.

Margaret herself seems to have had a fortunate capacity

for living in peace. Her position could not have been an easy one between her stepson and her niece, his wife. This "flower of France," as one of the chroniclers names her, leaves the fragrance of the good woman behind her on the page of England. She still has, in constant attendance on her, her minstrel, Guillot ; he leaves with her for France, and with his royal employer returns again to England. The minstrel is a man of substance too, the owner of shops and houses in the City. To-day, were the sites of them carpeted with gold the ground-landlord would hardly feel temptation to dispose of them.

The two young princes, Thomas and Edmund, had already been provided for by their father, Edward I. Edward II gives further estates, and by the time the elder is eighteen we find him as Earl of Norfolk and Earl Marshal of England. Edmund Plantagenet is Duke of Kent; one of his descendants, as Richard II, is to wear the crown of England. He and his brother serve their half-brother loyally. We find them journeying to Scotland to fight for him against the rebels there.

Their mother did not live to see their prime, for her gentle life came to an end in 1318, when she was still under forty years of age.

Some of the relatives of the new king had found favour in his sight.

We remember Ralph de Montemery, the knight who married Joan, Edward's elder sister, after her first husband, the Earl of Gloucester's, death. Joan was dead, but Lord de Montemery, as the widower was styled, and his children by the princess, were objects of royal favour and confidence. A marriage is arranged between his daughter Mary and Duncan, Earl of Fife, and we hear, too, of his sons, Thomas and Edward. Later on he is the ranger of the forests south of Trent, and in 1319 has married again, without royal licence too, Isabel, the widow of the Lord de Hastyngs. The pair managed to patch up their misfeasance, for in 1325 they were made custodians of Edward's daughters and had the use of some dwellings within the royal castle of Marlborough for themselves and their charges. After Ralph's death, his widow continued to be custodian of the princesses.

When Joan, the King's sister, had married Ralph Montemery, her son Gilbert, now Earl of Gloucester, was a minor. His stepfather was appointed as his guardian, and by a curious fiction of the times he was styled, *pro tem.*, Ralph Montemery, "Earl of Gloucester and Hertford." Gilbert de Clare was still under age when his uncle, the King, summoned him to go with him to Scotland. In 1313, he had come into his inheritance, and a year later he crossed to France in the train of Queen Isabel. In the same year he died, leaving a young widow, Matilda, and some prospect of an heir. After a time, these hopes having come to nothing, his estate was divided between his three sisters, the widow receiving as her portion the dower granted to her on her marriage.

The three sisters of De Clare, Eleanor, Margaret, and Elizabeth, all made marriages with subjects of their uncle, the King, who were destined to be involved in treason or sedition. Eleanor became the wife of the younger Despenser, son of the Earl of Winchester. Margaret, after Gaveston's death, was wed to Hugh de Audley. Elizabeth, already twice widowed, married thirdly Roger Damory, another, on whose head attainder fell in years to come. There was also a half-sister, Isabel de Clare, by their father's first wife, Alice, whom he had divorced. She married Maurice Berkeley and was less implicated than her half-sisters of the blood in the factions of the reign.

Of greater interest than the foregoing is that forceful personality, Mary, the royal nun. As she had been the object of her father's solicitude, so now we find her that of her brother's. Her provision of wine and firewood is confirmed : she receives a further grant of landed property to enable her to "support her state suitably." Dame Mary is no ascetic nor yet a hermit. She has some trouble with her property, on which some ill-conditioned fellows trespassed ; but here she suffers no uncommon thing, for King and Queen, prince and noble, alike are subject to the same annoyance. Edward himself, in a riotous freak, had, as we remember, broken into one of Bishop Langton's parks in the last reign. Mary's authority was upheld before the world. She received power to use the smaller seal of Bristol (called the "cocket") in dealings with her debtors. Most interesting of all is her visit, in 1313, to Windsor Castle, which she had probably not seen since she was seven years old. Here she would find the baby heir-apparent and his elder sisters, Eleanor and Joan, and would have a view, if a restricted one, of the great world. Perhaps she came upon some business of the convent, for nuns did sometimes come to announce to the sovereign the death of a superior and to obtain his letters-patent for a new election.

We have no record of her adventures or her impressions, which must, all the same, be painted thick on the most reticent imagination. Priceless, indeed would be the *cahier-bleu* of the Lady Mary of Woodstock, but, upon reflection, it faces us that quite probably writing was no easy task to a Plantagenet princess. Mary the nun did not go away empty-handed. Her charges of the journey for herself and her equerry, and hay and fodder for her mount, were provided at the King's command from the issues of the counties which she traversed. The sheriffs had the thing in hand. She rode, maybe upon the "woman's saddle" which had come into use. Perhaps she spent her Christmas at Windsor, perhaps she returned for the Lord's birthday to her cloister. There must have been talk for many a day; the innocent echoes must have heard the tale of a world so new, so full of acute impression on the unblurred consciousness of this convent child, then thirty-three years old.

Again, we see in Mary her father's qualities; the leadership of men; an energy for business, for organization; a desire for dominance. The Abbess of Fontévrault (nowhere have we found so much as an initial of her name) is not, at times, at all events, on easy terms with her royal daughter in religion. There had been friction between the mother-house and Amesbury in the last reign; again we find, four years after the visit to Windsor, implications of a deadlock, and again the sovereign's intervention.

The royal nun had, on some earlier occasion, made a visitation of the houses of the order in England. To her own thinking, and to King Edward's, all had been carried out judiciously, with advantage to the internal discipline of the establishments. Yet we must surmise some failure, from the monastic point of view, or some ill-disposition in mother-abbess beyond the seas towards

Dame Mary. Clear it is that Edward wrote, requesting her to appoint his sister for the work and expressing surprise at the delay of the abbess in giving her orders upon this head. Kings might not safely quarrel with these great *religieuses ;* Rome would speak ; that was a material point ; again, it would be an outrage on the brides of Christ. Thomas of Canterbury was an eternal remembrance for the crowned of England. Yet Mary clearly held her brother's, as she had held her father's ear. Edward comes pretty near to regal sarcasm. He reminds the abbess that her prestige cannot suffer, as she has not hitherto made these visitations in person. The abbess, indeed, was to be made to feel that she was something of a dog-in-the-manger. The power, if granted, could be withdrawn at any moment, he reminds her further. Finally, he sends the letter-close to the Dean of Angers by the hands of one of the royal chaplains, urging him to take the abbess in hand and also to hear further what Master John Ildesly shall tell him *viva voce.*

The rest is silence. Dame Mary may have got her way or the abbess, equally masterful (or perhaps a sour curmudgeon was it), may have come herself to England, as she or a predecessor had done to fetch the heart of dead King Henry.

There is a wholesome whiff of energy about the Lady Mary's apparition. She makes a contrast to the maudlin King. Yet Edward, separated from the poisonous friendships and the domestic rebellions of his career, might have earned some little impressiveness. He was, though not of splendid aspect like the baleful Piers, a personable man. He had chance enough of being in the public eye, for his reign, like his father's, was full of warfare. Usurping Bruce absorbed the energies of

English arms. Already, in the first summer of the reign, immense stores are on their way to Scotland. Beans and bacon, barley-malt, wheat in grain and wheat ground and sifted and packed in barrels, are provided. For camp and palace use, thousands of salmon are salted beyond Tweed, "red" herring and sturgeon too, in lesser quantity, come from English fishing-grounds and from French ports. Nantes sends a contribution of the choicer lamprey to the Scotch borders.

To-day, fat pork and beef are chosen to be salted for the harness cask on shipboard, then, the royal estates were systematically hunted by a pack, under the King's verderers, to obtain fat venison, which, salted and packed upon the spot in casks, was forwarded from the shrievalty of the respective counties. At Gravesend is a royal rabbit-warren. The King's ferreter had orders to take the little rodents for the royal table.

The swan was still the special dish. The burgesses of Lynn provided it for a royal visitor ; Queen Isabel was not bereft of it in her forced retirement at Castle Rising.

A great fish called a "porpais" is cast upon the royal foreshore ; it is valued as high as sixty shillings. Its liver might have been recommended for the King's experiment. If the sovereign waived his right to the whale cast on the land of some tenant-in-chief, he yet required the tongue, as a *bonne bouche*, or as a royal reservation. Henry I thus granted whales to the Bishop of London and the Dean and Chapter of St. Paul's. Perhaps this was forgotten by the reign of Edward II, for a whale, thus stranded, was handed over to the King, but subsequently claimed by the churchmen under the aforesaid charter.

The East Anglian coast, ever a centre of the herring fishery, is visited by the King's servants to make provision for the Lenten fast, six months ahead. Salt is ordered in great quantity, both in its coarser granulation from the pans and in a finer kind which appears in the royal provender about the time of Edward's accession.

Sore dearth was in the land in Edward's reign. The laws against foreign imports are relaxed. The merchants of Amiens have leave to trade in England. The Italian guilds are still foremost in the foreign trading-world. Andrew de Pessaigne, of Genoa, is the King's merchant, his seneschal in Gascony, and confidential agent. He sends honey, wheat, and oil to the King of England in the time of famine. Ginger, cloves, pepper, saffron, and *materia medica* are shipped to England, and, to supplement the shortage of the dearth, or as a rarer savoury, perhaps, come herrings preserved in fat.

Sugar-loaves are mentioned, perhaps for the first time.

The departments of the household become more defined as years go on. Ralph Spray was once buyer for the kitchen ; the King's "larderer" next deals with flesh and fish. The pantry, buttery, saucery and scullery are the charge of separate caterers, who journey throughout the realm to acquire the raw material from the sheriffs or from the royal deer-parks and fishponds.

As time goes on the "clerk of the kitchen" is the receiver of supplies at Windsor. Wine is bought for the palace and the royal castles. In the latter strongholds is stored, as well, provision for the contingency of siege. Spent and even "putrid" stores are to be sorted out and sold. From the timber of Llewellyn's hall in Conway, pulled down by the King's orders in 1316, is built a storehouse for provisions in Carnarvon Castle. Wine, too, is taken for the King as excise in kind. The " King's prise" is made in various ports under different high functionaries. Gaveston thus makes perquisition in the Devon town of Dartmouth. The smuggler's joy of evasion leads to artful dodging of the "customs"; the King's officers await in vain, at Ipswich, freights which have been craftily landed at Harwich, at the river's mouth. So it was in Edward I's day.

Edward II grants to an old servant casks of wine from the "prise." The lighter wines were perishable. In the last dreadful days of the reign, when his power was tottering, when his very head was shuddering on his shoulders, Edward gives command by letters-close regarding the wines which Bennett Fulsham, the royal Butler, cannot keep "by reason of their weakness."

At Boston Fair the vintners make a "ring" so that the King's Butler cannot buy of them, and proceedings are taken against them on that count.

Wax continues to be used in large quantities, though for lighting purposes tallow is also in request; wicks and other requisites pass through the office of the Chandlery.

"Candle-ends" are not so insignificant but that they can be included in the emoluments of the King's marshals.

One of Edward's former chaplains, besides his board and bedding, robes and shoe-leather, is to receive a nightly tallow dip for his bedroom.

Edward II pensioned off quite an astonishing number of old servants in the religious houses of the kingdom. His father's cook is sent to Osney (Oxon.); his own, Gilbert, is superannuated at another monastery. The

King rates the Abbot of Tavistock for declining to receive one *protégé* and requires an explanation, which sometimes was sufficient, the pensioner being passed on elsewhere.   Thus, the rejected of Tavistock found shelter at Bodmin Priory.

Women sometimes are the objects of the royal interest.   Evelyn la Petite is sent to the hospital of St. Leonard at York.   Where under the same rule there were nuns, the women pensioners would receive a chamber within the monastery, but the request on one occasion is that the female pensioner may be granted a house without the abbey gate.   The allowance is generally stipulated for as the same which would be granted to a monk in the same house.   Royal and noble prisoners were committed to the care of nunneries.   Margery Bruce, in the last reign, we see at a Yorkshire convent.

Elizabeth, wife of Robert Bruce, was a state-prisoner at Windsor Castle in 1312, under Warren de l'Isle, constable of the castle.   Then she was removed to Rochester, and on her way was a visitor of the Abbess of Barking.

At Rochester she was to have the service of a maid and two men, and to receive the not inconsiderable sum of twenty shillings a week for her maintenance.

Margaret de Clare, as the wife of the attainted Hugh de Audley, was sent by Edward II to the Abbot of Sempyngham, and a mixed house in the North of England receives Cassandra, widow of Walter de Ros, among the brethren and sisters.

Margery Mortimer goes to her durance with a train of attendants.   Through England she travels to Yorkshire, with her damsel and her equerry, her groom, her page and laundress. A mark a week was her stipend from the King during her stay in Skipton Castle. When liberated, she did not use her freedom well, for two years later, the King has heard that " divers suspicious assemblies and gatherings of men are daily made by her," and she is ordered to betake herself to a convent near Bedford, where houses within the walls are to be made ready for her, and the abbess is enjoined to forbid her to pass the gates or to hold any kind of meeting without royal licence. The royal allowance must have been cut off as well, as Margery is ordered to reside at her own costs among the nuns.

The shingled roof is being replaced by stone tiles as time goes on. Queen Margaret's houses are being thus renovated, also the roofs of some of the castles in different parts of England. In rarer instances a leaden covering is employed. Yet Westminster Palace is being largely built again of shingles, whether for roofing or for a timbered façade, remains in doubt. The great stone conduits, which served as sewers, are the objects of repair in one of the royal castles. Rarely does royal mandate lead to the cleaning of the moat and of the ditches, into which we must surmise that the sewage of the fortress or the palace was discharged.

Within, we have not many signs to tell us of advance in elegance of living. Rushes still strew the floors, and we cannot picture here that artful affectation of simplicity which covers our own with the woven products of the marsh, with substance and costliness almost equal to that of a pile carpet.

The royal plate-coffers received an accession during this reign, when some of the costly property of the deceased Bishop of Durham was purchased for the King at an outlay of over £1,836. We may believe that Edward had nothing to surpass the show of silver and gold dishes, cups and spoons, or ewers and tankards which Anthony Dunelm. left behind him.

There is an increase of elaboration in the drinking-cup and tankard of the King. There are cups on stems, with covers more or less enriched with boss or battlemented work in gold and enamel, yet free from any florid superfluity. Ewers go with them in pairs; the individual wine-jug, it would seem, from which was served the King, or other royal diner.

Queen Isabel had her own plate of silver or of gold, simple or wrought to some extent, or enriched with enamel work. One ewer is adorned with impish figures, which doubtless claimed kindred in the grotesques found upon the monkish page.

Jars of some kind are purchased for the office of the Buttery. Goats are captured from the herds in the Forest of Dean to supply milk for the royal dairy.

The office of the Marshalsay covered the department of the Master of the Horse of to-day as well as others, and included also the royal "lock-up."

The monastic houses could probably outvie the royal palace in their gardens. At Windsor, horticulture must have been of simple kind. A vineyard figures there, and there is the "garden without the castle," for which one gardener seems to have sufficed. Edmund and John appear, and Adam is there for several years, but of their helpers we hear nothing. Were they single-handed then, and if head-gardeners, consider then their wage! For Adam's twopence *per diem* is recorded on the close-roll. And what of Hamo Chambers, who kept both gates, or Edmund Aldgate, who at another time held the same post at such a modest hire ? To-day the palace *personnel* may smile at such a record. The rations and apparel of these servitors was supplied to them under exact prescription.

Two chaplains served the chapel-royal at Windsor.

Bread and wine were provided for the ritual uses of the Mass, oil for the ever-burning lamps of the sanctuary, and other necessaries such as the services required The missals and other books, in manuscript, passed from the care of one head chaplain to another.

The royal menagerie was at the Tower. In the by-gone 'fifties of the previous century Louis the Saint had sent an elephant to England, " a beast most straunge and wonderfull to the English people, for that seldome, or neuer, anie of that kinde hadde been seen in England before." The elephant had died or disappeared, but Edward II had his lion and leopard in the keeping of Peter le Fevre, and for the former royal beast a quarter of mutton daily was supplied. Peter received twopence *per diem* for his care of them until his death, which happened about 1316. The lion soon disappears from the royal records, but the leopard had survived Peter, and sixpence a day is granted for its support. In the earliest entry, we have found, this amount was twopence until after Lent, when it was raised to sixpence. Can a fast have been imposed upon the captive carnivora ?

War and the chase were the main occupations of the Plantagenet Edwards. War, indeed, to those early English sovereigns, must have supplied an occupation— a very pastime—apart from any questions of political necessity. Edward sends abroad for war-horses, perhaps the Flemish breed. The cruder complications of the day were met by sword and pike or "engine" for the siege, hurling stones against the foemen on the walls or battering down the masonry with such mechanism as may have figured at the siege of Jerusalem, and being, indeed, of inferior execution.

The infinite complexity of modern international affairs is met by a correspondingly developed system of diplomatic tactics. The treaty-room, the hall of congress are in the picture, rather than the field of battle. The English sovereign of to-day labours far more strenuously to head off bloodshed than did his Plantagenet predecessors to head their lordlings into battle. Few, if any, are the hours which sovereigns of the twentieth century can call their own, but we are urged to the conclusion that the Plantagenets, war failing, would have found time heavy on their hands. The courtiers, too, without the call to arms would have had much yawning time. The tourney was prohibited, though sometimes we perceive evasion. Thus a knight is pardoned for his share in the forbidden feats of arms.

Edward II, like Louis XIII of France, was fond of music. Two of his minstrels, if not more, are known to later centuries. There is *notre menestrel* Reymund Cousin early in the reign, and again, nearer to the end, comes William Morley, "called *roi du North.*"

Our insistence on the fighting avocations of our Plantagenets and their courtiers must be further tempered by the knowledge that they had some indoor games. Here is one courtier at least who owns a curious chessboard of ginger-root and nutmeg, with chessmen made of crystal.

The King as *ex-officio* guardian of minors we saw in

the last reign.   Edward II, in this capacity, arranges a marriage for his little great-niece, Joan Gaveston, with young Thomas de Wake, but the youth, preferring another bride, pays down 1,000 marks as fine to the sovereign whose *partie* he has declined.   Elsewhere, we find a youthful widow apparently resisting a match desired by the King.   The King wishes to do well to one Arnold de Durfort, who has served him faithfully, by arranging a marriage between him and Katharine de l'Isle.   Sir Bernard Jordan is requested to use his influence to persuade the lady, presumably a kinswoman, to look favourably upon the aspirant.

A work of importance was set in hand during this reign when orders were issued for the cataloguing of the muniments of the Exchequer and of the duchy of Aquitaine, which were stored in the offices of the Treasury and the Wardrobe.   Books, which seem to have been chiefly Latin works on law, were removed in 1313 by royal command from the Exchequer to Windsor Castle under the care of a Carmelite monk.

Armour still figures as kingly wear more than softer goods, and is more largely found in relics of the time than more perishable garb.   We remember the royal tailor in the previous reign and his task of choosing cheese of Brie.   Here is the tailor of Edward II confessing to a debt to another of his craft in the City of London.   "Dog eats not dog," but the City tailor-man was less sparing of Henry of Cambridge, the royal warrant-holder.   The debtor admits his liability, recorded on the close-roll.   *Sartor resartus!*

CHAPTER VI

THE HOUSEHOLD FOES

THE coming of his children and the saner devotion of his fatherhood did not avert from Edward of Carnarvon the aberration of friendship, nor release him from the drainage of the parasite. Gaveston had plunged rapacious fingers in the treasury, Hugh Despenser was to incite the monarch to put the guiltless to the sword. For, under Hugh's dominance, they were held traitors who sickened and rebelled at the association of the sovereign with the man of evil-living. The Despenser saw to it that such as spoke and moved against him had soon their tongues set fast in death.

Isabel, the Queen, too, had in him a bitter enemy: so she believed, though Edward, in weak effusions sent to her across the seas, declared that his " dear nephew" had never willed nor manifested to her any enmity. She, the Queen, had grown from the petulant girl, jealous of Gaveston's greater hold upon her husband, to be a woman, lovely and full of energy, mingling with her voluptuous impulses some sovereign dignity and capability. She it was who forwarded the treaty made with France in 1325.

Perhaps from her influence a slight advance in the

refinements of the table and the toilet took its origin. France may not have been the leader of cut or fashioning. Perhaps Florence it was which gave the tone to mantua-making. Yet France would be ahead of England. Isabel sent to her own country for some part of her attire. Mary, Countess of Fife, is also seen sending her servants abroad to obtain apparel and other objects for her adornment.

From Anthony, the merchant of Genoa, are purchased pearls for the Queen to the value of forty livres.

The King's captives in Yorkshire or at Rochester Castle had an outfit or a dress-allowance. Margery Mortimer received ten marks a year for her "robes," but her daughters, imprisoned in various nunneries, were allowed one mark a year only.

Taxation and protection are laid on English cloth and wool. The merchants of the Staple are prominent among the trading guilds of the time. The King's, or standard balance, for weighing wool is kept in the Port of London. Officials are charged with the collection of the tax, royal promulgations are aimed at the ill-doers who, as in the case of the crown wine-dues (the "prise of wine"), seek to evade the impost. Nor must the foreign clothworker send to England for native aids of his industry. Neither teazle nor fuller's earth, nor the native vegetable dyes of blue and crimson may be exported.

When we compare their methods of travelling with our own, we must be struck with wonder at the journeys of the King and of his subjects and allies alike in those long-past Edwardian days. The very spices used in the royal dispensary bring with them the aroma of far-off climes into our kingdom.

Have we asked perhaps how these products of the East found their way to us ? We are answered by the following passage relative to trade with the East in the time of the Crusades.

"Although we have no pilgrim diaries of the century during which the Turks became rulers of West Asia, we know that Latins were visiting the Holy City in ever-increasing numbers. Trade with Asia was carried on by French and Italian merchants.

"A fair was held annually at Jerusalem on September 15th, and the traders of Pisa, Venice, Genoa and Marseilles bought cloves, nutmeg, and mace brought from India ; pepper, ginger, and frankincense from Aden ; silk from China—whether by overland caravan or by the Chinese junk, which appeared in the Red Sea during the Middle Ages—sugar from Syria, flax from Egypt, with quicksilver, coral, metals, glass from Tyre, almonds, mastic, saffron, with rich stuffs and weapons, from Damascus.

"The Jews paid a heavy tax to secure the monopoly as dyers, and Jewish dyers still lived near the Tower of David in 1163 A.D., as mentioned by Benjamin of Tudela. The sugar-cane of Tripoli is noticed by Albert of Aix, and sugar-mills set up by Moslems and afterwards used by the Franks still remain in ruins at Jericho. Jerusalem was famous for its sugar as early indeed as the tenth century." [1]

Royal journeys were a costly thing. The King and Queen, with their train of nobles, visited France in 1313, and the cost of going and returning came to more than £400 of the contemporary currency.

From various ranks of society went pilgrims to the

[1] *The City of Jerusalem.* Colonel C. R. Conder, R.E., LL.D.

shrine of Santiago or to the Holy Land. Queen Isabel heads the list.

Missionary friars receive the royal " safe-conduct " when visiting the realm of the King of Georgia, while another apostle of Christianity goes to convert the Tartars.

In 1325 there came that fateful journey of Queen Isabel's to France, made under cover of seeking peace with the French King, who was invading Edward's French possessions. Young Edward joined his mother there. The sisters, Eleanor and Joan, were with the widow of Montemery at Marlborough Castle. John of Eltham, the younger son of Edward II and Isabel, had provision for his household, but figures little in the tale.

The King of England had alienated alike his people, his nobles, and his queen by his nauseous subservience to the hated Despenser. Democracies are the first to decry the overstepping of the boundary line of royal restrictions in the matter of the personal friend. To the nobles, the unhealthy business was repugnant ; reptiles such as the younger Despenser rouse the gorge of healthy men ; the prestige of the crown, and of the sovereign's lieges alike, was flecked by this fatuous association : few there were who failed to spit at it for a more evil thing.

Isabel, with a more fiercely seething hatred still, had turned her back on the husband who shamed her by his open absorption in the favourite rather than in the wife, and who deprecated her angry resentment at Despenser's insolence. " Hugh, our very dear and faithful nephew." How the woman, quick of wit and ardent of blood, would tear the words in hissing mimicry between her teeth ; her being writhing in revolt against the unregal wearer of the crown—against the perverted husband.

Then she had turned, had thrown herself into the passionate intrigue with the rebel Mortimer. He, thrown into the Tower for treason, was not to be separated from the lovely and loving woman. He fled the Tower by night ; John Cromwell, the Keeper of the Tower, notwithstanding. The King had no enthusiasts on his side, the rebels many ; the Cinque Ports, primed with spies by royal command, failed to arrest his flight : the convenient myopia of the King's malcontents may be assumed. Roger landed on French soil ; he was " received and cherished in the lordship of Picardy," whines Edward.

Isabel does not return, in spite of her lord's protestations. In 1325, Prince Edward crossed to his mother. On the way he lodged with his suite at the Maison-Dieu at Dover. The thirteen-year-old boy went to do homage to the King of France for the French possessions of England, which his father had conferred on him in the forlorn hope of buying off the hostility of Isabel's relations. Edward had no grasp of the larger issues in those days of boyhood. Between the feeble, whimpering father and the vivacious, brilliant, and capable mother-parent, his young eyes, his unripe apprehension, had to choose. In his ears were the whispers of his mother's partizans ; few plucked his sleeve to listen to the contrary tale. The Bishop of Exeter stood solitary, in the days of deposition, for the King's allegiance.

King Edward writes at length, to every one in turn. To Isabel herself, the *casus belli*, to the King her brother, to a great French prelate, and, most exhaustively of all, to Edward, Prince of Wales.

Charles le Beau is conjured to procure Isabel's return to England, without having regard to the " wilful pleasure of woman."

Then the tale is written to the Bishop of Beauvais. " It is well known how Queen Isabel stays in France, withdraws herself from the King and adheres to Roger de Mortimer, the King's deadly enemy, under attainder."

Last of all, it is to young Edward that the King pours out his tale in pages-full, adjuring him with proverbs from the Scriptures ; then resorting to threats that " if the King find him contrary to his will, he will ordain so that Edward shall feel it all the days of his life, and that all other sons shall take example thereby of disobeying their lords and fathers."   He must not marry without the King's consent.

For Isabel had been matchmaking during a stay in Flanders, whither she had betaken herself, so it is said by some of her chroniclers, because her brother was feeling her presence in Paris rather awkward.

There had been earlier proposals of marriage between the Prince of Wales and a daughter of Hainault as well as with other princesses.

Edward was himself in treaty with the King of Castile in reference to marriages proposed between King Alphonso himself and Eleanor, Edward's eldest daughter, and also between Prince Edward and Eleanor, Alphonso's sister.

There had been another project for betrothing Edward to Iolanthe, daughter of James, King of Aragon, but from this, or from some coherent stipulations, James had withdrawn.

The King of Portugal was also sending letters regarding alliances between his children and those of England, but without that " punctilio " which was fitting to so

great a matter, it would seem ; for Edward requires that
envoys of more prestige shall be sent before the matter
can be considered.

Then there were the girl-cousins, daughters of the
Count of Holland and Hainault and great-nieces of
Edward II.[1] A dispensation had been already discussed
with reference to Margaret, the eldest, but when young
Edward, with his mother, went on a visit to the count's
dominion, it was Philippa who struck the prince's fancy
and affection, and Philippa it was who responded to his
attraction.

The King of England all this time rains letters on
the respective parties, still urging the return of Isabel.
And at length, in the summer of 1326, Isabel did return.
No tender spouse returning to her lord, but an open
traitor, Isabel took ship at Dordrecht with several vessels
bearing foreign knights and nobles who had placed
themselves under the Queen's allegiance, all prepared
to take arms against the English sovereign and against
his parasite. The English ports were not in obedience
to the King. Edmund, Earl of Kent, King Edward's
half-brother, was Warden of the Cinque Ports. He,
too, at length, had become disaffected. A year before,
Edward had been " much perturbed " that the Constable
of Dover should allow religious to go to France without
royal licence, they having already been forbidden to do
so. The provincials, and the heads of the great religious
houses, were inhibited from going beyond seas to attend
the chapters of their orders. He had none to trust ; the
very ground of England trembled beneath the miserable
degenerate, her King. The sea alone, so often henchmaid

---

[1] William, Count of Hainault, was a son of Elizabeth, daughter of
Edward I, Countess of Holland and Hainault by her first marriage.

of the kingdom, bestirred herself; the fleet of Isabel, which
had sailed in fine weather from Holland, was caught by
tempest, "un grand tourment les prit en mer." They
were driven far out of their course and completely lost
their reckoning. Two days later, when the weather
moderated, they found themselves off the English coast.
The sailor-men, at hazard, for none knew their where-
abouts, ran the ships ashore in shallow water upon a
sandy beach, and here, on short rations, they worked for
three days discharging the horses and their mailed equi-
page. Then, on the fourth day, they took steed and cast
themselves on Providence and on St. George, in the
desperate plight of them who had suffered hunger by day
and cold by night, with terrors past and yet to come.
And so rode they, says Froissart, over hill and dale, and
hither and thither that, at length, they came upon certain
hamlets, and then to a great abbey of the Blackfriars,
under St. Edmund's patronage (at Bury St. Edmunds),
"et s'y hérbèrgerent et rafraichirent par trois jours."

" Rumour flies swiftly though the cities."

At Bristol, the miserable King has now his back
against the wall. The aged Earl of Winchester, now
nearing ninety years of age; his son, Despenser, the
major cause of all the hideous household turmoil; a
handful of knights around them—these are all, these
only, hold the realm—hold Bristol Castle, the last
stronghold.

The ports, the nobles, wife and son, the foreigner
from Flanders and from France, are leagued against
the wretched King : the failure of the storm has been
the final triumph of Erynnes. Even the frigid parch-

ments, so aloof, in general, from all emotion, seem here to bestir them with hysteric foam : the last ineptitude froths in the letters-close which bid the Chancellor of Oxford to keep sure guard upon Smithgate, that there may be no entry for "Roger Mortimer, or for other rebels, who have entered the realm with a multitude of aliens."

Edward's reign is at an end.   We have now to deal with young Edward as the sovereign and his mother as the regent.   Despenser, the younger, has been slain, the adherents of Edward II receive punishment or pardon, as being enemies of Edward III and of the Queen-mother Isabel, the regent.

Behind the walls of Gloucester, or of Berkeley, Castle the deposed King was enduring a persecution in which is reflected the savagery of the age, run wild in its particular detestation of the miserable invertebrate there captive.   His gaolers, with the Queen's tacit commendation, some say with her connivance, sought to hound him out of life by every rigour and indignity.   A great churchman, so they gossiped, sent letters in which ambiguous alternatives, contrived by an absence of punctuation, intimated the death solution.   To the miserable captive, pleading for warm water that he might shave himself, they brought the turbid solution from a ditch.   Their victim, forced to tears, redeemed his manhood by one doleful spark of repartee.   "See," he exclaimed as the tears streamed down his wretched face, " here—natheless—is warm water ! "

Other wretched wives have craved the death of husbands ; sometimes with remorse, sometimes with unappeasable malignity.   Isabel was gall through-out.   As her voluptuous instincts broke bounds

in her association with the paramour, so did her
venom concentrate itself against the despicable consort. The rebel Mortimer was at least a man. She
would not visit Edward II herself nor let the young
King do so. Yet the wretched prisoner did not die.
It was not quick enough—the Queen was heard to say,
or so they believed that her words would have been.
A dreadful contemplation! For cruel are the libertine
and the wanton when their passions make short circuit
to crude animalism. We have no need to involve the
Queen in the particular horror of the end. The hideous
contrivance by which his gaolers destroyed the viscera
of the tortured King without producing outward wound
—the formal viewing of the body by a packed jury
of Bristol citizens, for we can hardly take their inquest
or their verdict as aught but mock solemnities—these
things which sicken our contemplation may yet have
held an impulse, not of absolute devilry, but of retribution. Despenser had died, marred hideously, for crimes
which the cry of the nation had, truly or not, attributed
to him, and Edward of Carnarvon may have paid the
cost of evil deeds laid at his door in the insidious horror
which brought him to his end.

The masters of the situation overdid their rôle. Reaction followed. The long-drawn horrors of his end
moved the people to commiseration; in later days a
section of them even sought, though without effect,
to convert the dead King's tortures into the sufferings
of martyrdom.

EDWARD III

THE CORONATION OF EDWARD III

CHAPTER VII

THE MOTHER AND THE SON

WITH the mere name of Edward III we breathe a saner air. From the miasmic atmosphere of the invertebrate, we turn with refreshment to the healthy type of fighting Englishman who stands before our face in the grandson of Edward Longshanks.

Though he could have had no veneration for his father, and though his mother and her adherents remained his oracle, young Edward was yet unwilling to take up the sceptre until his father should resign it to him.

In his captivity, the miserable King had no real option. Pressed against the wall, he at length consented to abdicate formally, accepting the situation, say some, as due to his wrongdoing. And so the third Edward began his reign and was crowned King in the early days of 1327.

The young life, the mother-hand as well, are alike an ever living suggestion of the olive-branch. And so the early days are filled with pardon of the civil enemy, such as took part against the invading Isabel, and with treaties for truce abroad and over the Border.

The Council of the Realm is occupied alike with the negotiations with Charles le Beau and the Scots.

John Cromwell, Keeper of the Tower, through whose fingers Mortimer had slipped, is reinstated in his post upon a five years' tenure.

Young Edward's thoughts were also with the girl Philippa across the North Sea, and in October negotiations for the marriage were on foot, and not long after Philippa was Queen and was crowned on Sunday-before-St. Peter's-Chair, 1330.

The customary dower at the church door does not seem to have been bestowed on the girl-queen, but early in the year following his marriage, Edward gave an undertaking to assign her lands for that object. There was some delay in carrying out the arrangement.

On New Year's Day, 1331, manors and castles to the yearly value of £4,000 were granted to her with the assent of Parliament. This, however, not proving enough for the maintenance of her establishment, a further sum of 500 marks was granted some fifteen months later, a sum "which the Queen believes will meet the deficiency." Philippa was a less acquisitive person, it would seem, than Queen Isabel, or even than the nun of Amesbury.

Round them at the court, in these their early days, Edward and his young wife had the Queen-mother, the heir-presumptive, John of Eltham, and the King's two sisters, Joan and Eleanor.

Early in the reign the nurses of the young royal people were handsomely pensioned off by Edward, and in 1328 measures were on foot for Joan's marriage to Robert, King of Scotland, son of the Robert Bruce of Edward Longshanks's reign. Her dower from the Scots

King, fixed at £2,000 per annum in lands, was received on her behalf by two commissioners who travelled to the North for that intent. As Queen of Scotland, to her faithful servants rewards were given by her brother of England, John de Bristol receiving custody of the King's park and warren at Liskeard, while a bounty is conferred upon a lady of her entourage who had journeyed in her train on a visit to England.

Eleanor, the younger sister, began to receive her own "dress allowance" in the fifth year of the reign, the Keeper of the Wardrobe receiving royal commands to supply John Thresk, her tailor, with cloth and fur for her use.

By this time marriage arrangements had already been under consideration for her as well as for Prince John. First, the eldest son of the King of France was proposed as bridegroom; a year later, Peter, heir-apparent to the King of Aragon. Later still, the Count of Gueldres is in view, and this marriage project was carried out in 1336. The King had again recourse to borrowing for the expenses of his sister's wedding; more than this, he obtained as gifts from a number of the religious houses of the kingdom sums of various amount towards the same purpose. The Abbot of St. Mary's at York was appointed to collect the gifts, which were, in some cases, given with free hand, but in others, apparently, extorted from an unwilling or impoverished community. The Abbot of Croyland obtained indeed a royal guarantee that his grant of ten marks on this occasion might not be established as a precedent to the injury of himself and his successors.

Eleanor went to Germany escorted by English ecclesiastics as her guardians. Her account-book has been preserved to this day, relates an entry in the *Daily Mail* in June, 1910.

"For £47 the original household book of accounts of Eleanor, daughter of Edward II, on her journey to Verlie for her marriage to the Earl of Gelders, was sold yesterday in the Phillipps MS. collection."

For John of Eltham, a daughter of the French King was first proposed. John was fulfilling his part as "handy-man" to the King-brother. He acted as regent when Edward went privately to France to fulfil a vow, made in a moment of danger, or to do homage to his uncle of France for the English crown possessions.

His separate household was now kept up and the arrears made good for his maintenance, from the previous reign, when the general disorder of the realm had brought everything into confusion.

John was sent to Aquitaine on the King's service. Again, provision in the good old style was made of bacon and of beans, and of the fish called "hak." English feeding pursues him across the Channel.

He was created Earl of Cornwall, and received the office of Keeper of the Scottish Marches. He obtained the sovereign clemency on behalf of several criminals as an appurtenance of his royalty, but his own life was but a short one, for he died on September 13, 1336.

Margaret, Duchess of Brabant, daughter of Edward I and aunt of Edward III, was still living in this reign, residing in her son's dominions, which were contiguous to the countship of Hainault. Early in the reign, she was called upon to give security for some Englishman who had got into trouble in the Count of Hainault's territory in a trading dispute.

It is with real regret that we come upon the last days

of that vivid personality, Mary, the nun of Amesbury. She, too, had suffered from the disorders of her brother's reign. Her firewood failed ; the Chief Butler had forgotten her.

With her nephew's accession, Mary the nun is soon upon the scene. Richard de la Pole, the new Butler, received the royal mandate to make up her arrears of wine to the " uttermost farthing," [1] and from several counties oak logs were again furnished for her cell, together with all arrears of them. For the theft of cattle from one of her manors, Robert Crawley was wrongfully arrested, but contrived to leave the court "without a stain," as modern justices would put it. Before the tribunal of Edward's time, Robert was said to " purge his innocence."

An inference as to a foreign sojourn may be made from the fact that two of Edward's subjects are empowered to act as attorneys in England for his aunt Mary for two years from 1330. Of any such journey, however, we have no certainty, nor anything to tell, and the alternative suggestion is that she was entitled to give powers to the persons in question for matters within the kingdom. Perhaps she went on visitation to the French houses of the order. We remember her brother Edward's correspondence with the Abbess of Fontévrault upon the subject of such visitations in the past reign. Perhaps, again, she went to reside for a time at the mother-house. Perhaps she merely was in failing health, and unfit to deal with her estates in England, though the implication is not so strong, for various reasons, as the former, or so it appears to the writer. Then, in 1332, we find that she is dead. Of her fifty-

---

[1] To half a pitcher the compilers of the Calendar of Close Rolls tell us.

three years of life, all but the first seven were spent amidst the retirement and restriction of the cloister. Yet she leaves, in the few glimpses of her personality, a far more stringent impress on the page of England than many other royal women, or even men, of the Plantagenet house.

Isabel, the Queen-mother, was, in the early years of her son's reign, a being of splendour and prestige. Regarded as the saviour of the realm and as the successful nego- tiator of French treaties, Parliament and her son alike could hardly do too much for her. Her dower was raised to the sum of 20,000 marks a year, a splendid income for a queen of her times. In the full strength of her beauty and her charm as a widow of some three-and- thirty years, she fell, as time went on, more and more under the spell of Mortimer, who was marching on in the very footprints of the dead Despensers, to an arrogant assertion of power over the whole kingdom. This man, much older than the Queen, was rapidly completing the subjugation of her being to his dominant personality. Children, and even grandchildren, might provide for him a tacit implication of grey hairs ; yet Roger and the Queen were absorbed in their reciprocal attraction, exchanging the endearments of lovers. The miserable Edward, pent in Gloucester, or Berkeley, Castle, deposed from his sovereignty, might crave the nuptial visit of his queen ; Mortimer, with fierce physical jealousy, deterred the Queen from any impulse to compassion—from any inter- view with the forlorn captive—by assurances of the danger she would run from the discrowned King and his vengeful dagger.

A little later the wretched inmate of Berkeley Castle had shrieked out his existence—his miserable failure of a life —and the whispered horror had made men question whether the new lordship of the realm were not also an evil, successive on the former tyranny of the Despensers. The people, who, with dazzled eye, had acclaimed in Mortimer the deliverer, now turned, with growing perception, a hostile face upon him as a fresh usurper of sovereign dues.

Nearer home, the young King's uncle, Edmund, Earl of Kent, had become an object of apprehension to Isabel and her paramour. His eye must mark, his judgment must condemn, this wanton in high places and her ill-spirit, Mortimer. In his early prime, for he had the years of the century, the Earl of Kent had the robuster qualities of the Plantagenets. His father was the virile Edward I ; for eighteen years he had received the care of Margaret, the " sweet flower of France," his mother. Now, against him, they poured into the ears of his young sovereign fear and suspicion. The poison worked, and Edmund was put to death ; although, says Mr. Joshua Barnes in his history of the reign, " I find no real stain fixed upon him by any."

The earl's death only waked more vigorously the resentful voices both of nobles and of commons. Last of all, upon young Edward's belated perception was this horror thrust. The mother, beautiful, his champion, his idol, was this thing to which all sonship strives to close its eyes. In the rage and anguish of his recoil the King sought to press the thing home, to confront the Queen-mother and the Earl of March in their flagrant hour. Roger, aglow with the new honours of his earldom, was with Isabel at Nottingham, securely established in the castle. It was no part of her son's plan to pay a sovereign's visit there, to be received with all the circumstance of a king's entry, with every fierce utterance of outraged sonship falling flat upon the arrayed front of conventional decorum.   No ; his quest was plainly for the Earl of March, and those in the secret were ready with suggestion for the trapping.   In Saxon times there had been tunnelled a subterranean way into the castle to give a burrow to hard-pressed warriors.   Unused of late, half choked, this dank and musty passage was shown to the young King.   Through it he hurried, escorted by traitors from within and by his own attendants.

Isabel might lay her head for sleep upon the bolster, beneath which, nightly, she placed the castle keys. Earth opened her mouth, and neither she nor Mortimer knew of the ancient way beneath the keep.   The King's followers, swarming in, laid hands on Mortimer, not where they most expected him to be, in the Queen-mother's room, but not far off, and in company which should give a varnish of respectability to his presence in the castle.   It was with the Bishop of Lincoln, a member of the Queen-mother's cabal, that he was found.   Isabel, trembling in her bed, had become aware of her son's presence within her gates.   The scuffle with his attendants for the capture of Earl Roger, a struggle in which the earl's servitors received some wounds, struck her with fear for the fate of her lover.   To her son, or to his henchmen, for the tales are various, she cried for pity on " gallant Mortimer."   She was unheeded.   On the London highway, the aged Earl of Lancaster, who had suffered sorely at the hands of the now captive Roger, tossed his cap into the air with cries of triumph.

Within six weeks, the overbearing favourite was a prisoner in the fateful Tower of London.

Before Queen Isabel there stretched long years of state imprisonment in Rising Castle.

CHAPTER VIII

THE CHILDREN OF THE KING

NOW that this miserable business was accomplished Edward could give himself to happy domesticity. The young Queen, with her charming face and healthy physique, was consolation for the melancholy episode. In the autumn of 1329 she had undergone a narrow escape from serious injury at a tournament held in the City.

Near Eleanor's Cross, in Cheapside, a splendid pageant was displayed. Knights of England challenged their fellows or those of France to the encounter of skill. The royal family was there, and the Queen with her ladies was seated upon a temporary wooden staging. In the midst of the excitement and glitter of the scene of chivalry, the Queen's platform gave way, and she fell, together with her ladies, amidst the broken timbers. Edward, with the hot blood of his grandfather, was furious with the master-workmen who had put up the insufficient structure, and would have had them killed or cruelly punished. But young Philippa played here the part, in which she has become immortal, of suppliant for her husband's pardon to the wrongdoers. As in after-years she clung to the knees of the conqueror of Calais to plead for the doomed burghers of that stronghold, so now she craved her husband and her King to pardon the defaulting carpenters. The King was appeased by the tender hands and the soft voice, and the British workman escaped his penalty.

Philippa received no hurt, and in the following summer bore to her husband Edward, the eldest of the family of twelve which justified the envoys who had drawn up the marriage treaty, and who had enlarged upon the young princess's opulence of form as of good maternal augury.

Children came apace and war did not lag behind. Foreign hostilities of various kind took Edward and his Queen across the Channel. Philippa was left in some place of non-combatant security while Edward led his armies, of English subjects or hired mercenaries, into the field.

Philippa, in her retirement, was "not idle." At the Premonstratensian Convent of St. Michael at Antwerp she gave birth to Lionel, her third son. Little William of Hatfield, her second son, had died in childhood, but Lionel was to live and found a family to which, more than a century later, was born Edward IV of the House of York.

Edward III, returning to her there, made handsome offerings to the monastery in commemoration of the birth and baptism of the infant Leon, and Philippa remained with the hospitable monks during her succeeding pregnancy.

In the spring of 1340, Edward and Philippa were both at Ghent, the Queen remaining there after Edward's return to Antwerp to continue his arrangements for war with France, and here she became the mother of John, known ever since as John of Gaunt, a perversion from the Latin or the Flemish name of his birthplace—John, who, acquiring the duchy of Lancaster by right of his wife, Blanche Plantagenet, daughter of Henry, Duke of Lancaster, was to be ancestor of three reigning houses of England, and a progenitor of fire and bloodshed in the realm for a hundred years on end.

Tales of the "warming-pan" and changeling kind cluster round the birth of John. The Queen having, says one rumour, brought forth an unwanted female child, exchanged it for a male, to avert her consort's disappointment.

Another story has it that she overlaid the babe, and, in her fear of Edward's anger at the accident, procured an infant from outside as substitute for her dead off-spring. But all such tales must be discounted in the light of the fierce enmity between the descendants of the babe of Ghent and those of his elder brother Lionel, the "legitimate" claimants of the English crown. Even the monkish chronicle was conceivably "faked" by partizan scribes, and the issues clouded even more by the time-server.[1]

A fine and lusty boy, he slumbers in his cradle or in his mother's bed, heedless and unknowing of the rose which should put forth its white and crimson challenge to a kingdom.

The fifth son of the King and Queen came to celebrate an interval of peace. War for the time was at an end; the sovereign and Queen Philippa had returned to England, and in the summer of 1341, at King's Langley, was born Edmund, known as Edmund of Langley, who was to be a common ancestor of York and Tudor kings.

[1] See Introduction by Sir E. Maunde Thompson to *St. Albans Chronicle*. Record Series.

The neighbouring Abbey of St. Albans was the scene of the young prince's baptism.

There were other sons and daughters, too, besides these more eminent and fateful ones. Some leave a name, and no more, in their swiftly-ended lives.

Joan, the eldest daughter, born, like her aunt Joan, Queen of Scotland, in the Tower of London, became the wife of a sovereign of Spain.

The second daughter, Isabel Plantagenet, like her great-aunt Eleanor, Duchess of Bar, seems to have taken a good deal of giving in marriage before, at thirty-one years of age, she finally became the Lady de Couci.

Flanders had played a trick in the boyhood of Edward II. The King of France had been the *diabolus ex machinâ* on that occasion.

Again, in the reign of Edward III, a king of France was to abet the trickery of a count of Flanders. For Edward was ready to negotiate a contract between young Louis of Flanders and Isabel, then in her early teens, and somewhat older than the count. The count, indeed, was then in durance to the King of England, but all was to be adjusted by this family enterprise. Behind the scenes, however, John, Duke of Brabant, and Philip, King of France, had an understanding relating to a desired marriage between the duke's daughter and the youthful Count of Flanders.

The King of France was in with John. The Flemings, however, were all in favour of the English King, and they cordially invited Edward and his queen to bring their daughter along with them to a place of meeting to which they would bring their lord, and there conclude the marriage contract.

" Now you must know that the King and Queen were

at these tidings mightily rejoiced, and said the Flemings were fine fellows."

To the Abbey of Bergues, near Gravelines, came then all the notables of Flanders, with utmost pomp and circumstance, escorting their youthful lord, "who courteously bowed himself before the King and Queen of England, who had already arrived there in great state.

"The King of England took the said count by the right hand most gently and stroked it as he spoke ; and then declared himself innocent of the death of the count's father ; saying, for so help him God, that neither on the day of Creci nor on the morrow had he either seen nor heard of the count his father."

Young Louis feigned a credence of the statement. He went beyond and agreed for " Madame Isabelle." Days passed, and at length the Flemings escorted their seigneur back to Flanders, while Edward and Philippa returned *moult aimablement* to Calais and the siege thereof.

The Flemings held the thing for sure, which showed, remarks Jean Froissart, that they did not understand their lord, "for he, whatever was his outward seeming, held within a courage purely French."

The count then, with his unmelted-butter air, betook him on a certain day in Easter week, 1346, to the sport of hawking. Uttering the huntsman's "halloo" of the day, Count Louis spurred his steed and gave his guards the slip. So he came into France and to King Philip, " to whom he related his adventures, and how, *par grand' subtilité*, he had escaped alike from his own subjects and the English."

The King of France, as may be well believed, *en eut grand' joie*, but the English naturally felt they had been "had." Edward, however, was too just to blame the Flemings, whom he knew to be *moult courroucés*, and their excuses, which they made, he readily accepted.

In 1346, when Edward had gone off to France, he left his second surviving son, Lionel, as regent of the kingdom. The boy, then about eight years old, spent some time during his parents' absence at the manor house of Beames, in Wiltshire, with his younger brothers and sisters, and there the peace of the royal children was rudely disturbed by one of the fiercely lawless episodes of mediæval England.

For on Good Friday morn of 1347, before dawn, there came a bold and wicked knight,—John Dalton was his name,—and carried off the lady of the manor, Margery de la Beche, a widow, then betrothed, as it would seem, to Gerard de l'Isle.[1]

A crowd of persons belonging to the estates were placed under arrest, as well as some adherents of the knight.

His father, Robert Dalton, was among them, also a parish priest. For the abduction had been forcibly opposed, and in the scrimmage wounds and even death had been dealt out. Michael Poynings, "le uncle," had been killed in the *émeute*, and Margery's chaplain had died of fright. Orders were issued far and wide. Edward of Scots, as Keeper of the Scottish Border, received a mandate to arrest the knight, who might be making his way towards those parts. The sheriffs were apprised, the hue-and-cry was raised from end to end of England. Sir John Dalton got away, however, to some Gretna of the time, for he married Margery and she outlived him. The father, Robert Dalton, went over seas and sur-

---

[1] She is spoken of in one instance on the Rolls as "lawful wife" of De l'Isle.

rendered to King Edward, and the greater number of the persons implicated in the affair were able to prove their innocence, having been in the position merely of the man who deserved all he got, said Lord Beaconsfield, if he were arrested on a scene of riot.

Great stress is laid, in the account of the affair, on " the terror of the Keeper of the Realm," but we have found no record of the amount of damages exacted from the creator of all this shocking uproar.

He was indeed a very wicked knight !

At the time of the incident young Lionel had been already for five years betrothed to his cousin Elizabeth Burke, daughter of the Earl of Ulster, whom in due time he married, obtaining, in right of his wife's heirship, the family earldom of Ulster and the remoter honour of Clare, or Clarence.

It was, however, by his second marriage, with Violanta of Milan, that Lionel Plantagenet became ancestor of the York dynasty and of Edward IV, and thereby also of King Edward VII.

Edmund of Langley, Duke of York, was yet another victim of the King of France's interfering proclivities in matters of England and Flanders. He was proposed for a daughter of the Count of Flanders, but Charles stepped in, and in the end obtained the Flemish marriage for his brother, Philip, Duke of Burgundy, while the Duke of York, as husband of Joan Holland, became, in common with his brother Lionel, the progenitor of the royal lines of York and Tudor.

The heroic figure of Edward the Black Prince is in the eye of every child of England from his earliest schooldays. His black armour, his doings at Creci, watched by his father from a windmill, his three feathers annexed from the blind King of Bohemia, his high bearing to his captive, by whose splendid steed he rode "on a little black palfrey" : these are willingly remembered among more urgent matters of crude exactitude.

Young Edward was a lusty and a splendid babe, and his welfare, as well as that of his younger brothers and sisters, was the special object of his mother, who herself nursed her own offspring, not relegating them, as was the common manner with royal infants, to the vicarious attention of the wet-nurse, as we know that Edward III was relegated.

The glow and glamour which surround Edward Plantagenet in our earliest arbitrary impression are not swept from our vision by a nearer seeking into his records. From his stripling days he is the frank and generous prince and kinsman. His appanage is drawn upon for many gifts. To his mother he presents a sumptuous garment. Philippa has still youth enough to deck herself delightedly in gauds—at the hands of such a first-born, too. Could any mother be aught but young in love for such a son as Edward ? The young Prince of Wales—so he was created at thirteen years of age—lived in his London mansion on the marge of Thames, where his swans mirrored their whiteness in the waters of the stream, clearer then than now. Cannon Street must run through his erstwhile demesne, through his gardens perhaps, which were not scientifically tended nor regarded, for if John or Adam could deal with Windsor, we need not look for a large or learned staff at the prince's town abode.

The Black Prince's years were, like his father's, filled with the cry of battle. Generously did the King of England share with his heir the glory of Creci.

Edward knew his son, and would not interfere with the meed of that day's valour. The anxious military staff would even dare to urge reinforcements, but the proud father stayed his hand. " Let him win his spurs ! " he cried to those who trembled for the prince's issue from the strenuous conflict.

For light amour there could have been no great space in Edward's time. Two, beyond his legitimate children, are credited to him. Even the necessities of dynasty did not press him into marriage till his third decade. And then it was no alliance of diplomacy, no closer linkage with a foreign Power, that Edward made. The Black Prince fell a victim partly to the charm, partly to the delightful wiles, of a cousin rather older than himself, Joan, daughter of the Earl of Kent who had been put to death by Mortimer's influence early in the reign. Through the death of her brothers, Joan had succeeded in her own right to the earldom of Kent. Lovely and well-dowered, she inspired and reciprocated amorous emotion. Indeed, her experiments in matrimony were great in their complication.

She was already an object of design on the part of the second Earl of Salisbury when his squire, Sir Thomas Holland, had sailed in before his lord and annexed the fair Joan, sealing her for his own in a manner indisputable and irrevocable to boot. A contract stood for the public side of the affair when Holland had to leave his bride, who was also essentially his wife, though nuptial Mass and benediction had not as yet been uttered over them.

The beautiful Countess as a grass widow was no less provocative than as a maiden to the Earl of Salisbury. Joan, indeed, was torn in two by her lovers,

for Salisbury claimed her with fierce mediæval owner-
ship and ardour for his own. He may, indeed, have
laid hands on the entrancing countess and carried her
away. We have already come upon high-handedness of
such a kind among names less notable than theirs.

Salisbury alleged a promise, but, fiercely, Holland
opposed his "contract" and the unanswerable clinching
of the fleshly bond. The Pontiff and the Papal Curia
were the sole effective arbitrators in so poignant an
impasse. Rome decided in a manner perfectly logical.
The essence of the nuptial sacrament itself lies in the
free-will rendering of each to either : the solemn
contract verged so near that it constituted *per se* an
impediment to other marriage. Adultery would have
lain in cohabitation with the earl, not in the ungar-
nished incipience of the relations between the knight
and his lovely mistress.

"The Pope took her from the Earl of Salisbury and
gave her to her gallant, Sir Thomas Holand," is the quite
inaccurate version of a later chronicler.

Court circles did not, of course, encourage such
flinging of the cap over the windmill. Still, Joan was
not cut by her relatives. Her cousin, the young Prince
of Wales, stood godfather to one of her sons. The
countess is believed to be that "Jeannette," his kinswoman, to whom the open-handed prince presented
"a large silver beaker enamelled at the base, provided
with a cover having crenellated ornament, and parcel-
gilt withal."

There came a day when Joan, with her little family,
was left bereaved. Holland was dead, yet to be a
"widow indeed" was not the way of the Fair Maid
of Kent. Another suitor had entered the lists, a hench-

man of the Black Prince.   Edward took upon himself to
plead the wooer's cause.   The young widow, however,
had quite other visions in her mind.   "Never," she
declared, "would she wed again to one less than herself."

"If haply such a knight as yourself, Sir Prince ; yet
failing this, I entreat you not to urge me to other
wedlock."

What was left for this sun of chivalry but to shine
responsive on the lovely widow ?   Joan, with her for-
givable ensnaring, her "come-hither-in-the-e'e," was
irresistible to the heir-apparent, as he stood before her
full of the vigour of his thirty years of splendid manhood.
There was, however, a crowd of impediments to be got
rid of before Joan could become Princess of Wales and
second lady in the land.

There was nearness of blood, for Edward was her
first cousin once removed, and a still further complication
was that of spiritual affinity, for her son had "been
raised from the font" by the prince.   To Rome appeal
was made.   There was work enough provided for the
Holy See by Joan and her marriages.   All was brought
through successfully, however, and the new Princess
of Wales was alike the guest and hostess of the King and
Queen of England a short time after the marriage.

Of Joan's appearance, except that she was beautiful
and melting-eyed, we can tell nothing.   Indeed,
chroniclers, being mainly austere and learned monks,
who would not suitably be concerned with study of
fair ladies, are almost dumb upon the subject of the
features of the royal ladies whom they write into their
annals.

So whether they were Saxon blond or Norman
dusky-haired we have not often found, nor if their eyes

were hazel or blue, or the violet, which is azure seen through the trellis of black lash.

Chaucer, whose heroines more than once possessed "an ey as gray as glas," is reticent about these court ladies, whom yet he must have known with some intimacy.

A sculptured head of Joan is told of, but without an *imprimatur* of authority.

Sorrow fell upon the home when the eldest child of Edward and of Joan, a boy Edward, was cut off in early years.

Richard, their younger, born in France, was to wear the crown after his grandfather, the third Edward, and to be the last of the reigning house of Plantagenet, though the blood was to continue in the usurping Lancastrians and the rightful Yorkists.

CHAPTER IX

WARRIORS, KNIGHTS, AND THE ORDER OF THE GARTER

WAR, one of the horrible necessities of Time, has been amply treated of by many chroniclers and critics ; not least as it relates to Edward III, great among warrior-kings of history.

It is enough for us to skim over the tale of battle with a touch or two, to give us a rough background for the more detailed scene of peace.

The insubstantial amnesty with Scotland, made at the King's accession, was soon split. The King of Scots had died in an early year and was succeeded by his brother David, and soon the seldom sleeping antagonism was on the upspring.

Then came the wars with France and Edward's claim to sovereignty in that realm in right of Isabel his mother, based on the non-judicial character of the Salic custom, which barred female inheritance.

We have heard and read of the confusion of ideas which led Edward to argue his claim upon a basis which, if allowed, would have put a female cousin of the Valois family on the throne of France without more pother. We are not here to enter on such already threshed-out questions, but to see something of the by-play of royal personality.

While Philippa brought future warriors into the world, Edward, the King, was at the head of armies on the fields of France.

Here is Peter Byne, a great merchant of the society of the Bardi of Italy, receiving, with his fellows, a royal command to buy, in places "convenient" for the King, good and reliable armour for a hundred men.

Peter is greatly to the fore; he seems to have supplied the place of Andrew de Pessaigne, the right-hand man of Edward II. Sometimes he is Italianized as Byni. He may have been one of the Sussex family of Byne, who are already heard of in Plantagenet times. Other Bynes are heard of too, one as a collector of the customs at "Troy Town." [1]

Peter and his guild received royal licence to export wool from England at a time when it was generally forbidden, even to the merchants of the Staple.

Our King had come to great renown when he was appointed by the Emperor of Germany as his viceroy. Though, as a political event, this may fall without our present scope, yet we must not pass over the picture of old Froissart, who covers many sins of inexactitude by the naïve and vivid offerings of his pages.

It was at Herck, in Flanders, that the viceregal installation took place in October (Froissart has it at Martinmas).

"You must know that when all had assembled there the town was filled to overflowing with lords and knights and squires, and with people of all condition; the market-hall, where bread and meat were sold, was draped with splendid hangings, even as though it were the King's chamber; and there sat the English King, and

[1] He was collector for Plymouth and Fowey.

on his head his golden crown *moult riche et moult noble*. And there, raised five feet higher than all others, he sat upon a butcher's block, just where the butcher cuts and sells his joints. Never was market-place so honoured."

Money was often "tight" with the King of England. Wars drained his coffers. The fifteen months' hostilities, between July, 1346, and October, 1347, which included the siege of Calais, involved a special stringency. As in a host of instances, the religious houses and the secular prelates of England were called upon for loans. In the year of Calais, Edward was borrowing all round. Both the great gold crown and the crown of Queen Philippa were in pawn on several occasions and for long spaces of time.

The Archbishop of Treves advanced 25,000 Florentine florins on the one, while one of those merchant princes of Italy, Anthony Bache, lent 34,000 florins for the hire of mercenaries to fight "beyond the seas" in 1340.

In May, 1347, the great crown had safely returned to England, through the efforts of William de Melchbourn, the King's merchant, who had carried through the business of redeeming it from pawn and had conveyed it to England. An annual pension of £20 awarded to him speaks of a not unreasonable relief and gratitude on the part of the sovereign.

The siege which gained Calais for the English crown and made it a possession of England for two centuries, absorbed Edward's energies for more than a year and involved him in immense expenditure. Even as late as August, 1347, Edward is borrowing all round. We find him urging on the clerics of England his supreme need—"as necessity pushes him harder, and peril will overtake the King, the realm, and the Anglican Church if the King be obliged to withdraw from the war; and he cannot continue it without larger subsidies."

The loans or grants were not refused, and in October, 1347, Edward was established before Calais till it should surrender. And to give all furtherance to this end he built his ex-mural township, Ville-Neuve-la-Hardie, between Calais and the river, " fit to last a dozen years and munished with all the equipment of an army and far more. . . . Here was a fixed place wherein to hold a market on Saturday and Wednesday, and there were mercers' shops and butchers' stalls and the halls for cloth and bread and all other necessaries, and all these things were brought in by sea from England and from Flanders, so that they were well supplied with victuals and with wares.

" Now the captain of Calais was a doughty knight of Burgundy, a fighter of renown, called Messire Jean de Vienne."

And when the governor saw Edward's preparation for a ruthless siege he ordered all such people as had no means of livelihood to quit the town without delay. Men, women, and children in uncertain number were thus expelled. According to one, five hundred, from another point of recollection nearly two thousand. These did the doughty Jehan in the cruel strait send forth among the foe. And in his grim plan could have been no great tincture of hope that they might meet with mercy, for the age in general would put such wretched *expurgata* to the sword. Nearly three centuries later than this indeed, in France, were the Béarn townships burned during the civil revolt and their inmates put to the sword.

Great is the conflict of account as to the end of the extruded burghers. One says that, unable to pass the English lines, they died of winter cold and of starvation. But let us look upon the page of Froissart and read his tale of Edward's magnanimity. For, says he, " They left the town upon a Wednesday morn and entered the English camp. And were there asked wherefore they had evacuated. They answering said that they had no subsistence. Then the King granted them safe-conduct through his lines and gave them all a dinner, plentiful and good, and after dinner to every one of them two *esterlins,* the which grace and bounty was esteemed *moult belle : ce fut bien raison."*

Froissart, we may admit, was, as one in the service of the English court, a prejudiced recorder, but other foreign chroniclers note the English custom of sparing the life of enemies once vanquished, instead of putting them to the sword in the manner of the European Powers in general.

With every month, with every week, the city-circling English drew the noose of fate more closely. The little sloops which, in the laxer days, had slipped down from Boulogne, hugging the coast, to bring provision to the city could no longer cheat the picket boats. King Philip's tactics had failed to relieve the pressed and starving garrison. The governor planned a desperate sortie, willing to fall sword in hand, with glory, rather than to die of ignominious starvation when the rats, the horses, and yet more final nourishment was at an end. Froissart, who elsewhere has a surprised word to say of the rough English army provender, the dry biscuit, the carcass roasted in its skin, could find no *plat* so filling, and so savoury even, here in Calais. The rat-ragout of the besieged, did it not even fail at length, maybe for lack of fuel ?

The final arbitration of Pope Clement VI had come to naught ; the Bishop of Tusculum and Cardinal Aubert had failed in the object of their nunciature, for Edward, like his fathers, was not easily amenable to the Holy See in temporal affairs.

During the earlier part of Edward's absence, Philippa was engaged on his behalf in combat with the Scots, with whom the oft-renewed hostilities were then on foot. Valiantly she played her part with the King's forces. Whether she did indeed appear in person on the field of battle on the land of Neville we may leave to the academics of criticism, for, even without that final touch to the picture, we have in the combat one typically representative of martial event in those Middle Ages out of which England was even then passing, and that, in the words of a Froissart attuned to the naïve story-telling of the age. For Jehan makes us see, encamped at a distance from Newcastle of *trois petites lieues anglesches, le roy d'Ecosse et tout son ost* in colours which know no tarnish from the hand of time. And when her work was done, the valiant Queen went across to Calais, "not without trial and danger," to join her husband.

And there, in a scene which will never grow dim in the picture-gallery of our imagination, Philippa knelt before the King her husband and wrestled for the lives of the doomed burghers, headed by Eustache de St. Pierre, who waited in shirt and halter to die for the people. Eighteen years had passed since, in her wedded girlhood she had knelt in Cheap to pray for the master-carpenters. She had borne Edward many children, and journeyed many long days' journeys. Even now, she was awaiting maternity at an early day.

"Lady, I would thou hadst not asked it of me," protested Edward, but the day was won and the six condemned were clothed and feasted.

It is true that property forfeited by one of them was granted to the Queen, but an extremist only would cavil at so common a custom of the time. In his deprivation the burgher was honoured by such a successor to his share of the soil of Calais.

If the reign of the third Edward resounded with the clash of arms, it uttered also with the softer voices of the arts and crafts of peace. Of the one, Calais and the triple plume were monuments. Windsor displayed the fairer edifices of peace. For here, where this great Edward had been born, from which he took his local epithet, Edward de Wyndesore, and where, in the royal chapel he was baptized—here he caused to rise the chapel dedicated to Our Lady, St. George, and St. Edward, upon the foundations, or as an enlargement, of the chapel built by his ancestors. Here he founded a secular community of twenty-three canons to serve the chapel, and set a warden at their head, that they might act as chaplains to the now collegiate church in place of the two chaplains who had served in the preceding reigns. And to supersede the stipends given by the sovereigns, he endowed the community with lands in several dioceses, promising to make up their yearly grant to the value of £1,000.

Some years earlier, Edward had been occupied, among other works at Windsor Castle, in building what was perhaps the Round Tower there.[1] The chroniclers talk

---

[1] See on this point a letter in Bodley's Library, Ashmolean MSS. 1131, f. 264.

of his Round Table, set up as a successor to that of King
Arthur ; also they tell of how the King of France set up
one too, and endeavoured to attract the knights of Italy
and Germany to the rival board. The easiest solution
seems to be that the Round Tower was built with the
motive, primary or secondary, of serving as a scene for
the meetings of the Table Round.[1]

When the collegiate chapel of St. George was established there was set up in connection with it the little
company of twenty-four poor knights of Windsor, of
whom, though their establishment is set forth clear upon
the records, we remember little in comparison with that
glowing Order of the Garter, the origin of which remains
still wrapped in fable. For though historical critics, or
critical historians, will destroy the nursery legend, so
attractive, of Lady Joan's garter, dropped at the court
ball, yet they have constructed nothing convincing, or
even plausible, to fill its niche.

The lady may or may not have been Joan Plantagenet,
Countess of Salisbury. It is uncertain that she danced at
a court ball or that the dance was understood in such a
connection in the reign of Edward III.

Was she a fair flame of the King, and did the courtiers
smile their covert, knowing, smile, convinced of amorosity
on Edward's part when he stood holding the garter shed so
inopportunely by the shamefaced lady ? Or did the King
simply desire to cool her blushes at her own mishap,
without any question of rebuke to the beliefs of the
beholders on that other score ? Whatever may be said,
it is no ill origin after all of a glorious order that it should
have been thus rooted in pure chivalry. Queen Philippa

---

[1] "Rex Edwardus . . . cœpit ædificare domum quæ Rotunda
Tabula vocaretur."—*Chronicle of St. Albans.*

it was, say others, who was the heroine of the dropped garter, which came off as she left the King's chamber. The courtiers would have kicked it on one side, but the King, taking it up, said he would yet make a garter a thing most glorious before them all.

A writer of the seventeenth century plunges back to classic eras for the origin of the ligature. It was the fillet of purple dye with which men girt themselves below the breast as amulet against the perils of the deep.

Others it would better please to think that Edward nailed a garter to his pennon and made his battle-cry on some great day therefrom.

The wearing of the gem-set band beneath the knee is undoubtedly a curiosity. Had some noble lady given her girdle for a gage, we might, in fancy, see the sovereign fastening it, too small for his middle, but fitting to his lower limb, and adopting it thus for part of the insignia of a new order. Or, again, there would be plausibility in the hypothesis that some gentle feminine assistant in the background of the field of battle may have made use of her garter to bind the wounds of a prince or of his liege. Of all this there is, however, no least ghost of record. Again, if the garter had been evolved from the ring, at which knights tilted, its adjustment to the knee still remains unclear.

It was on St. George's Day, 1349, that the Order of the Garter was formally initiated, when Edward and the knights-companions went together in solemn procession to St. George's Chapel.

They were clad in robes of russet and mantles of fine blue cloth powdered with the Garter, and wore the collars of the order and two long blue silk cords depending from the collar ; and the other badges, which are, however, not exactly specified. Within the chapel, the Bishop of Winchester, who was the first appointed chaplain to the order,[1] sang Mass, and the installation followed. After the more solemn ceremonies were over, the King entertained the new knights at a splendid banquet, and for several days after there were gorgeous tournaments.

It remains more lustrous to-day than ever, an honour welcomed by crowned heads no less than by great nobles. It has been the choicest offering bestowed on foreign guests of special eminence. The Duc de Chevreuse was a recipient at the time of the marriage of Charles I, for whom he stood proxy and whose ancestry he shared.

Queen Victoria reminds a correspondent of the reservation of the dignity which had precluded her from bestowing it even on illustrious relatives. Each sovereign of England becomes *ex officio* sovereign of the order. The sovereign's place is the only one which remains unaltered in position, and, in the earliest day, that was not so, and the King sat according to his chronological status. The Lady of the Garter is now the sovereign's consort,[2] and this by no inherent claim but by bestowal. In earlier times, however, other royal ladies sometimes received the honour.

---

[1] At a later date the Bishop of Salisbury disputed (as diocesan ?) the right of holding the appointment.

[2] The reference here is to H.M. Queen Alexandra.

CHAPTER X

THE DECADENCE

THE glorious reign of Edward III had reached its apogee. Reverses on the Continent were not more symptomatic of the turn of glory than were the abuses to which a plethora of prosperity had given rise in the internal economies of the kingdom. The coffers of the knights were glutted with the loot of French campaigns ; they " were pestered " with the very multitude of their acquisitions. In every English household appeared some token of these imports, whether in fine linen or in feminine jewel or finery.

The general standard of living had gone up. For though it might be a fable of the gods which Chaucer sings—

> " Of down of pure doves white
> I will give him a feather-bed
> Rayed with gold and right well clad,
> In fine black satin doutremere,"

it was but an apotheosis, doubtless, of the luxurious bedding which replaced, at the court of Edward III, the ruder sack of straw which had furnished earlier Plantagenets.

Certainly the linen of Brittany was in use, as famed as Irish is to-day :—

> "And many a pillow, and every bere [1]
> Of cloth of Rennes, to sleepë soft."

The merchant class evinced the tendency in apparel, or in silver-plate ; even the labourer's cottage saw meat and drink of more luxurious kind than formerly.

The King sought to amend the condition by sumptuary laws—always most irksome of enactments—and by even more domestic legislation.

Even the peasant's board was invaded by the new restrictions. A limit was to be set to the costliness and refinement of the viands which piled the trencher or of the draught which brimmed the beaker. An autocracy of the breakfast table, in very truth, was here. For kings' daughters, it is true that beeves and bacon had been the mainstay of the wedding-feast till recent years at least. What was the style of living that had called down the royal ban ? Had the light wine of Gascony found its way in place of the small beer ?

The Nonnë Preestë in the moral tract with which she told the tale of Chantecler and "faire Pertelote"—to which the twentieth century has added French perversions and that "strange woman" *la Faisane*—this pilgrim, as she beguiled, or bored, her eight-and-twenty fellow-travellers on the Canterbury road, pictured the perfect thing in widows :—

> "No wine ne drank she, neither white ne red ;
> Her board was servèd most with white and black,
> Milk and brown bread, in which she found no lack,
> Sound bacon, and sometime an egg or two."

---

[1] Pillow-slip.

In the *Romaunt of the Rose* we find the alluring tale
of contrast :—

> " But they defend hem with lamprey,
> With luce, with eels, with salmóns,
> With tender geese and with capóns,
> With tartës or with cheeses fat,
> With dainty flawnës broad and flat,
> With caleweys or with pulaille,
> With coninges, or with fine vitaille.
>
> *   *   *   *
>
> Or but he wol do come in haste
> Roe-venison ybake in paste."

Table manners were receiving attention.   Madame
Eglantine, the prioress-pilgrim, is our example.   For,
besides her other accomplishments—

> " Full well she sung the service divine,
> Entuned in her nose full seemly ;
> And French she spake full fair and fetisly,
> After the school of Stratford at the Bow,
> For French of Paris was to her unknow."

We are further told—

> " She let no morsel from her lippës fall,
> Ne wet her fingers in her saucë depe ;
> Well could she carry a morsel and well keep,
> That no drop ne fell upon her breast.
>
> *   *   *   *
>
> Her over lippë wipèd she so clean,
> That in her cuppë was no farthing seen
> Of grease when she drunken had her draught."

As with the crown of the lady in Piers the Ploughman's
Vision—

> (" The King hath ne better ")—

so the palace can scarcely have surpassed the refinements of this Chaucerian heroine.

With regard to dress, restriction was aimed necessarily at material and adornment, rather than at any generalities of "cut" or *façon*. For there was, especially in women's dress, a certain uniformity, and less caprice of Lady Fashion than in later times. There is, practically, no difference in general outline between the dress of one of Edward's daughters and her "damsel's."

The princess might wear the richer material, trimmed perhaps with "breast of miniver," a fur which was also the right of legal dignitaries.

Her train was longer, her jewels more famed and resplendent. Yet the simple skirt and the bodice cut low in the bust—the opening being veiled with a "modestie," not revelling in "frou-frou" but austerely extended between the *revers* of the bodice—in the general fashioning of it all there was small distinction.

Nor did the royal lady's headgear stun the sight with any splendour which was not to be found in that of her lady-in-waiting or her handmaid. For the towering sugar-loaf of black taffaty, or lesser stuff, backed possibly with the same stiffening that fortified the Garter, displays no individualism. The veil, or wimple, which floated from the peak, abraded or acute, was no doubt distinctive in some gossamery quality in the royal or noble lady.

Velvet, serge, and russet cloth might mark the three estates of the realm. Yet of the latter we speak with no assurance, for the Knights of the Garter wore "russet" mantles, and whether the distinction indicated, in this place, related to colour, or to textile variety, it would be rash to say.

The robes of chivalry and the sheath of armour

A PRINCESS, HER LADY AND HER LUGGAGE
FOURTEENTH CENTURY

remained the common garb of the upper ranks of society. The jerkin and tightly fitting small clothes are seen on the ordinary citizen. Squires attend their lords in boots reaching to the thigh, the Wellingtons, or Bluchers, of Plantagenet days. The surcoat, of which a modification survives in the herald's tabard, was a gorgeous donation of colour, even on the field. No khaki tints for mediæval warriors! No thought to cheat the eye when, breast to breast, crossbow-men twanged their strings, and a half-pike's length alone intervened between the mounted knights and their fell adversaries.

Even the "engins," the *machines* or the *springalds*, hurled their bombs of stone at near range against the walls of the besieged city and the enemy upon them.

The resilient power of these engines of warfare must have been largely obtained by the use of horsehair; 600 lbs. of this are ordered by the King to be sent for the purposes of his "springalds" in the Tower.

The naïve artist of exquisite miniatures, in contemporary MS. histories of sieges, pictures the besieging forces squeezed up against the lower courses of the fortress, directing on the inhabitants, who yet are taken altogether by surprise, a piece of ordnance which, as the late Mr. H. Noel Humphreys humorously remarks, "looks as likely to be detrimental to themselves as to their adversaries."

Though we still find that the old servants are sometimes sent to end their days in monasteries, there is not such a wholesale relegation of them to those retreats as in the days of Edward's father. It is a happy picture to come upon that ancient man, Richard

Clebury, who had served as cook during the two preceding reigns, and who receives sick leave with full pay and his clothing, and then, if too infirm to return to work, is to have his wages paid at the Exchequer.

Agatha, the washerwoman, who is too feeble to cross the seas with her royal master, is granted 4½d. a day till his return.

Wages became higher during this reign, either on account of long service or in concord with a general advance in financial conditions.

The gardener at Windsor Castle, John, who, if he be the John of Edward II, had served a quarter of a century, had a "rise," his wages being 2½d. instead of the earlier 2d. a day.

A new gardener is appointed, and his name is Alexander.

The most striking increase is in the wages of the keeper of the beasts at the Tower, for Berenger Caudrer was in receipt of 12d. a day for wages and of 2s. 1d. for the maintenance of the lions and leopards. These must have multiplied either by nature or by purchase, one most suppose. Berenger's wages fell into arrears at times, in the press of foreign or Scottish campaigns, and here once more comes in Peter Byne and his colleagues, who pay the arrears due to Berenger on the King's behalf.

Elizabeth, wife of Lionel Plantagenet, gives a present to the keeper of the lions on her visit to the Tower.[1]

The stocking of the game-larder gives us suggestion of sport at its most picturesque, when Robert Curzon, the bishop's "yeoman," journeys forth with his gay goshawk and furnished with "safe conduct," to take

[1] *Life Records of Chaucer.* (Chaucer Society.)

pheasant and partridge for young King Edward and his Chancellor (Hotham, Bishop of Ely).

Royal wines were not all suited for laying down during this reign, any more than they had been in the preceding one. They suffered too from causes quite extraneous to their lack of "body." For here in a quiet Wiltshire village is an outburst of most rude depravity on the part of the yokels; rural high-waymen indeed, who seized upon two wagons of the Queen's, each drawn by a team of six and laden with two great casks of wine, valued at £40, belonging to the Queen. The rustic freebooters kept the goods and wagons for so long, from mere ruffianism it would seem, that the wine entirely "perished." The wretched teams, more sadly, also "perished" — of hunger.

There were vintners, too, who were up to wicked faking of their liquor. They and their "tied houses" would mix together wine of good and feeble kind, selling it as "fine and fruity" or "grand wine"—in terms of mediæval equivalent. Edward calls upon the mayor and sheriffs of London to see that "such malpractices cease."

The high living, or something, had an ill-effect upon a good many of the provision merchants of the time. Here is a most sweeping indictment from which none seems to be excluded.

"The butcher, the baker, the candlestick-maker," to-gether with the fish and poultry mongers, brewers, and tavern-keepers, are all found wanting: they are "lax in their misteries"; while evil persons march with swords and staves through London City, beating and ill-treating the single passer-by.

The fearful pestilence which visited England in this reign was, like other mediæval scourges, mainly a filth disease.

Again the Mayor of London is at fault, again the King calls him to order, contrasting his neglect of sanitary regulations with his predecessors' vigilance. In 1349 the Mayor is called upon to clear the streets of the City of filth and human *excreta*, and remove all to a distance, and to see that both City and suburb are kept as clean as in the time of preceding mayors, the danger being all the greater from the contagious sickness then prevailing.

Plate does not reveal any feature of great development during the reign of Edward III. The most curious article encountered is the griffin's egg mounted in silver gilt, belonging to a citizen of Bristol and taken into the King's custody on behalf of the owner. Golden buckles set with a great ruby and with one large emerald and a smaller one, flanked with diamonds, are among the jewels of Joan and Isabel, King Edward's eldest daughters. The spoils of foreign conquest would introduce *art nouveau* into the designs of the English goldsmiths. The latter figure in an early deed of Edward's reign, which enacted that none of that "mystery" shall keep shop anywhere but in Cheapside.

The Girdlers' Guild received protective grants from the King, regulating the degree of base metal which should be employed in ornamenting girdles of silk or wool, leather or linen ; beaten work or open work of steel or iron might be employed, but the sham of lead, tin or pewter, used by rivals outside the civic bar, to the great damage of the craftsmen of the City, was declared illegal, and all girdles so ornamented were to be burned.

Chaucer, who was the court poet of the reign, as well as Master of the Household, sings of the knight, Sir Thopas, whose

> ". . . fine hauberk,
> Was all ywrought of Jewës work,
> Full strong it was of plate,
> And over that his coat-armour,
> As white as is a lily-flower,
> In which he will debate.
>
> His shield was all of gold so red,
> And therein was a boar's head,
> A carbuncle beside ;
> And there he swore on ale and bread
> How that the giant shall be dead,
> Betidë what betide."

The knight had not set forth, indeed, without a cheering cup—

> " They set him first the sweet wine
> And mead eke in a maselyn
> And royal spicery
> Of ginger-bread that was full fine
> And liquourice and eke cummin
> With sugar that is so try."

And through many verses the tale of the good knight had been heard. But Sir Thopas fell upon a day of austerity—

> " Himself drank water of the well,
> As did the knight Sir Percival,
> So worthy under wede,
> Till on a day ——"

[Here the Host stinteth Chaucer of his Tale of Thopas.]

And this is not wonderful, seeing the injury to business that would result from a teetotal Thopas.

Of Chaucer's life at court and his disgrace, of his wife and of her reputed relationship to Katharine Swinford, John of Gaunt's mistress and later wife, all that is as yet known may be studied in the works of the Chaucer Society.

When John of Gaunt addresses him as cousin it may imply a family relationship, but it is also, not impossibly, an allusion to a joint spiritual sponsorship.

If the little wheels in the arms of a later Chaucer, whose kinship to Geoffrey has not, however, been proved, are allusive to the *rouet* and to the De Roet descent of himself from a female of the same family as that of which Katharine Roet (Swinford) was an heiress, or whether Chaucer's wife was related, not to the Roets directly but to the Swinford family—these are points giving a large scope to the leisured investigator.

To the reader in general who enjoys the pithy tale of this fourteenth-century poet the question is a secondary one.

From these general aspects of the social state we must come back to Edward III himself, now sinking into years and mental decadence.

Domestic sorrow had pressed in upon the ageing King.

Philippa, the sharer of more than forty years of wedlock, had passed from the side of her husband and from the midst of her children.

The Black Prince, who had never recovered from an illness taken abroad, and, of course, ascribed to poison, but which may, in fact, have been some form of renal disorder—he, too, had passed from his family and from the nation.

These were the days when the " strange woman "
wound her blandishments around the senile residue of
a great king. Alice, wife of my lord Windsor, whether
as the mistress or as the greedy parasite, brought tarnish
to the great Plantagenet in those last years of gloom.

Edward had not, as did his grandfather, taken a second
wife. No younger family woke the echoes of those sere
years of his fifth decade. But Alice, with the breast of
woman and with the claws that naught relinquish,
hovered round the stricken warrior.

How far was she of harpy-kind, how far created by
monster-breeding clamour ? She appears, in solid being,
as a litigant at Westminster, the wife of a great servant
of the crown. Anon, she swells like any Eastern jinn,
fertile in crime. The haze of fable quivers round her.
To restore her to her bottle is beyond the coldest of the
archivists, to write her down for what she was indeed.
Sweeping aside examples which make an everlasting yea
in such regard, some commentators, "rushing out of
doors," deny that Edward had with this woman amorous
relations ; she was merely an avaricious lady of his court.
There are always champions prepared with a blind eye
towards the sexual point in their heroes. Yet with what
general futility ! Alice Perrers, as the mistress, kept
within her bounds, would have affected little, if at all,
the major issues of the final years. To the clerics she
would be, it is allowed, always the woman with feet pre-
hensile upon hell ; to the court, less definitely uniform
in evil ; to posterity, a fact to be accepted with a
shrugging of the shoulders. Who cares for the evils
wrought by the debauchery of Henri de Navarre ? His
genial form, the Ivry pennon, the economic enterprises
of his reign, gleam on the sight ; the visual nerve is

heedless of the darker forms which loom behind.
Creci and Calais make the same fire-curtain to our
retrospect. Edward might gleam in spite of Dame
Alice were it not for the *avilization* of the Plantagenet
King's whole personality. A senile dotard, robbed in his
very bedchamber—this makes the picture for contempt.
Henry of Navarre might hang his chains of pearls
round the neck of a mistress born of the people, but
from the fingers, enervated by death, of Edward Plantagenet the Alice tentacles have drawn the rings—the hero
has become the quarry of the carrion-bird; it is sordid,
effete, a paltry bit of scenic failure. The Bourbon King
died at a blow, arrested in the fullness of his glamour;
the Plantagenet dies the common death upon his bed,
the husk of his once vital fruition. Henry is glowing
still upon the staging of the years; Edward's one aberration blots the last page with stains which have become
ingrained in the national retrospect. And it is not the
question of the Gallic frame or of the British one alone,
though such setting does affect the values too. It is the
larger fact that tells—which is that our logical valuation
may suffer lesion with less resentment than our hunger
for the picturesque. Henry's splendour, if often a simula-
crum, has contrived to prevail; his varnish glints upon
the eye. Edward, sere, effete, stricken with unpoetic
malady, is a picture grimed with the sordid cobweb
common to all flesh.

Even the Church must hold aloof till the concubine-
woman has been dismissed. Then, when Edward, half-
unconscious, could not bar her entrance, Alice Perrers
must still find her way into the death-chamber, giving
colour to the supposition that even then the dying King
had not broken the bonds of sin. And so, in the ulti-

mate extremity, when the hovering woman had nothing more on which to lay her hand, this Edward of Creci and of Calais lay with locks limp with the dews of death receiving the last rites, administered, almost furtively, by a solitary priest, a stranger to court dignity, whose sacerdotal faculties natheless could shrive the now repentant soul.

The curtain falls on the last Edward of the Plantagenets, for the next king of his name, though of their *gens*, comes under the heading of the reigning house of York.

EDWARD IV

EDWARD IV

CHAPTER XI

THE WHITE ROSE BLOOMS

IT is more than eighty years since the curtain was rung down upon the reign of Edward III, and now it rises upon the fourth one of his name, a Plantagenet of the "legitimate" branch, which for over sixty years had been kept from the throne by the usurping progeny of John of Gaunt, the fourth son of Edward III. During those years, with which we shall not deal, the clash of combat between blood-kin had sounded from one end of England to the other; roses, red as blood, and roses, pale as death, had been the badges of the followers of those respective descendants of the third Edward who had made of sovereignty an open wound for the larger part of a century. The prestige of the conquerors had waned. The splendour of Henry of Agincourt might beguile the eye of even Yorkist champions, but Henry of Winchester with his feebleness had irked the realm beyond the possibility of readjustment. And now "that puppet of a king" is thrust out and Edward enters London in the early days of March, 1461, welcomed by all the population and appointed sovereign "at the demand, nay by compulsion, of well-nigh all present both Lords and Commons."

On the face of the records, Edward's triumph seems of

suddenness beyond belief. Here at the close of 1460 was he, receiving office and emolument from his kinsman, the supplanter, Henry VI. In February of 1461 even, after his father's death in Wakefield battle, Henry was turning to the son, now Duke of York, "to stand by him against those who should be our lieges, and in number not a few, who, led away by devilish deceits, are arrayed in war in several counties of our realm of England." Yet it is but twenty-six days later that, *regnante Eduardo quarto*, the new king hands the Great Seal of gold, already inscribed with his own sign, to the Chancellor, George, Bishop of Exeter, his own near kinsman. In the family mansion of the Yorks, Baynard's Castle in Thames Street by the river, did this significant ceremony take place ; the Seal, in its bag of white leather, being then transported by the Chancellor to his episcopal mansion of Herbert House in the City. On Wednesday, March 11th, it was used upon the first letters-patent of the reign.

It is bewildering ! Was Henry duped to such a point or was his appeal but a last bait to win the adversary's allegiance ? A chronicle of France gives us the clearest insight into the position of this sovereign overthrown. For, after the battle of Northampton, where he was taken prisoner, he was conveyed into the town in the custody of Edward and of the Earl of Warwick, the King-maker.

"Il fut moult ebahy quant il se trouva en leurs mains nonobstant que il n'avoit pas le sens de concepvoir les grans maulz qui en advendroient."

Stunned he was, this soft-brained king, though having not the wits to reck of the great evils which should follow on.

The battle of Towton was the final clearance of the *via regia*. The red rose dyed the stream of Wharfe ; by tens of thousands in the crucial strife did the Lancastrians give their blood for their lost cause.

Edward had begun his reign, yet the pageantry of accession was not prolonged, for the reign of Henry, in the eyes of a faithful remnant, was not ended. For a space, indeed, a spell of Henry was in later years to make irruption in the story of the kingdom, to renew for a short space King Henry's chequered sway.

Margaret, the "man-woman" in the North, the league of the Lancastrian forces with those of Scotland, could leave to Edward no hope of breathing yet awhile the peaceful air of an established rule. He was again upon the highway of battle.

There is a pause at midsummer, when he is crowned. He creates his young brothers, George and Richard, Dukes of Clarence and Gloucester.

The coronation banquet follows, and the champion flings his glove in challenge. The Mayor of London comes proffering the City sword, which Edward handed to a knight, who held it behind the King during the banquet, after which Edward himself returned it to the Mayor.

The *ancien régime* is restored : precedent dates from the last year of Edward III and, with rare exceptions, the enactments of Lancastrian kings form no basis for those of the restored monarchy. Edward, greeted with vivacity by his subjects, had, in his turn, the gracious task of rewarding faithful servitors.

Court appointments were distributed among the henchmen in degree. So busy was Sir John Wenlock, Chief Butler of England, laying in a store of wines for the coronation that it was necessary to provide him with a subordinate. Thus Richard Stowell was appointed "yeoman" because Sir John was "fully occupied."

The salaries of most of the new officials were settled on the same scale as had prevailed in the last year of Edward III, a long time in the reckoning of the wages-table. We wonder indeed whether the new officials may not have yearned a little for the "rise" which sixty years might have reasonably brought them. Yet, if the scale of wages was conservative, archaic even, we seem to find an evolution in the court appointments themselves. Officials of higher quality and style now presided over the departments of the royal household, having menial subordinates to fulfil the practical duties of the same. For knights and squires succeed Tom, Dick, and Harry.

Here is Ralph Hastings, an esquire of the body, appointed to be custodian of the lions, lionesses, and leopards at the Tower, and for these animals two plots of ground within the fortress were assigned. It seems as though a check were to be placed upon the claims for sustenance of the tawny beasts, for the Chancellor was empowered to inquire from time to time into the number of them. Before the reign was four years old, the royal letters, granting the appointment to Ralph, were "casually lost," and a sworn undertaking was put in force pending the time when the missing grant should again turn up. Within the Tower accommodation was found as well for the makers of the King's bows and of his arrows.

England remained still sore and perturbed from the wounds of so much civil conflict. Edward himself is "a poor man"—lord of a land which has been bled by sword and pestilence and famine. The "Third Estate" is staunch in its allegiance to the crown, for the Commons vote an "aid" of £37,000, not forgetting indeed an odd halfpenny at the tail of sterling. For this Edward thus they raise finances, this Edward who, they tell us, had such outpouring of both hands from the jade Fortune, and who knew so little how to flank her gifts by steadfast purpose of his own. His physical beauty—"he was the handsomest royal person of his time that I have ever seen," says a French chronicler—and his manly form, so lavish an addition to his kingship, made him only too successful in the matter of fair women. Ever ready was he for amorous experiment.

All looked forward to a queen and offspring who should confirm the restored line ; but years went on and the nobles were uneasy, for they knew well that Edward was no ascetic, and feared illicit dealings with the feminine.

Warwick, who had made him King, was ardent now to make a match for him. With Louis XI of France, the King's servants conspired towards this amiable end. Sir John Wenlock went to France, was met by Louis and conducted to Dampierre, where the Queen, a princess of Savoy, received him. With her were her two sisters, one of whom Louis XI desired to see sharing the throne of England. He broached the subject to Wenlock and displayed the damsel. Beautiful and charming was Bona of Savoy, without doubt, "bien digne de royal lit."

The Chief Butler was well impressed, and Warwick opened up negotiations in which, at the outset, Edward himself seems also to have been favourably involved.

Then, in an assembly of the lords at Reading Abbey, in the fourth year of the reign, they pressed the King to take unto himself a wife, and to add to the lustre of

England by an adequate alliance. They were too late, and now, pressed into a corner, Edward revealed a secret now some months old.

The tale begins years back in the Lancastrian days, with Jaquetta, the widow of the Regent Bedford, who married, as her second husband, Richard Woodville, either the Duke of Bedford's chamberlain or a son of his.[1]   It was a *mésalliance* truly, for Jacqueline (we will take leave to call her by the softer Gallic version, though "Jaquete" was her signature)—Jacqueline was a great lady, the daughter of the Comte St. Pol, and well-fitted herself to mate with royalty. The marriage was a secret one, and cost the bride (for Woodville could hardly have produced the sum) £1,000 as fine to Henry VI.

Richard Woodville and the duchess had several children, among them, Elizabeth, who married a young Lancastrian knight, John Grey. Two little sons they had, and then John Grey was slain in a battle of the Roses. Elizabeth went home to her mother's house, or was at all events a guest there, when the new king called one day and honoured Duchess Jacqueline with a visit.

The royal favour warmed the women to a venture. Elizabeth cast herself upon her knees before the King and prayed his clemency for her little sons, Thomas Grey and his younger brother, who were without inheritance

---

[1] There being authorities of weight ranged on the side of Woodville the chamberlain as being Jaquetta's second husband, and, as well, on that of Woodville's son, also a Richard, being the true person, the author's position is somewhat invidious. It might appear that the chamberlain would have the better opportunity of acquaintance with the wife of the Regent-in-France. On the other hand, there is no indication as to the freedom of intercourse which may have existed between Jaquetta and the families of the officials of her first husband.

through the attainder of their father. The beautiful
young widow, in her garb of woe, for widows did not
lightly cast their weeds in earlier Edwards' days, knelt
before a man to whom women and beauty were ever
irresistible appellants. Hot blood beat in his veins, "he
could refuse her nothing." But, as with lesser men, King
Edward had his price, and one which fair Elizabeth declined to pay. For though, she pleaded, she knew her unfit-
ness to be a queen, yet was she of blood too proud to be
a mistress even to a king. And whether she really would
not profane her pride or whether she saw that Edward
was enthralled beyond recovery we know not. But what
the outcome was they tell us. For Edward, to whom her
beauty and appeal had become, at any cost, a necessity,
resolved to offer marriage where first a lesser price was
named. Affairs were urgent at the time, and it was only
by pretext of a hunting party that Edward stole away on
that May day from his nobles, and made Elizabeth his
own by a secret marriage. None but the bride's mother
knew at all of that furtive honeymoon of a few hours
when Elizabeth stole to the King's chamber, whence, ere
nightfall, Edward must emerge to gallop back to his
awaiting court.

The boy Grey was restored to his father's honours and
estates, but it was some time still before Edward avowed
his marriage. Then, when the importunities of his
followers could not be longer fenced with, he avowed the
deed and bade their presence at the public spousals.
But the nobles did not appear with unanimity at the
King's command. Some felt they had been fooled.
Margaret of Scotland, who had been sought as bride for
the King of England, had alleged a prior betrothal
to young Edward of Lancaster. Isabella of Castile, who

"was o'er young to marry yet," had, nevertheless, married Ferdinand of Aragon, a greater *parti* than the English King. And now Edward had left them and the negotiations with the Princess of Savoy in the lurch to marry a subject, and the widow of one of the opposite faction. The wrath of the King-maker outdid that of them all. For he had not alone to face the *impasse* with Louis XI and his queen, but had, it is alleged, a blacker cause for rancour against Edward. The King had offered insult to his own young daughter, and now he had espoused in valid bonds this Elizabeth, with her upstart relatives and her sons, the offspring of the attainted Grey.

The tale is discredited by some on the ground that the King had only too many at his call among fair women to need to offer violence to the Neville maiden. Yet even wiped away, it leaves us with the Princess of Savoy and the ruptured marriage plans. However, the thing was done. "Goody" of Savoy married, instead, a Duke of Milan, and Elizabeth Woodville and her family were installed at court and raised to honours of which the chamberlain Woodville had never dreamed.

Elizabeth may have been about the age of her husband or a little older, but she cannot have exceeded the age of twenty-seven at her marriage, while Edward was about twenty-two at the same time, his elder brother, Henry Plantagenet, dead many years before, having been born in 1441.

In April, 1465, Queen Elizabeth was crowned in the Tower of London, a few weeks after the birth of her eldest child, that Elizabeth Plantagenet through whom the Plantagenet descent was carried down to our King Edward VII.

The mother of the King had not lightly swallowed down the deed of the *mésalliance* with a Lancastrian coterie. She had moved heaven and earth, alleging Edward's pre-contract to a lady of the Talbot family. By the time of the christening, however, the Duchess of York had been compelled to accept the situation, and she stood with Jacqueline, duchess, and the Earl of Warwick as sponsors, while for the confirmation, which, after the manner of those days, followed immediately upon the other sacrament, the Duchess of Buckingham was godmother.

Warwick stood by the font, but his wrath was smouldering, and not long after this he withdrew himself from court, and planned his treason against the King whom he had helped to raise to power. Other nobles of distinction followed in his train. Edward, seen by foreign vision, is "durement courouchié" by these events. Yet he did not apprehend the wisdom of keeping out the ill-loved taint of nepotism. The Woodville pensioners clustered more thick as time went on. The Queen's father, now Earl Rivers, was made Treasurer. Her brother Anthony married a wealthy heiress and became, in right of her, Lord Scales, and for the many Woodville sisters brilliant marriages were arranged.

Sir Thomas Grey, the elder son of the dead Lancastrian, was created Marquis of Dorset, and for him a marriage was arranged with Edward's niece, the heiress of the duchy of Exeter.

The Commons, reflecting doubtless on their thirty-seven thousand sterling, looked sourly on these greedy devourers of loyal subsidies.

Some of Edward's sisters had been already married

when he became King. Margaret, who was about fifteen at the time of the accession, was the next to be considered. For her a match was devised with the Comte de Charleroi, already twice a widower, and for whom a third alliance with Madame (Anne) of France had been mooted. Louis XI kept on putting off the comte with the pretext of madame's tender youth; the story of Isabella of Castile seems to be repeated, and Madame married some one else eventually, though not until long after the match between the comte and the English princess had been arranged and carried out, the contract being signed at Kingston early in 1467.

Before the marriage could take place, however, Charleroi had succeeded his father as Duke of Burgundy.

Philip the Good fell ill at Bruges upon a Friday in June of the same year. So ill was he on Sunday that messengers were sent in hot haste to tell his son at Ghent. Charleroi mounted and rode away for Bruges. Furiously did he ride, so furiously that it seemed as though he must even cleave his horse's hoofs, and but four or five knights of all his train could keep up with him as he thundered through the villages. Next day the duke was dead, and Charles le Téméraire was Duke of Burgundy.

He was of large frame, this Charles le Téméraire, with bronzed skin and thick dark hair and beard. His natural man disposed him to hot deeds of anger, and the rest. Strong were his passions, but he was "seigneur de soimesme"—he broke himself in by virtue and the fear of God. They tell of his clear eyes—these not an asset of the libertine.

If Edward's marriage was bereft, by its clandestine

shade, of glow and colour, we lack nothing, in these regards, in the case of Margaret, his sister. Her first reception, it is true, across the North Sea, seems to have been almost too ponderous with solemnity to hold a tender welcome for the girl-bride. For, though the Duchess Isabel, the dowager of Burgundy, journeyed to Sluys to receive her new daughter-in-law upon her landing, it was not until next day that Charles arrived at that place to visit his betrothed. Then, too, how are we to read the story of his slowness to carry out the nuptials? The Bishop of Salisbury, who had come over with Margaret, seems to have felt constrained to bring the duke up to the climax. For, falling on his knees between the "high contracting parties," the urgent prelate pressed his point from that obsequious level. On which the duke averred that it was not for him to choose the moment, and referred to Margaret, who, as we seem to see, would not let it be her fault if the stolid suitor were not forthwith nailed to his undertakings. For no other end had she come there, declared the lady. Marry-and-come-up it was, and then and there the bishop carried out the solemn espousals, leaving the nuptial Mass and benediction for a later day.

Duke Charles, though, at a distance of 450 years, he may seem to have displayed some lack of zeal in accomplishing his espousals, had been no laggard in the preparations made for his English bride. An army of workmen had accomplished structural alterations at his own palace and at the lodgings of the foreign guests at Bruges. The austere cloisters of the Carmelite monastery rang with the sound of building operations and of woodwork construction. Four vast brick ovens were to cook the ordinary meals of the English nobles and their suites. Larders were added to contain the store of flesh and fish. In the great hall, where the lords of England were to dine, a "dresser" and long tables were put up to hold the viands for their feasting, with carving tables for the service.

In the quadrangle were fed their servants and the common people in their train. Within the monastery, rooms were set aside for the various domestic offices and fitted up with buffets, trestle-tables, and other necessary arrangements for the store of silver and of wine, as well as for the humbler bakery and still-room products.

While the ducal bridegroom was coming and going—for he made two visits before the bishop's intervention—Margaret remained at Sluys, where she had landed. On Saturday, July 2nd, she, with her train of English nobles, moved on to Dam, near Bruges. The Queen of England's brother, my Lord Scales, was foremost among the company.

On the following morning all were up at daybreak, for at five o'clock the wedding took place, after which the bridegroom rode off to Bruges, there to await the bride's arrival at his *hôtel*.

The officers of his household then set off for Dam to fetch the duchess, and she entered " moult notablement" into ancient Bruges.

First came the duke's great steward and others ; then drummers, trumpeters, minstrels and players on the clarionet, and the heralds of the duchy.

And then came Margaret of England in her litter, richly draped with cloth of gold and crimson velvet and surrounded by a company of knights ; and the bride was dressed in cloth of gold and silver, with a court-mantle of crimson golden tissue. Her lovely hair flowed loose, and on her head she wore a glorious crown.

Behind her rode her maids-of-honour on cream-coloured hackneys of pure blood.

All the great trade guilds of old time followed in the procession—Florentines and Lombards, Spaniards, Esterlings, and English, and the rest.

By companies they marched, bearing in their hands flaming torches of meet colour with the uniform of their society. The white and blue, the red and green, so on, until the chronicler is tired and the unimportant English are left without description.

In the streets, wild beasts in effigy spouted wine or hippocras or milk, and at the crossways *tableaux-vivants* were displayed.

Coming to the duke's house, Margaret was received by Duchess Isabel and the little Marie of Burgundy, a daughter of Duke Charles; the bridegroom awaiting her in his state apartments; and here was spread the wedding-feast.

Court artists had bestowed their talents on the banqueting-hall and on the wedding-feast alike. Six banquets within one week called for their versatility. It would end in weariness to some if we were to give account of all their works. Yet, as we have no power to tell anything of those furtive wedding celebrations of Edward and his queen, we may fill that vacancy with some of the marvels of the wedding of the King of England's sister. For, after the dinner, followed jousts, in which Lord Scales of England tilted, but not with the Bastard of Burgundy, half-brother to Duke Charles, as he had done at Smithfield but a little time before. At the wedding-supper we read of thirty model ships, each seven feet long, with masts and sails and fully rigged. Of each the hull was black and studded with gilt nail-heads; the mainmast and the mizen, cordage and gear all gilded with fine gold; the sails and pennants were of silk. Their sides were washed by mimic waves of silver, which were curbed within a rocky barrier, devised in wood of various tinting, among which waxen algæ flourished, while, to add the never-failing quip of the grotesque, devouring beasts lay here and there within the crevices.

On these craft was served the *pièce de résistance*, the *rosbif* of the feast—the *gros rost* they called it there. Four little boats were tenders to each larger vessel, and carried their miniature crews of sailors and marines and a load of lemons, capers, olives, "et semblables menus metz"—the right condiments to the various roasts which were the cargo of the tended ships.

A great gold lion displayed the bridegroom's arms as its caparison, while on its back was seated a female figure bearing the flag of the Princess Marie of Burgundy in one hand and in the other the name-flower of the bride— a marguerite, richly wrought in gold.

A unicorn of silver was draped with silk bearing the arms of England, while upon its back, astride, rode a leopard displaying our royal standard.

Bruges indeed had expended itself down to the simplest form of decoration. Reams of paper and gallons of *colle forte* were fashioned into daisies to compliment the bride of England.

Charles of Burgundy had made his wedding-feast a sumptuous one, but even he had not attained to the features which distinguished a banquet once given by his father. For there was seen a monster pasty, and " when the pie was opened," within was found an orchestra of twenty-eight, who burst into a concert before the guests.

There too was seen the representation of a woman clothed alone in her own flowing tresses and a sumptuous hat, and from her breast flowed hippocras all supper-time. He would have been valiant who ventured near her generosity, for to a pillar close to her was chained a living lion, while on a placard was the warning, *Ne touchez à ma dame.*

The housing of the lesser officials at Bruges, during the wedding festivities, was very inadequate and led to much murmuring.

Said one :—" As for bedding, Lyard, my horse, had more ease than had some good yeoman, for my horse stood in the house and the yeoman sometime lay without in the street. For less and [than] 4d. a man should not have a bed o' night. Lo ! how soon they could play the niggards."

A shoulder of mutton sold for 12d., so dear in Flanders was meat at the time of Margaret's wedding. Ill feeling between the English and Flemings kept hot even after the return to England and there was a brawl between them at St. Mary Over Hey (Overy), which led to bloodshed.

Thus was wed the Lady Margaret of York, who in days to come was to espouse the cause of Perkin Warbeck and to be a thorn in the side of Henry Tudor, whether from a true conviction of the claimant's right (such things have been seen in our own times) or from a design to harry at any cost the Welsh usurper. Margaret visited England during her brother's reign, and was able to provide Warbeck with circumstantial detail relating to the court and family of Edward IV towards the end of the reign. Her presence has been denied by some eighteenth-century historians, but Sir N. Harris Nicolas has adduced a very strong case for her being in this country, on the evidence of the preparations made, and furnishing provided for her residence and her chapel at Coldharbour. He omitted, or was perhaps unaware of another possible piece of evidence, namely that in the same year, 1480, Margaret received royal licence to buy in this country a thousand oxen and two thousand rams and to "take them to the Low Countries." This licence, it must be admitted, was not necessarily for use in person, and Margaret did receive another one when in Flanders. This was after Charles le Téméraire had died, leaving, says a French historian, warfare in Europe for two hundred years.

CHAPTER XII

THE TENTH YEAR AND ITS CLOUD-BURST

THE lustre of enthusiasm which had made so brilliant young Edward's entrance into the kingdom of his birthright had suffered tarnish swiftly.

To Edward all had looked to bring triumph and stability out of the chaos of the battle and of the feebleness of Henry's sway. A strong yet genial rule was called for. England's need was urgent ; she was sore and breathless from the terrible convulsion of long-lasting civil strife. So exhausted was the country, avers an Italian witness, that had France and Scotland but combined they could have crushed her dead between them. They did not make this combination, but had their separate dealings with her, and the land seemed ready for the new era of prosperity. It was her King who failed her. The angry nobles at Reading we have seen, fooled by the sovereign who was to knit the bonds with France by a royal alliance. Not lightly did they deal with the revelation of the hidden marriage. They sought, and Edward's mother with them, to find a means of rupture, some flaw afforded by a pre-contract. There was Lady Elinor Talbot : she, however, saved the King's skin by a solemn denial of any contract, though she could not save her own fair name. The Lady Lucy was another implicated. She was the alleged mother of King Edward's son, Arthur Plantagenet, who lived on into the boyhood of Edward VI. At one ceremony of affiance it was averred that the Bishop of Bath and Wells had been present, and this was quite enough under Catholic discipline to establish a bond unbreakable. Joan Plantagenet and her lover Holland had, in the days of Edward III, involved themselves in a contract by a less formal association. Out of the rumour—false though it may have been—arose evil long stretched out after Edward's death. This we shall see in its own place.

The marriages of the Woodville sisters did but introduce further traitors against a future day. Warwick was revolving in his angry soul the failure of his splendid scheme. The King whom he had set upon the throne, who was to blaze before the Powers in the new age of England's rising glory—what was he but a gay-faced hedonist, frittering in libertine diversions the hours, the faculties, destined for regal valours? Elizabeth Woodville had warded off his illicit enterprise with such *aplomb* that she had gained a crown. She had to live through various episodes of her husband's light amours. The lady of the hour was not, perhaps, thrust upon her consciousness; the harem arrangements of the Bourbons were not fore-dated at the English court; still, Elizabeth must have had knowledge of the facile caresses which her lord bestowed elsewhere. Lady Lucy, or another, had borne him Arthur; this was a liaison after the pattern of royal manners for all time, it might be said. Edward kept open-house in his desires for the feminine in varied strata. The loyalty of London, said the gossip of the hour, was, in half at least, insured by the admiration of her burgess dames for their King of the genial smile. They coaxed the purse-strings of their spouses to loose themselves for Edward's monetary needs. A merry widow of uncertain age offered her tribute of £20 to the royal wallet, and moved the King to so much gratitude that he bestowed a kiss upon the benefactress. Warmed in her waning years by this delightful recompense, the lady added a second £20 in homage to the caresser.

At a time when a solemn alliance had been secured between the sovereigns of France and England, Louis XI offered a cunning bait to bring King Edward on a visit to Paris.

"Come," said he, "and if the beauties of our court make too great inroads on your continence, there is Cardinal Bourbon, a most genial prelate, ready to give you absolution."

The jest was one after King Edward's heart ; his eyes shone with their response to the allurement. Did he not, jesting, boast that he owned three concubines, "one the merriest, one the wiliest, and the third the holiest —— in his realm " ?

Then there was Jane, the wife of worthy Master Shore, with her curving outlines, the fair pallor of her exquisite skin and her tawny tresses. "One would have wished her somewhat higher." Gay she was and open-hearted and not over-greedy, though the King was ready with his gifts. Nor did she use her royal lover's infatuation to gain her own ends in any marked degree. She was the ready accomplice of his erotics and scarcely more. Smiling and simple-hearted, Jane seems to have had little of the *femme funeste* about her, yet she was to be branded as a witch in after days; but that was by the mouth of Richard, the King's brother,—*sournois*,—warped in mind and frame. Witchcraft was an allegation not brought against the Third Estate alone, for was not that great lady Jacqueline, Duchess of Bedford, mother of the Queen, indicted similarly?

Jane's story did not end with Edward's reign. Upon her, in her days of shame and penance, we shall look once more.

The time came when all this frittering away of royal zeal in light-toned dalliance had undermined the public patience. Scarce had the seas of blood, through which Edward had gained the throne, been cleared of their fierce crimson when the King was seen plunged into gallantries, volatile, light-hearted, forgetful of his calling.

There were nearer foes than the masses or than Warwick. There was young George, created Duke of Clarence at the coronation, now entering manhood and leagued with Warwick against the careless King. Clarence, now twenty years of age, crossed over to Calais with the King-maker and there wedded a daughter of the earl. Now, on both sides of the Channel, treachery ran rife. Hearts were turning again to the Lancastrian side. Henry might be a nonentity, but there was Margaret; still more, there was her son, young Edward, who still displayed the ostrich plumes of a Prince of Wales; and Elizabeth the Queen had borne no son in half a dozen years of marriage. "The name of Edward drew all men like an adamant."

The careless King had no firm hand in dealing with the situation. A little coaxing of the errant ones seemed to him enough. To the young Duchess of Clarence, in France, he sent "a gentlewoman" upon some ostensible pretext, but the secret mission of the envoy was to advise the duchess to divert her husband from his allegiance to the ex-King Henry and his son, when he would again receive Clarence into favour. Such tinkering with so great ill was by the time quite futile.

The Earl of Warwick's chaplain at Paul's Cross cried to the crowds that Edward was a usurper. Perhaps already in the adolescent brain of Richard, Duke of Gloucester, was hatching the foul brood of horrid accusations against his mother's honour which later he put forth to support his frenzied imputations upon Edward's birth.

In the black midst of all these treacheries gleamed one light of friendship. Charles of Burgundy, the strong man whose recreation was business, whose pleasure was in extension of his dominion, held a helping hand to the trivial brother-in-law of England. He kept Edward posted in affairs at the French court, where Edward's cause ran risk of being overlooked in favour of the rebels. It was a nominee of the duke's who was Governor of Calais when Warwick appeared before that port and sought admittance in company with his daughter, the Duchess of Clarence. But there was no admittance there for the enemies of Edward. , They were rebuffed, although the sore strait of the young duchess was adduced, she in the very hour of childbirth. At most, a few bottles of wine were sent off for her in the emergency.

Clarence, now landing on the English shores, had stirred up disaffection in the West. The fourth Edward, like the second, knew the depth of household treachery.

Woe followed woe within the kingdom. The Archbishop of York, always a waverer, seceded from the

King's allegiance; more direful still, his brother, having, in King Edward's name, raised six thousand fighting men, turned them over to the Earl of Warwick. Pressed on every side, Edward lost his nerve. Leaving his Queen and their young daughters in the Tower, he went forth upon a desperate venture. Caught by the King-maker, suffered to escape as in some game of cat-and-mouse, there now is neither doubling nor burrow in the realm. What desperately resolved, chaotic, plan now rises in his soul ?

II

Within one decade of his coronation the King who had come into his own must flee the country. The *coup d'état* has all the suddenness and violence of a Bourbon downfall or of a *crise Napoléon*. It was stolid England, in the dawn of her modern era, who saw this overthrow, this confusion staring to the arc of her grey heavens.

It is the flight of the desperate. The Wash, so male-ficent to John, his ancestor, did not spare Edward. With the loss of half his panoply of battle in the fateful inlet, Edward the *débonair* gains Bishop's Lynn.[1] As merely man stands England's King, bereft of power, of treasure, even of the crown, for all he knows, in this his catastrophic hour. Without so much as a carpet-bag, or its equivalent of that age, without the minimum of baggage, he, with life alone still in his hand, puts out

---

[1] The author is aware that Ipswich has been mentioned as the port of embarkation, but inclines to the belief that Lynn is the more likely place as regarded in connection with other data of the flight.

to sea. Three ships, two of them Dutch, received the
King and his last faithful ones. Lord Scales is one,
young Duke Richard is another, and Hastings third
among the minished band.

Even as the North Sea made interval between King
Edward and his rebel kingdom, and as the vague and
brumous land-line of the Netherlands was sighted by
the mariners, a further peril hove in sight. The sails
of Esterlings were espied; those freebooters whose
piratical misdeeds were tolerated by Flemish rule
because they had their value in keeping strangers
from the coasts. Their lesser draught and the pro-
pitious concurrence of a tide were alone the salvation
of the vessels of the refugees. Piled up in the shallows
they had a few hours' respite from the pursuing Esterlings. With the next flow the enemy would have them
at their mercy. But now upon this way to Jericho of
theirs arose a good Samaritan. Louis, the Lord of Gruythuse, Chamberlain to Duke Charles, happened to be in
the vicinity of the stranded ships. He heard the story
of the hunted King, and at once sent out his orders to
the Esterlings to desist from their harassment. They
owed too much to Flemish toleration to disobey. They
gave safe passage to the ships.

For the charges of his passage, Edward had not one
solitary coin of his own currency to bestow, but he
handed to the shipmaster a cloak with lining of sables,
and, once ashore, the Seigneur Gruythuse gave him, of
the bounty of a generous host, entertainment and the
means to make his journey to the Hague.

There, in the Netherlands, shorn of everything, with
his style as King of England even in abeyance, and with
the sky falling on his head, did Edward hear the news

of the birth of his first son, heir to this sum of cataclysm, born in the common Sanctuary at Westminster, to which the Queen had fled from the Tower ; baptized with the maimed rites of mere essentiality, that tragic-fated little Edward whom we hardly deem a king, remembering more constantly him and his equally doomed brother as " Princes in the Tower."

Thus, in a few short weeks, came a turning-point in the King's affairs, for one must, in the advent of that little son of sanctuary, see a power to move the malcontents to new reflection. Henry and his son might still be reversioners, for the claims of feminine primogeniture were little regarded, but the immediate power of that other Edward, him of Lancaster, suffered a set-back.

Events moved rapidly, astonishingly so when one considers the comparative conveniences of travel and the courier.

Edward's flight was near to Michaelmas, 1470. Warwick and Clarence had brought out captive Henry from the Tower and conducted him in state along Cheapside to the palace of the Bishop of London. The rush and tangle of events are bewildering.

" Warwick conquered England in eleven days," says one recorder, " Edward regained it in twenty."

Here, early in Lent, is the King, who fled hot-foot to Flanders, landing again on his own shores. Now is turn and counter-turn ; the shifting of the factions is beyond understanding.

Lancastrians essay an appeal to the people. The Archbishop of York rode with Henry through the streets of London, crying to the populace that they should be true to King Henry. It was an act over which the sword of Damocles was suspended. The

ELIZABETH WOODVILLE

hour brought forth the man, and Worswick, the recorder
of the City, had proclamation cried that all armed men
should go and get their dinners.   Then, when the streets
were divested of this danger, King Edward made a
sudden entry into the Bishop of London's palace and
placed Henry and the Archbishop under arrest.

The feeble traitor, Clarence, was lured back to his
brother's side.   On the other hand, there was the strange
defection of the Governor of Calais, who, so short a time
before, had trained cannon upon Warwick, and who
now went over to his side.   But Warwick's end was near.

Edward returned to his palace, and, as he came by
Westminster Sanctuary, Elizabeth heard her husband and
his followers and ran out of the Sanctuary to greet him.

Edward's return to his kingdom and to power brought
new and direful measures against the temporary usurpers
of the realm.   With the cruel streak, which often lurks in
the easygoing, the King swung to the further limit of
recrimination.

Barnet had worsted Margaret and her son, and
Tewkesbury saw the last remnant cowering in sanctuary,
which Edward would have violated in defiance of a
custom infinitely sacred.   But a churchman dared the
King to profane the ultimate asylum, and it was only
when, by base strategy, the refugees had been lured
forth, that they were put to death.   Gloucester and
Hastings butchered young Edward Lancaster as he fell
into the toils.

And now no more should feeble-minded Henry,
hidden in the Tower, be made a figure-head for the
Lancastrian cause by that *maîtresse-femme*, his wife.

Of the exact means and acts which brought about
King Edward's ends we have no clear account.   Deeds

like these are not proclaimed *à haute voix* nor super-scribed upon the royal sign-manual. Rather are they set in the sentence of *double entente*, as with the wretched Edward of Carnarvon, or their responsibility shifted on to other shoulders, as with the warrant by which the head of Mary Stewart rolled in the dust at Fotheringhay, under the rule of Elizabeth.

So with Edward's resolve to deal with Henry we may conceive that formalities were exiguous. Scarce would his meaning be articulated, enough for the eager acces-sories were the lifting of an eyelid.

The sinister shadows of the Tower hid the deed of blood as they hid so many more, as they were, in horrible repayment, to hide the innocent blood of that little Edward, then newborn, the heir-apparent.

The very stones cry out; the people murmur that Henry has been slain. Yet on the heels of it there treads that further rumour which, proven false, checks us in our haste to accept the death as necessarily violent—that Margaret has shared her husband's fate. " In short," writes a contemporary to the Papal nuncio, " King Edward has elected to crush the seed."

Margaret, it is true, survived, and was in the end, by the intervention of France, restored to her father, René of Anjou, upon a ransom which almost beggared the wretched prince.

Rumour still growled about the wretched Henry's *exitus* from his ill-fated life. From the corpse, as it lay in state in St. Paul's, gushed streams of blood, crying to Heaven, in popular belief, against his murderers. The body was taken by the Thames to Chertsey, and there buried, and did not for many years reach its final resting-place at Windsor.

The black tragedy roused a general feeling of re-vulsion; there was a momentary glare of storm. Yet, as it lacked co-ordination, the movement sank to earth : "there being neither head nor tail, the thing was soon suppressed."

Barnet field had seen the end of Warwick. There, too, had been left for dead the Duke of Exeter, Edward's rebel brother-in-law. Yet he had revived from his real, or simulated, insensibility, and had, it has been judged, fled to the coast, for his corpse was found some time later on the Kentish shores. Again they say that he fled to sanctuary, hoping that his duchess would prevail with her brother for his pardon. But the King's sister and her husband had been estranged for years on account of the duke's adherence to the Lancastrians, and whether she were unwilling, or unable, certain it is that Exeter received no royal clemency.

The Earl of Oxford too had fled to France after Tewkesbury and stayed there for two years. But Louis XI was ready for an alliance with the King of England, and now Oxford embarked upon a fierce and desperate venture. He returned to England, and with a mere handful of men, some seventy-five, he attacked and took St. Michael's Mount. Against him, Edward sent royal forces, and the little band, powerless to hold the marine fortress, swiftly capitulated.

The earl was imprisoned in a fortress near Calais, his goods attainted, his wife, a Neville, beggared. In the last years of the reign, we find that she received a grant from the King.

The ringleaders had paid the price.

CHAPTER XIII

OF HOUSEHOLD THINGS

WHILE prosperity and cataclysm were succeeding one another, a large young family was springing up round Edward and Elizabeth. Several daughters had been born before the flight to Flanders and before the birth of little Edward in the darkest hour.

Elizabeth, the eldest, as historical developments have shaped themselves, became the most important of the ten children of the fourth Edward, for, as consort of Henry VII, she carried on the legitimate line, and is an ancestress of our present reigning house.

The Duchesses of York and Bedford, mothers of the King and of his queen, respectively, were godmothers to her and the " King-maker " her godfather.

In a pageant, given by the loyal inhabitants of Bristol to celebrate a visit from their King, appeared St. George and the Dragon, while the King and Queen were represented " on high in a castle and his daughter (Elizabeth) beneath, with a lamb, and, at the slaying of the dragon, there was a great melody of angels."

Elizabeth was about two years of age when her father made a grant for her maintenance, and in 1468, by letters-patent, an allowance of £400 per annum was assigned for the expenses of Elizabeth and Mary, her next sister, "until other provision" was made. Then came Cecily and Margaret (who died in infancy), and Anne, who married one of the Howards, but whose children died in their early years. Katharine was married to a son of the Earl of Devon ; we shall find her descendants at court in the time of Edward VI.

Bridget, born near the end of her father's reign, became a nun and lived on in her cloister till the reign of Henry VIII.

Of Edward and his brother Richard we shall tell in the scanty story of the fifth Edward. George, born late in the reign, died in childhood.

Domestic comfort, both in the palace and in the mansion of the country gentleman, had attained to a standard considerably higher than that we left behind in the reigns of previous Edwards. Rushes still prevailed as the more general floor-covering, at which we need not wonder, for the drainage and the metalling of roads were absent, and the importation of mud into the interior of a dwelling must have been considerable, and must have called for the aid of a floor-covering of renewable kind, though rushes even had to endure much wear before they were replaced.

Carpets were placed before the chairs of the King and his consort, or were seen as hangings to cloak the grim exterior masonry on gala days, or, again, upon the naked walls of castle-hall or of the Queen's bower or private chamber.

Arras hung in general in living or sleeping rooms or formed the hangings of the beds. The subjects of its designs were commonly drawn from the chase and its appurtenances—the huntsman and the hart, the gentlewoman and the whelp, appeared in their variations. Scriptural scenes had the next place, and, again, heraldic emblems appeared as border or diaper work.

Beds and bedding had become quite luxurious. In the chamber of the first York sovereign we find beds with ceiler and tester, the upright and horizontal hangings which survived in their kind into the days of Edward VII's earliest life. From the ceiler hung rich curtains of velvet, white and pale blue, or of silk with broidery, and there were counterpanes also embroidered or worked with bullion and small metal *plaques* or spangles. Feather beds, and bolsters and pillows stuffed with down, furnished the great state beds. There were pallets too, a "shake down" for the servant or for the younger members of a family, with rougher mattresses, and, here and there, we come across the mention of a leather pillow.

Silk cushions appear, and they would find a place beneath the royal foot as much as in the chair.

Dutch linen could not be obtained in breadth sufficient for the sheets, and several widths were joined to make up the necessary sizes, two sheets being used to cover the head and foot portions of the bed or mattress.

Though linen might be imported from the Low Countries, English linen was not without renown, nor were queens without a share in the household handicraft. An honoured guest at Windsor slept in linen of the "Queen's own ordonnance," perhaps woven under the eye of Elizabeth herself.

Where records of the palace outfit fail us, we may safely supply the vacancy from accounts of the household stuff of the great nobles or of substantial country magnates, who then, as now, were not behindhand in possessions. So to the pillow stuffed with down, on which kings laid uneasy heads, we may add the "little pillow of green silk, full within of lavender," which was one asset of the great Sir John Fastolf in his Norfolk residence. The lavender pillow is found in several records of the times.

The "yeoman of the beds" had supervision of all these things in the royal stores ; of the down-filled beds and pillows, of the sheets, and of the fustian coverings and the finer blankets of white wool.

Upon the sides of bedsteads and of tables and of some other furniture were fastened hangings of arras or of more costly stuff ; these were the "costers," while those which hung upon the back of chair or bench were called "dossers."

Cords or rods were used for the suspension of the wall arras, and tenterhooks and rings played their part in holding up the same. Of nails great store was needed for such purposes and for attaching the "costers." Gilt-headed ones appear by hundreds in several places. John Coppersmith receives "for the amending of a broken chayer emended with small gilt nailles iii*d*." Yet another sort of nail was used for the draperies of the font at the christening of one of England's daughters. A claw-hammer was provided, as we find ; no doubt it had its predecessors.

Tablecloths and napkins were among the other items stored in the Great Wardrobe, also cupboard (sideboard) cloths and hand towels.

To keep moth and other destroyers from the stores of costly velvets and cloth-of-gold, and from the furs and royal garments, "little bags," containing aniseed and orris, were provided.

Clothing was advancing in elaborateness. The materials comprise the old baudekyn and scarlet of the earliest Edward's days; they were added to by camlet and other woollen cloths, imported in some cases from France, and by an increasing list of sumptuous velvets, shot silks, and cloth-of-gold in various colourings.

The doublet might have its sleeves slashed by the votaries of fashion, so might the long robes which were another wear.

The long years of warfare may have left the English people reduced to plain attire, but their neighbours of France were, at all events, in sumptuary prosperity: "there was not the merest little journeyman who had not his long cloth robe reaching to his very heels."

The beautiful French velvets and brocades, the shot silks and the cloths of English or foreign manufacture, were enriched in the making with embroidery and bullion and lined or trimmed with fur of various kinds. Tags or eyelets, of metal, finished silken laces or cords and dangled from the garments in a profusion bereft of mere utility.

We find our old friend "budge," which we begin to put down as black lamb's wool, or wool in general as distinct from the hair or fur of animals. Sable, marten, the commoner varieties of that fur, ermine and miniver are familiar. There are still unidentifiable kinds; some of which may doubtless be classed under the contributions of the English wild animals, coney, mole, and others, now obsolete, or labelled under names which hide their origin.

The county families had their fine apparel: the châtelaine might possess an ermine bonnet, the round, tower-like headgear which seems to have survived from the high pointed structure worn by Philippa of Hainault, and which is dimly restored in the brimless casque of straw, or fur, or fabric worn in a short spell of fashion in the day of Edward VII.

The slower movements of *la mode* made of these garments of splendid fabric a lasting possession. They were bequeathed to daughter, kinswoman or servant, according to degree. For the last-mentioned a gown of "musterdevelys" furred with black and a black girdle, ornamented with silver-gilt and enamel, was a testimony of faithful service.

Uniform was provided for a great number of royal servants and dependents. Upon the entertainment of distinguished guests, fresh liveries would be provided, at all events for those assigned from the royal household to wait upon them during their stay. The royal glazier, working in his shed called "glazier's lodge," within the Palace of Westminster, had his livery coat at Christmas.

The royal footgear was most varied. There were high boots of coarser leather and boots of Spanish leather, lined with fur or silken fabric. There were shoes and "slops" and slippers and socks of warm woollen fabric. Gloves were rare and costly, but the King had a good allowance. The importation of them was forbidden, so any worn by the general public must have been of English manufacture. Sumptuary and economic laws, however, have generally included dispensations for the ladies of the royal family and household.

Thomas Grime, the yeoman of the jewels, had acquisitions to the valuables under his care during Edward's reign. Some of the deposed Henry's possessions came, perhaps passing with the crown, into the hands of Edward. Among them was a coronet of gold set with large "baleys" (balass rubies ?) and fine pearls, and a jewel of great value called the "fetter-lock," set with splendid gems, diamonds, pearls, rubies, and sapphires and others, and valued at £2,000, which would represent a substantial sum even for a regal ornament to-day.

Edward, too, upon the dawn of his good fortune, was able to redeem another jewel, a golden clasp with a great brilliant and the white rose of York in enamel, and another clasp, with the arms of his mother's family, which his father, Richard, had pledged to Sir John Fastolf.

Towards the end of the reign his agent was buying jewels for the King in foreign parts.

The royal commissariat is conservative, yet additions have been made to the food-stuffs and to the dishes served at the royal table. No bill of fare for a royal banquet served to Edward is forthcoming, but from accounts of those a few years earlier we may picture the dishes and the manner of their service. Capon, duck, and partridge figure, while rabbits are in demand, for a reserve of them, for royal use, is made upon the lease of one of the King's manors.

The regal swan and crane and peacock are still of special distinction. Poachers upon the King's swannery in Fenland rob the sovereign of eggs and cygnets. All kinds of little birds were served—plovers, quails, woodcock, snipe, and larks.

Fish is plentiful, of course, if only for purposes of Church abstinence from flesh. Two London fishmongers receive royal warrant to supply salted salmon, herrings, and other stockfish, and "sea fish"—in fresh state presumably.

Carp and bream and pike appear at a state banquet of the time.

Vegetables and fruit are in far less evidence. Herbs would represent the greater part of vegetarian diet, and these would have their most important functions in the preparation of " simples." Borage is a garnish to a dish of poultry. Strawberries and cherries may be guessed at, for they appear within a few years of the reign, at any rate. A quince *compôte* was known before King Edward's time, and oranges, dates, and almonds were found in the houses of the country gentry as well as in the King's palace.

Furmenty, a porridge of cracked wheat, with wine and spices, was sometimes an accompaniment to a roast of venison.

Sweet dishes were more elaborate in device than in materials. Some were of the nature of a jelly or fruit cheese, and took the forms of heraldic animals—antelope, or lion, or leopard. There were fritters, some distinguished as being " crisp," and " custard royal."

The " subletye" we have seen at the wedding-feast of Charles and Margaret of Burgundy. On the royal board of England we see representations of past or of contemporary sovereigns, the reigning King in his Garter robes, or of Our Lady and the Saints, which the simple habits of the day moulded from meats or jelly with no thought of irreverence, and which were still further embellished by pious aphorism or Church canticle.

From the account already referred to, of a royal banquet prior to King Edward's reign, we gather that the courses were arranged on quite a different plan to anything we are familiar with.

Each provided a great mixture of dishes set together

on the board and having no distinction from the preceding course.

Thus boar's head and herring, swan and custard, all found a place together among equally diverse dishes, and in the next course were replaced by a similar variety. Pig in dory, peacock, bream, were set down in company with a dish of sweets inscribed with the opening words of the Ambrosian hymn and with "Flampayne" (flan ?) powdered with leopards and fleurs-de-lis, and were removed by a third course in which we find roast venison and all kinds of little game birds hobnobbing with great birds (query, bustards), with fruit *compôte* and "Blaundsore."

No great variety of utensils would be required for the preparation of these feasts. The wealthy knight had his couple of dozen of pewter cooking-pots and a few brass ones in his kitchen. The frying-pan had been known in the last century. The "mistery" of the Pewterers received privileges under Edward IV. The marble mortar and pestle would serve to grind up spice and other seasoning. A few huge spits would carry the *grosse chare*, while on smaller ones would be impaled the many little birds which figured at the banquet. One splendid cooking-vessel there was in the palace kitchen, a silver cauldron valued at £100, but nothing else is mentioned of similar distinction.

The head cook of Edward IV could yield to none in splendour of his style. "Archicocus noster"—if many a butler reminds one of a bishop, this cook of Edward's is surely primate.

With the "yeoman of the pitchery" we seem to come upon a development of the offices. Much extra help was hired at the time of the coronation in the departments of the head cook and of the scullery. For the banquet on that occasion many trestle tables were provided.

We have, in an earlier chapter, seen Sir John Wenlock's added labours at the same time. The "better red wine of Gascony" still comes to the royal cellars, and there is sack and malvoisie, in a butt of which, according to a picturesque but ill-founded nursery story, the Duke of Clarence made his end.

"Bastard" was a sweet and inferior liquor. We hear of the Carthusians, weakened by their fasts and vigils, receiving a grant of wine "for their bodies." "Thank the Lord, He did not put it on the drink!" says the Irish story of to-day, in reference to fasting.

In the parish of St. Martin's-without-Ludgate was the King's brewhouse. "Les hoppez" are now included in brewing stuff.

During this reign, overseers were appointed to see that brewers in general used sound material ; good malt from oats or barley, free from weevils ; and also that the beer was boiled enough and not overcharged with saccharine matter. Nor might it leave the brewhouse for a week after its making.

After the peace with France in 1475, Edward received an annual grant from that country—he called it a tribute himself—with which he was enabled to raise his style of living. Christmas he kept, indeed, at Eltham in great magnificence, a wonder to the chronicler. The great Warwick, however, could outvie the sovereigns he set up and deposed. At his London house, six oxen were eaten at the morning meal, and any one having any acquaintance with his household might carry off on skewer, or dagger, as much of roast and boiled as he could thus impale.

There is a fair, though not lavish, supply of plate recorded. Some came from Henry's store, others from the possessions of nobles under attainder. Large silver dishes, plates and broth-bowls, and cups and goblets of all kinds. These were sometimes gilt and enamelled. English flowers gave the note for decoration. The hawthorn, rose-leaf, or violet provided a scheme for chased work or enamelling.

Often there was a cover to the drinking-cup, and a knob in form of acorn or garlic-bulb would serve for a handle. Bowls and ewers for table use and basins for washing were made of silver and decorated according to the honour of their use. Another may be found of semi-precious stone or spar, as the cup of chalcedony, enriched with gold and precious gems, and another one of fine gold set with pearls, diamonds, rubies and sapphires to a great value. Here are two figures which came to Edward with the forfeited estate of Henry, Duke of Somerset: a golden ploughboy set with diamonds, rubies, and great pearls, and a milkmaid, similarly resplendent, standing within park palings.

Elsewhere, we hear of spoons of various kinds,[1] little spoons for eggs, others gilded, for green ginger. There were also jars of silver-gilt for this same ginger and spice plates in which were served spices to accompany the cup of wine. Spices of almost every kind were supplied for the King's " privy spicery."

The saucer may have held condiments or con- fections ; it may have been placed beneath the drinking-cup, though this is doubtful. Certainly its now surviving use had then no place. There was no

---

[1] Apostle spoons dating from this reign are known. The author has, however, found no record until *temp.* Hen. VIII.

dish, or cup, of bohea in the reign of any Edward until the seventh.

Salt-cellars were still an important part of the plate outfit. They were surmounted with battlements, or graved with flower designs, with a richness equal to that of any other object of the table service.

For the King's private chapel vessels and vestments were also needed.

A gold tabernacle, sets of vestments and altar cloths are among the objects of which we find a record. The laity then, as now, obtained, by licence from the diocesan, the privilege of reserving the Sacred Host in their domestic chapels. For this purpose and for the offering of Mass, or the service of other sacraments, we find among their possessions the pix, which held the wafer ; chalices and patens, holy-oil stocks, stoups and sprinklers for holy water, the cruets for the unconsecrated wine and water, and the necessary priestly albs and other vestments, the corporal and altar cloths, and the portable confession-box. A bell, too, to announce the most solemn moments of the Mass, is met with in one inventory, while passed over in less exact schedules. All these objects and their uses are perfectly familiar to followers of the old religion at the present day.

A Paschal candle of extra size would be offered to some church in connection with a vow or petition of the donor.

The Queen's mother had a very complete outfit of church plate among the household stuff she brought from home on her first marriage to the Duke of Bedford. All this, with table plate and other valuables, was handed over on her behalf to the ducal chamberlain, that Richard Woodville to whom, unless it were his son, the duchess was afterwards married.

Two guests of much importance visited the English court during the last ten years of Edward's reign. These were Gruythuse, who came in 1472, and Margaret, Duchess of Burgundy, who visited her brother and his queen in 1480. For both, great entertainment was provided. Edward, indeed, could scarcely do too much, for Gruythuse had been a splendid friend. In that dark hour when, hunted and penniless, he ran upon the Flemish shore, Gruythuse had saved his life and filled his purse, and given him generous welcome at the Gruytehuse in Bruges. And now was Edward's turn.

At Windsor, the honoured guest was taken a-hunting in "the lyttle Park," and dinner, then a midday meal, was served at a hunting-lodge. The royal buckhounds and greyhounds coursed the deer and the royal sportsmen shot with crossbows. The Queen sometimes used a bow, and some of these were stringed with silken cord.

Edward himself showed his Flemish friend round his royal demesne, displaying proudly his garden and the "vineyard of pleasure" where Adam Goodall worked for the wage of the earlier Edwardian kings.

At night there was dancing, and little Elizabeth was first her father's partner and next the Duke of Buckingham's. The Queen and her ladies played at games, some kind of parlour ninepins. Evensong was chanted in the respective apartments of the royal hosts and of their guest, and at bedtime Gruythuse was escorted to the door of his apartments by the King and Queen, and was then attended by the Lord Chamberlain, who assisted him to undress ; and Gruythuse took his bath in so much state that it seems to have differed little from an investiture of the knighthood of the Bath, which was already in existence.

Upon a bed of softest down Gruythuse took his night's repose. The finest linen of Brittany, famous for a hundred years, as Sir Frederick Madden reminds us, composed the sheets. The hangings of the state bed were of "shining cloth-of-gold," its curtains of white silk; the counterpane of cloth-of-gold, edged with ermine; truly a kingly covering.

Edward himself had commanded the arras for the walls and the carpets for the floors of the suite assigned to Gruythuse.

A second couch provided with a canopy of netting (to keep off flies ?) served for the siesta of noonday.

Green ginger had become a standard confection in the palace, as in the country mansion. With it, sweet syrup, or a draught of hippocras, formed a cordial "nightcap" at Windsor, as elsewhere.

In the morning, the company attended Mass in the King's own oratory.

There was a splendid ceremony at Westminster when King Edward conferred on Gruythuse the earldom of Winchester [1] and presented him with a talismanic cup of gold set with a piece of the horn of a unicorn and with fine pearls and a great sapphire in the cover.

Then there was a banquet, and at the King's "cup-board," whereon stood the golden cups of wine, waited the Chief Butler of England.

Then in three places of the hall of Westminster Palace was "Largess !" cried, three times, by Master Norrey, "because Master Garter had an impediment in his tongue."

It was a great day for them all ; for Edward, restored

---

[1] This peerage was surrendered to Henry VII by a successor of Gruythuse.

to sovereignty ; for his guest and benefactor, the new Earl of Winchester ; for Elizabeth Woodville, and for the people, when the Speaker of the House of Commons, so seldom heard, voiced their joy at the birth of little Edward, Prince of Wales.

The Duchess of Burgundy was received in state. Edward, it is true, had been somewhat faithless to the memory of Charles of Burgundy and had failed to support the cause of his young daughter, the child of Margaret's predecessor. For to that cause Louis XI of France was hostile, and there was that very acceptable grant from him to be kept in mind by the King of England.

Margaret was lodged at Coldharbour in the City, and from the royal stores in the Great Wardrobe, not far off, all kinds of furnishings were supplied for the mansion during her sojourn.

Arras " of the story of Paris and Elyn " (the heroine of Troy is persistently without an aspirate), sheets and blankets, feather beds and bolsters, hangings for the state bed, of striped velvet and shot silk, trimmed with silk fringe, and a second set of white and pale blue velvet. Hangings for her pew in the private chapel were also provided, and more than two thousand nails and hooks were sent out for the fastening and suspending of the various fabrics.

The King's bargemaster and his crew were provided with new jackets adorned with roses in embroidery. The latter were separately worked, and applied to the garments. The King's embroiderer, a Frenchman, received fourpence for the royal badge, in the larger size, and one penny for the same in the smaller.

Even when she left our shores after this visit, in which

she had laid such a rod in pickle for Henry VII in the years to come, Margaret left full-handed.   Costly stuffs of every kind were apportioned to her servitors and to a train of English who accompanied her—purple velvet, scarlet, blue, and black cloth, and coats of blue and murrey-colour, similar to those issued to the royal bargemen, were bestowed upon the retinue.   Hear, too, the stuff which went to make a pillion ; the seat behind the rider on which a lady sat on horseback : three yards and a quarter of cloth-of-gold in blue and purple, with silken fringe in the same colourings and fringe of Venice gold ; while two yards of buckram were provided for the stiffening of the sumptuous fabric.

The jackets must have been of scanty dimensions, like a jockey's perhaps ; for no more than two yards of material was provided for each, the width of which is not, however, traceable.   Possibly they were sleeveless ; made in the form of tabards.

Edward had music at his court.   Minstrels and trumpeters are referred to, and one of these, John Hills, received ten marks *per annum* from the fee-farm of Bridport, Dorset, a town which had been in the dower of Edward I's Queen Margaret.

George, Duke of Clarence, the heir-presumptive, also had his minstrel.

The children of the Chapel Royal sang the Church offices and carols at Christmas-time, and their instructor received payment from the King.

One of the King's chaplains, Master Thomas Saintguste, Mus.Doc., was made Master of King's College, Cambridge, early in the reign.

The King had his physician, "sworn to preserve the King's body," and the Queen had her own female attendant, who assisted her at the birth of her children.

The practice of boarding out old servants among the monasteries seems to have died out or to have escaped record upon the rolls. Several persons are made poor knights of Windsor. Almshouses were probably being established, for in later years an old servant of Edward IV is found receiving support in one of these institutions at the hands of Edward's daughter, Elizabeth.

To Edward IV, religious beliefs presented, as to many they do, more opening for superstition than for faith or practice undefiled. His subjects would have shared the belief that the day of the week on which fell Holy Innocents was unlucky for any undertaking. It was on this account that the coronation in June, 1461, was deferred to a Monday, because the preceding Holy Innocents' Day had fallen on a Sunday.

Edward, it is recorded, had a great devotion to St. Anne. Yet he scrupled not to try and break sanctuary and, having been opposed in that, to lure the refugees out by false promises and put them to death after Tewkesbury, an intrinsic malfeasance which made devotion to a saint no higher than the lowest fetishism.

The intervention of the Church was sought in dealing with outlaws, who, it would seem to us, could have paid but little heed to such authority, were it not for our recognition of the fear, lying in reserve in every mind in days gone by, of dying without shrift. The most heedless ruffian might pause before such threatened deprivation. At any rate, when pirates of Plymouth had tired out the coastguards of the day, they were dealt with by a sentence of excommunication.

On the other hand, the secular arm was invoked in cases of clerical indiscipline. Thus, on one occasion, the King commands his sheriffs to arrest, if found, certain of the Austin Friars who had discarded their habit and were wandering about the country in manner most irregular.

The art of alchemy might be practised under royal licence. Thus Richard Carter receives a permit for two years to practise with minerals and metals on the King's manor of Woodstock, and two of Edward's officials were also licensed to transmute mercury to gold.

The royal abbey of Fontévrault comes once more to our notice when Edward IV confirmed the charters granted by his forefathers.

Another religious house, associated with earlier Plantagenets, came before Edward's notice for an infraction of the regulations relating to royal licence. This was Godstow, where "Fair Rosamond" traditionally expiated her liaison with Henry II. The abbess had received appointment from the Holy See without the requisite confirmation from the sovereign. She was "pardoned" for her *lèse majesté*, and received formal restoration from the King of the abbatial estates.

The great invention of William Caxton was to bring to an end the beautiful art of manuscript as practised by the skilled workers of the cloister and, though later, of some of the royal clerks. Yet down to the days of Edward VII printing has been banned for certain purposes. The petitions of subjects to the sovereign must still be penned.

Edward himself had his collection of finely illustrated MSS. Their binding and the tagged laces for the same are mentioned in some of the royal memoranda and accounts. The King had his copy of the Holy Scriptures—"a book called the Bible,"—his Froissart, and a few Latin works.

He was so impressed by the beauty of the illuminated MSS. of his Flemish host, Gruythuse, that, upon his restoration, he commanded similar works for himself.

The country gentleman had also his little collection —the works of Cicero, some romantic ballads and legendary tales, to which, as justice-of-the-peace, he had added the book of statutes of the current reign.

The father of the Queen celebrated the first anniversary of her coronation by the purchase of a choice MS., and her brother was among the earliest patrons of printing. Indeed, he was a pioneer author among those whose work was printed by William Caxton.

We can see clearly into some ways of the household ; by others, we are baffled. What, for example, of those "paris candles" which were given out by weight in the royal wardrobe ?

They do not appear to have had association with *la ville lumière,* nor can they be considered as a "pair of candles," as some have believed. Were they of moulded kind or of white wax, or, once more, a feasible suggestion, were they "pierce " or hollow candles (*concavus* is the Latin term employed), against which an Act of Henry VI, one of the few adduced by his successor, was revived in the last years of Edward IV ? (Pat. 19 E. IV. m. 13.)

Let us return now to the King who misused so ignobly the greatness of his opportunity.

CHAPTER XIV

THE FINAL SPELL

EDWARD remained through everything the incurably self-indulgent personality whose lightness cast so much good fortune, so much opportunity, behind him. His nature could not stand prosperity. Peace with France, auspiciously signalled by the white dove which perched upon a tent in the English camp, the rich subsidy, the birth of sons, inspired him, less with a resolve to confirm, by his own efforts, the happy situation and to hand it on to his posterity, than with determination to enjoy the fleeting hour.

Once more, the courtier and the citizen looked grimly on the royal amours, upon a king not sobered by the tottering of his throne in that tenth year. Around were foes, some open, some insidious ; his nearest kin. His Chief Butler had forgotten him, and had perished in the field with the Lancastrians, cleft in twain, says one account, by his new masters, who saw him waver in the charge. The Nevilles were now, by various marriages, related more nearly than ever to the King. Could they fail to weight the balance ? Could Anne, widow of the murdered Edward, King Henry's heir, have swayed her second husband, Richard, Duke of Gloucester, in favour of the brother whom he was already watching with a sinister gleam of hatred, even of latent insanity?

In the realm and without the realm rose images of bale.

Harry of Richmond had made himself a power. He, a descendant from John of Gaunt, through the offspring so tardily legitimated, by a senile marriage, of John and Swinford's wife, was a greater fear to Edward than any of the lawful reversioners of his crown.

John of Gaunt had kept his paramour, Katharine le Roet, through his two marriages and through her own. Who had thought that John, the offspring of this "double avoutrie," would, as great-grandfather, be ancestor of a sovereign of England?

"No thought of the crown had prevailed in the legitimization of these bastards."

The skies were set with omens. Already, before the flight to Flanders, there had been the "blazing star four feet high by estimation, going towards the North, and so endured v or vi weeks."

Another in the west with flame "like a spear-head" had, says the chronicler, led to the decision regarding the marriage of Edward of Lancaster with Anne Neville.

Again, after the return of the King, there was that comet whose movements are recorded by the rude observers of the age. In January, 11 Edward IV, it appeared in the S.E., then in the E., as "a white flame fervently burning, not upright, and a great hole therein, and the flame came out. Then it rose in the N.E., and so backer and backer."

Two summers later "Womere water ran hugely."

This woe-water was said to be a presage of death, and it was in truth a summer of dysentery and fever epidemics, but a heat-wave was more logically involved than the intermittent springs.

The woe-water still breaks forth at times; in Kent, where there were three examples of it in the days of Edward IV, and in other places.[1]

There were warnings more uncanny by far than these. "A voice in the air, between Leicester and Banbury, crying Bowes! Bowes! (Repent)." There and in other places it was "heard of forty men. Some said a headless man cried. A warning to amend living."

But omens, in the air and the earth and in the waters under the earth, moved Edward little. The King, gay, fine in his presence, loved, as the debonair is loved, without the chop of logic, died in the very prime of life, leaving the boding heritage of treachery and rebellion to that hapless child of thirteen years whose kingship ever lags behind the pathos of his childhood's doom.

[1] The writer understands that the spring which bursts in the early year at Winterborne, near Dorchester, is of this character.

EDWARD V

EDWARD V AS A YOUNG CHILD, WITH HIS PARENTS AT THE PRESENTATION BY
ANTHONY, EARL RIVERS, AND WILLIAM CAXTON OF AN EARLY PRINTED BOOK

CHAPTER XV

"A CHILD SET IN THE MIDST"

*"And the prince born.
And a black star."*

THUS, in the least of verbiage, is chronicled the birth of that child figure whose veiled fate, with his younger brother's, is ever with us, while everything of his true status has slipped by.

King as rightful, though uncrowned, he may have been as any of the list, from Saxon Edwards downwards.

Duke of Cornwall, Earl of Chester, Prince of Wales, all these his honours, congenital or created, he did not lack, and yet we have forgotten them for the vision of the little bodies, his and Richard's, with breath smothered out of them, in the unrevealing dungeons of the Tower.

In the Tower, he should have first drawn breath. In the Tower, his mother waited, with daughters only round her, for the birth of her fourth royal child. In the Tower she heard of the King her husband's flight across the North Sea. She trusted less the deepness of the walls, the strategy of the garrison, than the hallowed custom of sanctuary. Traitors had held the government before now, and Warwick was without, somewhere in the kingdom, levying men, and with a record of power over both sides, over royalist and renegade, over legitimist and usurper, over the white rose and the red.

Elizabeth, like David of old, elected to fall rather into the hands of the Lord than those of men ; she left the grey, relentless walls, and fled along the great bend of the river to Benedictine Westminster.

And there, scarce knowing whether she were still a queen, for Henry of Lancaster, her fellow-lodger at the Tower, had been brought forth by the Janus-visaged Neville crew, Elizabeth, in that hour of the rending of a kingdom, brought forth on a November day the first son she bore to Edward, a little child born " poorly and christened without the ceremonies due to a prince."

There, in the Sanctuary, he abode with his mother until that day of early spring when the glad shouting on the highway told of the return of his royal father. An infant of a few months, he neither knew nor recked of the meaning of that joyful clamour, when his mother and her courtiers streamed out to greet the gay young sovereign, scarcely sobered by the grim page of vicissitude he had just turned. Perhaps he did not even stir in sleep, this little Edward ; perhaps, fretted by the unaccustomed storm of voices, he raised an infant whimper. Avice Wells, his nurse, was there to comfort him with her adapted version of the glad day's meaning.

We have no record and no picture of that moment when Edward IV first looked on the face of the child who should come after him, and who now, after the blackness of his start in the sore world, was to be the object of the honour and formality due to his heirship.

Master Vaughan, his chamberlain, bears him in his robes of state next after the sovereign in those scenes of splendid welcome to the Seigneur de Gruythuse. Old enough he then would be to look with a child's delight upon the vision of gold and colour, upon the yellow pallid gleam of tapers and of torches, and to hear, with some small fear, perhaps, the more than common blasts of the trumpets and the shouts of kings-at-arms, at Westminster. There sat his father wearing his cap of maintenance, and there his mother in a jewelled crown. It was the proudest day, the one flawless day, in her chequered life-story, that in which Elizabeth heard the commendations of Parliament, uttered before the King, upon her "womanly behaviour and great constancy, he [Edward IV] being beyond the sea."

Her fortitude, the valour so often manifested *etiam in sexu fragile!* Poor Elizabeth! was not her whole career one of "womanly" behaviour? For, with the weapons of her sex, she, who had been offered the standing of the "leman," conquered the place of queen. She busied herself with place-seeking for her kindred, with the accomplishment of good matches for her sisters and brothers. Anthony she saw becoming husband of the first heiress of the nobility, and peer in his bride's right. John, in the cold-blooded manner of the age, wedded to Katharine, Duchess of Norfolk, "she $\frac{xx}{iiii}$ an. He xx," spits out a chronicler, " *maritagium diabolicum!*" "A hag of eighty," cries another voice. It was the Duchess's fourth essay in marriage.

Elizabeth's firstborn son, by the Lancastrian Grey, had been ennobled as Marquis of Dorset and married to Edward's own niece, heiress to the duchy of Exeter.

But all this womanly wire-pulling of hers, which had irked the court and the country alike, were for the moment overlooked as she stood, the mother of the heir-apparent, before all England on that October day.

In a more sacred scene we see the child Edward carried in procession to the shrine of the king-saint, Edward, in the Abbey Church of Westminster, before which the King and prince made oblation.

For a time he may have been under the surveillance of Lady Darcy, the *gouvernante,* or, as she is called in the English records, the " lady-mistress of the King's nursery."

Then the Bishop of Rochester was appointed tutor, "that he may be brought up in virtue and cunning."

He was in his fifth year when he received the gift of a dwelling within the precincts of Westminster, built by his chamberlain Vaughan at great cost, and presented to the King on his behalf. Soon after, the little prince was appointed regent during his father's absence in France.

The Archbishop of Canterbury is one of the trustees for his duchy of Cornwall. Here and there we have a glimpse of minor officials of his household. His yeoman-porter receives the office of Porter of St. Briavel's in the Forest of Dean, a royal castle to this day.

To join the group of older sisters, young brothers and other sisters came to Edward, Prince of Wales. To him most tragically linked was Richard, the second son of Edward and Elizabeth, born at Shrewsbury.

The date of this young prince's birth is uncertain. One chronicle says that it took place in the month of July, *anno xi.*

Sir N. Harris Nicolas, citing Hall's Chronicle, says that the prince was born, most probably, in 1472. The authority cited is not sufficiently reliable to provide us with any certainty.

The birth of a daughter in April, 1472, is allowed by Sir N. Harris Nicolas, and such an event is noted by a country gentleman, who writes from London at the end of April, 1472 :—

"The Queen hadde chylde, a dowghter, but late at Wyndesor."

This was Margaret, who died in infancy in the same year.

If Richard were born in July, 1471, there is a very short interval between the two births. Margaret may, however, have owed her early death to premature nativity.

Richard, at all events, was created Duke of York in 1474, and in January, 1477, his marriage to Anne, daughter of the Duke of Norfolk, took place.

Sandford, not an exact authority, says that Richard was a year and more younger than his bride, whose age he places at about six years. Anne Moubray was, however, according to more exact evidence, only four years and three months old at the time of her marriage, so that Richard, if born in 1472 (reckoned in Old Style from Lady Day), could not have been more than a very few months younger than Anne. If, however, he had been born in 1473, a year which, as far as the writer can ascertain, is not precluded, he would then have been her junior by over a year.[1]

The marriage of the children took place in St.

[1] The complexity of computing dates during this reign is considerable, on account of the various systems of reckoning. The regnal year, the year of our Lord (which began on Lady Day), the contemporary registers, some reckoning from the London Mayoralty, October 28th, O.S., and some from the Shrievalty, a month earlier, have all to be studied and collated, apart from any question of intrinsic accuracy in the various sources of information.

Stephen's Chapel in the Palace of Westminster, where, on very rare occasions, the marriage of M.P.'s, or the christening of their offspring, takes place in our own day.

There being blood-relationship between the bride and bridegroom, an ecclesiastical challenge was formally made upon their arrival for the ceremony, upon which the requisite document of dispensation was produced on their behalf. The contract, or essential sacramental rite, was then proceeded with, and was followed by a nuptial Mass at the high altar.

Gold and silver largesse was thrown to the general public who had gathered for the occasion.

Then direful Richard, Duke of Gloucester, and the Duke of Buckingham, another royal kinsman, led little Anne to the wedding-feast, which was served at several tables.

At one sat young Dorset, Elizabeth's son by Grey, surrounded by fair ladies.

The cup of spiced wine was handed, " as appertained to matrimonial feasts."

The bridegroom, in right of his consort, was created Duke of Norfolk. He was also made Viceroy in Ireland, and, as such, appointed Robert Preston, Lord Gormanston, as his vicegerent.

Edward, Prince of Wales, had also his commissioners, who dealt with certain insurgents in his principality in an early year of his existence.

When Edward IV seized the goods of Neville, the rebel Archbishop of York, and converted the prelate's mitre into a crown for himself, he handed over the plate and jewels to his heir.

When Aunt Margaret of Burgundy came to England the Prince of Wales, then in his tenth year, received from his father a piece of golden tissue in white colour-ing, while purple velvet was provided for his younger brother Richard, together with less gorgeous fabrics.

Richard, too, received his robes of the Garter in the same year, the mantle of blue velvet, the garter and the lace (or cord) of blue with gold buttons.

The Keeper of the Great Wardrobe, Peter Curtis, was a busy man that year, giving out stuffs and stores of every kind for the celebration of Margaret's visit.

We come, after this small tale of their boyhood, to the April day when Edward became a reigning sove-reign. Yet there is little again to tell of those short months of kingship.

Upon them is cast that baleful shadow of their uncle Richard.

The story of Edward V, is it not rather the tale of Richard, Duke of Gloucester, and of the growing obsession of his own right of, and capabilities for, king-ship?

Through all the years of his youth (for he was but thirty-one when Edward V began his reign), Richard had marked the insecure hold of the light-living King, his brother; had seen, too, the removal one by one of many barriers between his own self and the throne.

Richard, of whom so many dark things are related. His entry foot-first into the world, with teeth already in his head, accounted, for some reason, as unrighteous-ness in the common mind of his own day.

Afflicted with infantile paralysis; this we may, with reason, believe him to have been. He may also, in truth, have had the spinal curvature and the high shoulder fitted to him in every chronicle.

There can be little doubt that he also possessed that

inflated self-esteem which Dame Nature, horribly adjusting the balance, accords so often to the physically unfit.

Also, we can see in him to-day the taint of aberration, in the light of which so many of his deeds are rendered clear ; that suggestion of the border-line of sanity, the dwellers upon which are ever a surer menace to the community than the avowed victims of a restrained lunacy.

He was a seventh son and but a child when Richard, Duke of York, his father, swept through the kingdom in his struggle for the crown he claimed, and arrived in London at the opening of Parliament in the late 'fifties of the fifteenth century.

His father, who had looked forward to a royal reception, to the acclamation of the peers, but who had conceived too glamorous a vision. For, entering the House of Lords, the duke stood there for a time beneath the royal canopy. Yes, doubtless in their eyes he was the head of the legitimate line. Yet stood he there with no acclaim as king. He rested, indeed, his hand upon the throne, as one who waited for the word to take his seat there. But the Lords were wrapped in silence.

It grew upon him that here was no welcome to a king. In the suspense, his hand was outstretched till it trembled ; in the ominous stillness his own hastening blood alone made drumming in his ears. Then the Archbishop of Canterbury, the first by precedency then in that House, moved forward to the solitary figure, and, with a refinement of tactfulness almost cruel, inquired whether the duke desired to pay his homage to the King. But now, Richard, who hitherto had bitten his lip upon all betrayal of his ardent expectation and his resentful confusion, flushed blood-crimson with the resentful shame of the rebuff. Hot-tongued, his haughty answer darted—

"I know of none," said he, "to whom *I* owe that honour!"

With that, he left the Chamber and hurried to his own Baynard's Castle on Thames bank, and there he treated by formal missive with the repellent peers, while the Lancastrian and Yorkist parties tilted wordily over their respective propositions.

Richard II had resigned his throne, said the Lancastrians.

That might be, responded the Yorkists, but it was not in favour of the House of Lancaster in particular or any member of it.

Then it was averred that since Richard, Earl of Cambridge, had died attainted, his son and his posterity were ever barred.

This was certainly a very involved method of begging the question, the Yorkists might have argued, for the rightful blood may well disclaim treason against the usurper.

Then cried the Yorkist faction that the earl had been reinstated in his honours and confirmed in the duchy of York and the earldom of March both by the King and all the realm.

Then arose a plea of limitation, since, said they, the House of Lancaster had worn the crown for more than sixty years.

To which it was opposed that the succession to the crown was by the unwritten law of natural right and that there was no decree enacted which could annul the same.

Then the Lancastrian defendant partizans took refuge in play on the emotions, the desperate resource of counsel to this day. They painted Henry, the blameless figure, already, for eight-and-thirty years, a king. How cruel would be the hands which tore the crown from off that harmless brow !

To this unreason's more unsubtle weapon the Yorkists answered forcibly that Henry was unfit to govern, and that the crown would be preserved to him for the devices of Queen Margaret alone (whom some accused of bearing her son Edward by another father than the King) and for the ministers, who already took Henry's name in vain for their own ends.

Nor when all was said and done was it meet that for love of him the realm should perish; neither should injustice be committed in the name of charity.

Duke Richard did not live to see the end of the contention. Slain in the field, he left his claim to his eldest surviving son, Edward, Earl of March. Richard, his seventh son, was still a child when all this happened. A boy of nine, he stood with George, aged twelve, on the steps of the throne while " Splendid Brother " [1] was crowned before their eyes. There were good things for little George and Richard in that dawn of the York dynasty. We have seen their creation as royal dukes (in Chapter XI), and as years went on there were gifts of manors and emoluments from the King. Then Richard in his early teens saw the Woodville crew gain prestige at the court ; he heard the whispers against the careless, self-indulgent King ; he saw Clarence leagued with Warwick against him. In the dawn of his young manhood he fled with the King brother from the crumbling

[1] A theft which all will recognize.

sovereignty. He stood, at eighteen years of age, once more on English soil and saw the desperation of the red rose. He helped with his own withered arm, they say, to slay young Edward, Henry's son, and (did a savage love already prompt the deed of blood?) he married Anne Neville the widow of the young Lancastrian victim. Isabel, her sister, was already wife of Clarence. To both were born young Edwards. And now perhaps was growing strong that dark obsession of his fitness for the kingship. Before him, out of six elder brothers, the King, Edward IV, alone survived. Clarence, the traitor, had been put to death, Richard the right-hand man in the doing. Then, against the King, his benefactor, turned the blackened soul. The thwarted brain hatched its foul brood of cruel deeds, the offspring of aborted gifts. Richard held an index-finger to the lightness of the careless ruler. What could not his own powers do in the seat of sovereignty were it but his and not the elder brother's, or the crown his, instead of being thrown into the hog-trough of the libertine.

Then with Edward's death a wild rush whelmed him, the paranoia of kingship blinded and stunned all other apprehension. Those little lives, Edward's and Richard's (for Clarence's son was negligible), stood alone between himself and the throne.

Between streaks of untrammelled fury, the cunning of the maniac inserted itself. He must secure the persons of the young King and his brother. Elizabeth, the widowed Queen, had no illusions regarding Richard's feelings towards herself. Nor did she trust his aims with regard to her sons: Edward, with his uncle, was on the way to London. With her remaining children,

Elizabeth once more took refuge in the Sanctuary where twelve years earlier she had given birth to Edward, now the reigning King. There, none could touch her.

But it was, all the same, not fitting for the heir-presumptive to skulk in sanctuary. Richard prevailed upon the Archbishop of Canterbury to visit the Queen and to put before her the right course. Let her hand her sons over to the keeping of their uncle, who would see to the interests of all. The archbishop, in all good faith, made his way with the mission to the Queen where she " sat low upon the rushes."

He was of the same mind, he told her, as the Duke of Gloucester. He painted the rousing of loyal enthusiasm when the young King appeared before the peers, before the people. Elizabeth clung with tears and trembling to little Richard and at first refused to let him go. Then a fresh weapon was turned against her. It would be sad for the brothers to be separated, said the Duke of Gloucester. And this, also, the archbishop, in good faith, impressed upon the widowed Queen. Elizabeth suffered herself to be moved ; the archbishop was above suspicion, himself the unhappy dupe of the Protector. And so Richard went forth innocently to his doom.

Richard, the Duke of Gloucester, cries now against the claim of all. His own mother, yet living, he befouls. All her children save himself alone, he swore, were the offspring of her adultery, foisted on his father. Again he swore, a very superfluity of allegation, regarding Edward's offspring.

The marriage of Edward, so he cried, had been no marriage, for he had been pre-contracted to the Lady Elizabeth Lucy. Elizabeth Lucy had, as we have heard,

JANE SHORE

denied the contract, while admitting her own shame as mistress of the King. There was the story of the Bishop of Bath and Wells, who had been witness. All evidence, sound or unsupported, was dragged into the turmoil of the controversy.

Then Richard bounded at a tangent to fresh invective.

"The witch-woman, Shore, she has caused mine arm to wither."

And he bared the shrunken limb before the Lords.

The beholders could but gaze dumb-struck upon the Protector, for they knew that the undeveloped arm was no new thing nor due to Jane, linked, as Richard had declared, in evil understanding with the widowed Queen.

Jane had, they tell, since Edward's death been living under the protection of Lord Hastings and later still of the Marquis of Dorset.

On her was to fall the crazed retribution of the coming king.

For Richard III had her haled forth by the churchmen to do penance for her deeds of magic. Clad in her kirtle only, with candle in her hand, she went forth from the Bishop of London's palace, where she had been arraigned. The shame of her dire plight flushed her cheek with the rose tones which alone her beauty lacked, so that in her hour of contumely she showed the fullness of her beauty ; she stood there in the pillory of Shoreditch, which owed no name to her, for it stands in records penned before her birth.

She was to live on for half a century, dying in the reign of Henry VIII in sorest destitution. So runs the tale.

"They say she was fair that knew her in her youth.

"For now is she old, lean, withered, and dried up, nothing left but rivelled skin and hard bone."

On Jane had come in those after years the nemesis of those who live but in the flesh.

The Duchess of York, King Edward's mother—she whose outcry had been so loud against his marriage—was to outlive her son by fourteen years.

Elizabeth, the Queen, she, too, was to live on for further years. She was to see the casting down of all things. Her daughter Cecily, bastardized by Richard's machinations, was no longer a meet spouse for James III of Scotland. She was to marry into the Tudor party, whose chief, as Henry VII, was to be husband to young Elizabeth Plantagenet.

She had known the keenest contrasts of vicissitude, the trough of the waves and the crest of the seas.

She had seen her father and her brother perish at the hands of the Lancastrian rebels—her father, Richard Woodville, who, by his marriage with Jacqueline, Bedford's widow, became a direct ancestor, not only of King Edward VII, but of the greater part of reigning Europe of to-day. For he is the common progenitor of the King and Queen of England (T.M. George V and Queen Mary), of a German Emperor (Wilhelm II), of a Tsaritza (Alexandra), of a Queen of Spain (Victoria Eugénie), of a Queen of Norway (Maud), of a Grand Duke of Hesse (Ernest Louis), of a Duke of Coburg (Charles Edward), and, as well, of Crown Princesses of Sweden and Roumania, and others beyond number.

" If," cried Napoleon to a brother on the day of coronation, " our father could but see us now ! "

If Richard, Earl Rivers, could have received, as he perished by the hands of his enemies, so glorious a vision of posterity, might not he too have cried his conviction—

" Non omnis moriar !"

In the years of widowhood, in the retreat of the Abbey of Bermondsey, from which, occasionally, she came forth into the court scene, as at her grandson, Arthur Tudor's christening, such was the retrospect of Elizabeth, Queen and woman.

The story, resting on the slightest substance, of Richard's project for a marriage between himself and his young niece, Elizabeth, has become immortal from no worth of fact, but from its having been, in Shakespeare's hands, set in an everlasting poignancy of drama.

Sir Thomas More's [Morton?] account, incorporated in the Chronicle of Holinshed, from which Shakespeare drew his matter, has passed into a scene of terrible intensity.

The mother, gasping her anguished retort and question; the dark Richard, dowered with that strange and morbid influence which is a feature of mania in its incipience; the dreadful cajolery of his insinuations:

"Prepare her ears to hear a lover's tale"

—and who had known the importunities of urgent lovers as Elizabeth, the mother of the sacrifice, had known them? On her consciousness he played amidst the horror of her present outlook; she writhes under the conflicting movements—the grotesque oppositions—of the scene.

Her sons, unheard behind the unrevealing confines of their prison—their fate unknown; surmised, yet not established; and he who is their gaoler, yea, their murderer, whispers to her of amorous blandishment and of her maiden daughter.

Shakespeare owed something, it is true, to W. Raphael Holinshed; though his apostrophe of "Mr. W. H.," which has so exercised the critics, had hardly an application to the chronicler, being perhaps, after all, but a matter of sonnets written to the order of some court squire or lady. But, if he borrowed this small capital, has he not paid a mighty interest for the same throughout the ages?

And Richard, what of him in that black hour when his young son, that other Edward, whom he had created Prince of Wales, died before his eyes, and all the projects born of his terrible obsession, his long black brooding, were smeared from the tablets of the future?

Truly, the third generation fails those who have stopped at nothing for their ends. Richard III and Henry VIII, and, again, Napoleon, all of whom, in varying degree, sought to establish dynasty.

There were no children's children left to tell the tale of their forefathers!

CHAPTER XVI

"A WHEEN BANES!"[1]

"AND the two sonnyes of Kynge Edward were put to silence."

Of these two—the King, Edward V, for whom a bride had been sought in Brittany, and Richard, heir-presumptive, already wed and widowed—is there more to say than has been said in rumour thin and drear?

Nothing!

The confession of Forest and Dighton, so convenient for Henry VII, goaded by Warbeck and Margaret of Burgundy : the smothered corpses thrust into a chest, buried, and moved again beneath the stairway of a lesser tower within the fortress : then, two centuries later, that heap of bones of children, of the victims' years, found at a spot concordant with the story of the self-accused murderers, and the fragments of what might be a chest found with them. There is no absolute judicial proof in any of these things ; presumptive evidence alone waits on the pulverizing contents of the coffin buried with royal honours on the command of Charles II.

[1] Words uttered in a pathetic Scottish story by Miss Mulock.

EDWARD VI

Edward Prince

EDWARD VI IN INFANCY

HOLBEIN

CHAPTER XVII

THE PRINCE

IN the month of February, 1537, the Emperor Charles V, in a letter to a diplomat, states that, upon information gleaned in England, it would seem unlikely that the King would have any more children. This hypothesis, reared giddily on haze; upon some alleged gossip of " the concubine," as the Catholic Powers, with crude logic, called Anne Boleyn, had, even as the Emperor wrote, been menaced with extinction. On the Eve of St. Edward in the same year it received its dissolution when Queen Jane bore the son who was to be the last king of the Tudor House.

More than half a century had passed since the reign of the fifth Edward. As had happened before in the history of England, female heirship to the throne had been set aside by the usurper. Elizabeth Plantagenet, next by right of birth after her vanished brothers, had become, as consort of Henry VII, the ancestress of kings, but not their sovereign predecessor.

Her son Arthur had predeceased his father, Henry VII, leaving the Princess Katharine maiden-widowed, so was said at least, both then and in the days to come, on high authority.

Katharine, duly married by papal licence to Henry,

Arthur's younger brother, was to become Queen-consort of England, and then, with all her children dead, save Mary, was to be repudiated by Henry, supported by the authority of the schismatic Cranmer.

In the cruel wrong Katharine saw, says one reporter, the vengeance of Heaven on her father, the King of Aragon, for having contracted her to the son of the usurper, Henry Tudor, regardless of the claims of the Earl of Warwick, son of that Duke of Clarence who had, by legend, met his death in malvoisie.

The contention ignored the female claim residing in Elizabeth Plantagenet, which in our own day would be held superior to her cousin Warwick's.

Sentiment, the so-called "natural law," did unquestionably prevail. For, even if the Salic law (or custom ?) did not ostensibly obtain in England, it yet became effective, almost automatically, whenever royal heirship fell to the spindle side.

The reporter too, was of the family of the Earl of Warwick, and so, perhaps, would willingly see with Queen Katharine's eyes in this respect, if, indeed, his kindred had not themselves offered suggestive vision to the wretched woman.

Katharine then had been repudiated, and her surviving daughter bastardized. But her successor was not destined for any steady tenure of a dazzling destiny.

The beauty of Anne Boleyn's lady-in-waiting, Jane Seymour, had already allured the King of England's roving eye. The way was well prepared for those who carried to the royal ear the tale of Anne Boleyn's ill-doing, and of her infamous association with her next in blood. A brother leaning carelessly upon her couch —a word or look waylaid between the Queen and a court musician—Henry believed as he desired; perhaps, indeed, as he was impelled by the acrid promptings of his gouty diathesis. The head of "La Ana" fell within the Tower, with eyes and lips quivering reflexive after the stroke of severance. The King, they tell, made a mock of mourning in white garments, and next day married Jane. The marriage must at all events have followed quickly on the death of "the concubine."

Henry's first queen was also dead. The "princess-dowager," as Katharine was styled, had ended her sad life with the opening of the year. Jane, therefore, might have status as a wife that Anne had lacked, even if Rome could only accept with reservation the marriage of schismatic Henry, solemnized by an Archbishop of Canterbury whose faculties were in suspense. The marriage might, in the judgment of the Papal Curia, rank on a level with those of heathen, perhaps a little lower in point of intention. On the new basis established by the English King, it could, however, pass well enough with the clique who had seceded from the pontifical obedience.

Yet, again, the law of England could only accept as heir-apparent the offspring of Jane Seymour upon the invalidation of any claim residing in Mary and Elizabeth, Henry's older offspring.

With all the tangle and the speculation involved by this "confusion of wives" (a contemporary thus describes Henry's matrimonial experiments) we cannot deal at length. Jane was wed and her coronation was appointed for Midsummer Day, 1536.

Yet says a passing voice—"The King shall not have the prize of those who do not repent of matrimony," for within a week of the public declaration of the marriage Henry had seen and admired two other ladies, and made it evident " how happy he could be with either." Certainly, Henry VIII could not have claimed the Dunmow flitch.

His vacillation led him, it was also said, to postpone the coronation of Queen Jane, which had been fixed at first for Midsummer, till after Michaelmas, so that it might be seen whether she was likely to be a mother. Even in the New Year she was not crowned, but soon a hint of her maternal hopes was creeping through the inner circles.

In the spring of 1537 the rumour of the event had spread beyond the court. It gathered detail with the months. In July, the Queen is seen without the lacing which united the openings of her dress in ordinary wear. November is alleged as the birth-month. In the last days of September the Queen should " take her chamber" at Hampton Court, entering upon the customary retirement of the mother-expectant. Early in October she has definitely done so. In the beautiful rural palace she is safer than in London from the plague infection. Great mortality prevailed that year in many parts of England from the pestilence.

In the early morning hours upon St. Edward's Eve was born Prince Edward. On the same day (October 12th) Queen Jane's official letter conveys to Cromwell, the Lord Chancellor, the news of the birth of her son " conceived in lawful wedlock." The precaution of the statement becomes neither extreme, nor merely formal, when review is made of the history of Anne Boleyn and of the later Katharine Howard.

Rejoicings hailed the heir-apparent. From St. Paul's and lesser churches rose the hymn *Te Deum*; in the streets were bonfires and the salute of cannon; everywhere was feasting, while swift messengers hastened throughout the land to bear the tidings to every city of the realm.

The custom of short delay in baptism which prevails in the Catholic Church, and which Henry's schismatics had not altered, brought little Edward early to the font. Precautions against plague reduced the number of those who attended at the ceremony. The Marchioness of Dorset, sister to the King, who was to have borne the infant to the font, was staying at the time at Croydon, in the Archbishop's palace. In that district deaths were occurring daily from the plague, and the marchioness and her husband were therefore inhibited by the King from attending at court.

The marchioness writes her thanks and her regrets the day before the ceremony.

The peers who were to attend might bring no more than a stipulated number of followers in their train.

The occasion gives us a strange medley of the old and new. The ceremonial is Catholic in full appearance, it might pass in the main for the baptismal rite of a Dauphin of France. Yet the schismatic Cranmer stands as one sponsor and Mary Tudor as another. In a "salt of gold" the Earl of Essex bears the salt of exorcism.

The Princess Elizabeth, still a tiny girl, was carried by Lord Beauchamp and a lord-in-waiting. She bore the chrisom [1] worked with rich embroidery.

The Marchioness of Exeter took the place of Lady

[1] The chrisom is a white cloth, typifying innocence, which is laid upon the infant at one point of the baptismal ceremonies.

Dorset and carried the prince, whose trained robes were held up by two peers.

The *gouvernante* followed after the infant, and the nurse and Queen Jane's midwife walked with the train-bearers. Six court officials held a canopy above the child. The Earl of Wiltshire carried the candle, the "shining-light" of the ritual. Other torches of virgin wax were borne unlighted till the christening had been performed. Then all were lighted while Garter King-at-Arms proclaimed Prince Edward's styles.

The Sacrament of Confirmation followed the Baptism, the infant being prepared in a side-chapel. Then the Princesses Mary and Elizabeth and the officiating prelates were served in great state with spiced wine and with wafers. Hippocras, a kind of liqueur, was served to the general company within the church, while the commoners who were present were refreshed with bread and such sweet wine as ranked with the " bastard " and the malvoisie of earlier reigns.

The tales which made Jane Seymour die upon the morrow of the birth have long been riddled. Those which represent her as the victim, upon the King's behest, of the most desperate of obstetric resources may also be dismissed. Jane might have sent her official letter to Cromwell *in extremis*, it is true ; these things are managed by court proxy. But she was sending further her intimate and friendly news. John Scarlett bears her letters to Lord Lisle and others.

Within a week of the birth preparations are on foot for her " churching "—a term which has supplanted the "purification" of Philippa and other earlier queens.

Henry created two new earls in that same week. Lord Beauchamp became the Earl of Hertford, and

the Lord High Admiral Fitzwilliam received the earldom of Southampton. As there were not enough peers
present in their robes to present the new earls at the
same time, Beauchamp was first presented for the
dignity, and the Duke of Norfolk and Lord Exeter, who
had supported him, then presented Sir William Fitzwilliam.

It was only on the ninth day, or thereabouts, that
sinister symptoms appeared. A chill, improper feeding,
"she ate what she craved," unchecked by the faculty.
In the early morning of October 24th the Queen's confessor attends her sick-bed and the last sacraments are
administered.

In little more than four hours all was over. The baby
prince was motherless. Yet he was, all the same, a
lusty infant ; unconscious alike of his great estate and
of his misfortune, he " sucketh like a child of his puis-
sance," while the dead Queen lies, awaiting burial, first
in the throne-room of the palace and then within the
chapel beneath the canopy of the catafalque. Twelve
hundred Masses for her soul were commanded, through
the Earl Marshal, to be said in London, and on November 12th, after a fortnight of solemn Mass and dirge in
the Hampton Court Chapel, the body was carried to
Windsor in a stately funeral procession.

Heralds and *poursuivants* headed the train ; then came
the court band and the King's poor pensioners, who,
at the halting-places on the route, kept the way, lining
the streets and bearing torches. The great officers

of state followed, the Archbishop of Canterbury with the *doyen* of the ambassadors of the Emperor Charles V, then Garter and Clarencieux, and the Lord Chamberlain and the Earl Marshal were next before the coffin, alongside of which peers were bearing banners. King Henry had retired into "a solitary place to pass his sorrows," and Princess Mary was chief mourner. She was then about twenty-one years old. Her sad and sombre youth may well have been already printed in her face as she rode there upon her horse, caparisoned in sable velvet.

In litters followed peeresses and great ladies of the court. Lady Rochford, the aunt of the ill-fated Anne Boleyn, was there. We see the names of Dudley, Russell, Jerningham, and Fitzherbert.

The Queen's maids were in the last conveyance, Anne Basset, Lord Lisle's stepdaughter, then newly appointed, among them.

Lord Lisle was that Arthur Plantagenet, the natural son of Edward IV by Elizabeth Lucy (or Jane Shore), of whom we heard in his father's reign. By his first marriage he attained to the viscounty of Lisle in his wife's right. He married, secondly, a widow with several children, and one of these was already maid-of-honour to Queen Jane, while her mother, the then Lady Lisle, was seeking places for her other daughters with much push and energy.

It is startling to turn from the solemn pageant of the funeral to the account of the behaviour of some of the royal officers. We hear, for instance, that " Clarencieux was so distempered that, in coming out of Mr. Treasurer's chamber, the day after the Queen's burial, he fell downstairs and, had he not fallen against Garter and

Chester, he had broken his neck. The same night he fell out with his servant, who brake his master's head with a pewter pot, while Somerset, laying improper hands on the maid of the house, nearly strangled her. . . . Somerset has three wives, all living" (!).

They were, indeed, very "naughty persons," these gentlemen of the College of Arms!

The motherless infant is left in the care of his nurse, Sybil Penn, and of the "lady-governess." Dawning life finds him a healthy nursling, a jocund little fellow. At eight months he has already cut four teeth, "three full out, the fourth appearing." The Emperor's ambassadors report him as "the prettiest child we ever saw," and, but a little later, the Chancellor declares that he "never saw so goodly a child of his age, so merry, so pleasant, so good and loving countenance, and so earnest an eye," and he is little more than a year old when the wife of the Governor of Calais (Lisle), visiting in England, writes that he is "the goodliest babe that ever I set mine eye upon. I pray God make him an old man, for I should never be weary of looking on him."

But if the visitors were so delighted, Edward was not invariably reciprocative. On one occasion he showed his infant feelings very strongly when he received the Ambassador of Saxony and another, "when my lord prince could not be brought to frame to look upon those ambassadors and put forth his hand for no cheering, dandling, and flattering the nurse and lady-mistress could use, but my lord prince ever cried and turned away his face, and yet at the same time, to accustom him to a stern countenance and rough great beard, the Earl of Essex played with my lord prince, took him by the hand, put his beard near his face, which my lord prince took pleasure and was therewith merry. In the end, when the ambassadors could have none other sight of my lord prince for all the labours taken, my said lord of Essex came to my lord prince and said, ' Now full well knowest thou,' quotha, ' that I am thy father's true man and thine, and these other be false knaves.'

" Such speech escaped him suddenly."

Again, they tell a tale flattering to the royal father. " My lord prince hath as much of the King's Highness's good nature as ever had any child of his father."

His first New Year had brought him gifts—plate from the King and the courtiers. One gives " a bell of gold with whistle," the equivalent of the rattle of a later day.

Mary, sister and godmother, presents a coat of embroidered satin ; and little Elizabeth, some four years old, has worked a little shirt as, later on, she also worked a *brassière* with early stitches of her baby fingers.

Nurse Sybil was a person of influence. In the early days of her service she obtained a post for a relative in the prince's household, and, for herself, a grant of the lease of the monastery at Missenden lately taken into the King's hand. She is among the crowd of retainers who receive gifts at the New Year. Nor does she herself come empty-handed before her sovereign, but brings a gift of handkerchiefs with golden trimming.

The household of the infant prince was appointed in his nursery days. Cromwell signs warrants for the members of it in November, 1539.

Mr. Richard Cotton was Comptroller ; William Hastings and George Carleton were among his servants. His Wardrobe has departments for the robes and for the beds, just as the King's. A sinister, if superstitious, shadow fell on his days when but a year old. Gossip in the kitchen of an Oxford college (Corpus) spreads the tale, received from London, of a waxen image found in a graveyard—an image said to represent the prince—and with a knife sticking through its head, or through its heart ; "and as that consumed so likewise should the prince."

A year later, however, he is still "merry and in prosperous estate." His sturdy limbs cannot contain themselves when his minstrels play ; they dance to the joyous strains of vial and of sackbut, then newly added to the court band.

While the infant Edward slept in his cradle, or in his bed of "rich arras," bought from a great Flemish merchant, his father was already on the track of a fresh bride. The King of Portugal, it is true, declined to give his daughter to the English King, but continental match-makers had interested themselves in bringing about a marriage between Henry and the Duchess of Milan, a relative of his first wife, Katharine of Aragon. Henry had his eye also on the widowed Duchesse de Longue-ville, already, though some denied it, contracted to the King of Scots. "Would Henry wish to take another man's wife ?" asked French diplomatists. Had not the tall Duchesse a sister, Mlle. de Guise ?—in a religious house, it was true, yet not as yet professed. And there was Mlle. Vendôme as well.

James V succeeded in marrying his French widow, and a lull appears to have come over Henry's marriage projects for a time. In the May following Queen Jane's death, he had a severe attack of phlebitis. His gouty tendencies were becoming marked ; obesity was adding to his disabilities. On this account his clothes had to be enlarged in the course of the year 1538.

The Constable of France avers that "there is small speaking of any queen; . . . in any case it will be an outland woman and will not happen till the spring." This in November. Two months later there is a project for cross-marriages. One between Henry and a sister of the Duke of Cleves, and a second between the young duke and Princess Mary of England. Anne of Cleves was, according to one report, already betrothed to the son of the Duc de Lorraine. Henry was searching into this matter during the early part of 1539. His emissaries were commanded to require the Chancellor Olisläger, and the Dowager-Duchess of Cleves, especially the latter, to "open the bottom of their stomachs" regarding this question. The "old lady of Cleves" and the Chancellor must have succeeded in quieting scruples on this head, for in July, 1539, the negotiations are well forward, and in September the details of Anne's journey to this country are being planned.

The emissaries think the bride-elect should not come by "long sea," for, being young and beautiful, the sea journey may injure her complexion. So the shorter *trajet* by Calais is planned. In England the matter was kept somewhat dark. True, the Queen's apartments in the royal palaces were being put in order, and some of the great officers had bought "much cloth of gold and other gauds, unusual except for some great solemnity." Henry, too, they say, is longing for further children, as he has but the one son.

At Calais Anne arrived, tall and thin, but dignified in carriage. There she received a presentation from the wife of the Governor. Bad weather detained the bridal train, but, safely landed on the English side, the bride forgot "all the foul weather and was very merry at supper."

At Greenwich, where the King awaited her, barriers had been erected on Thames side by the royal carpenter to keep the people from falling into the river in the crush upon the bride's arrival.

We know the sordid tale of the marriage *pro formâ*, of Henry's physical distaste for the bride, of his unmanly aspersions on her pre-nuptial chastity, which he averred remained, in any case, *in statu quo ante* as far as he was implicated. Further desperate attempts were made, by the King's command, to establish the pre-contract with young Guise. In the end came the decree of nullity, and Anne, a lady phlegmatic to the utmost degree of Flanders, it would appear, settled down in the England where she was to have been Queen-consort, and appears content to wear "a new dress every day."

She had to sit at another table than the King's when at court, it is true, but was "as joyous as ever . . . whether from prudent dissimulation or stupid forgetfulness."

On such good terms were she and Henry that coarse tongues could even credit her with having become enceinte by the King at Hampton Court.

Henry's eye was already set upon another. Among the maids appointed for the new Queen was Katharine Howard, niece of the Duke of Norfolk, small and graceful rather than definitely beautiful, with a devilry and vivacity about her, and with, alas! a stained record in the secret pages of her ill-guarded girlhood. Already, in July of 1540, they talk of her being set "in the same honour" as the discarded Anne. One maid-of-honour gossips to another, "What a man is the King! How many wives will he have?" and the second answers back with praise of Anne and depreciation of Katharine.

Rumours float around of the marriage, said to be

already secretly accomplished. On the Feast of the Assumption (August 15th) prayers for the Queen are publicly offered in the churches, which makes the marriage definite.

Gossip flows on. Henry is tired of her already, wag the tongues of one faction, while another avers that the King has never been so much attached to any of his previous wives. They told also of her rumoured hopes of issue, and in April of next year it was reported that, if this proved true, Henry would have her crowned at Whitsuntide.

But in the autumn of that year dread shades were falling on the young Queen's reputation. A high ecclesiastic finds it his duty to apprise Henry of the sordid tale. The Queen's easy loves for the undistinguished are retailed; the co-respondents testify to their own even greater shame.

When in the house of the " old lady of Norfolk," her grandmother, Katharine would steal the keys from under the duchess's pillow and keep *rendezvous* with one and another. Sir Francis Dereham (Durand he becomes in the mouth of a continental reporter) was even, it was said, contracted to the girl, whose marriage with the King would thus have been invalidated. Henry Monnocks, who had taught her to play the virginals in her girlhood, confessed to other dealings with her.

A musician had been one of those implicated in the alleged misdoings of Anne Boleyn ; while Lady Rochford, who had been a principal agent in bringing accusations against that possibly guiltless Queen, was now arrested as an accessory to the evil deeds of Katharine as Queen. For by this relative's connivance, it was said, the young Queen had studied all the ins-and-outs of the dwelling where she might be lodging, and had thus stolen to meetings with the lovers of her girlhood and with others. Culpeper, a gentleman of the Bedchamber and keeper of the picture gallery at Greenwich, was another of the group. A libertine already, Culpeper had shamefully misused a woman of the countryside, and, in the scrimmage which ensued, had killed one of the rustics who sought to seize him. For this Henry had pardoned him, reserving his ill life for so dreadful a return of benefit.

For such a man as this Katharine had given herself away. In the miserable tale, in the confessions of the co-respondents, is no spark of chivalry or even of romance. When Katharine knew that she was betrayed by her very accomplices—elsewhere have men bitten the lie into their tongue rather than be the undoing of a woman—when the wretched girl knew the ultimate horror and treachery of her erst "lovers," frenzy seized upon her. They had to remove from her all things with which she might have herself done a violence.

What of Henry, on whom, so trenchantly, the tables were now turned!

In the madness of his wronged passion and his grief, he seized a sword, and would have killed the wife who had been so great an object of attraction to his sensuality. Quicker it would have been, a death less terrible, with shorter horror of anticipation, than the doom decreed. From Sion Palace, where she had been sent in the first heat of her *débacle*, Katharine journeyed to the Tower. Lady Rochford was also within its walls. Raving with the horror of her fate, her punishment became a thing of question in her madness. "God's fool" might yet escape.

Katharine had arisen from her first hideous surprise

and showed a front, half regal, half histrionic, in the face of doom. She was allowed for her apparel to have some of her dresses, but without precious stone or pearl. Clad in black velvet, she journeyed to the fortress of death. On the night before her execution she petitioned for rehearsal at the block. Lady Rochford had recovered sanity enough to share her mistress's doom. Together, they confessed their wrongdoing—together, their heads fell. May the touch of heroism in the gay Queen's end have purged her soul.

The miserable Henry, to his secret tumult of shame and resentment, must add the knowledge of a public pillory. The dishonoured husband was the laughing-stock of Europe. Some spoke their minds, and reckoned of his misfortune as a judgment for the treatment of Anne of Cleves. Two London citizens were cast into prison for such utterance. Some, too, in secret, must have remembered that earlier Katharine, " Princess-dowager," so greatly wronged.

Edward, if his baby apprehension grasped anything of the tragic end to his young stepmother, would receive a guarded version of the tale. Elizabeth, too, was still a child. But Mary must have known of Katharine's end—Katharine who had complained of her want of deference, and had, so Mary thought, been instrumental in the banishment of some of her attendants. She, in her twenty-five years of existence, had suffered wrong and sorrow and turmoil of the soul—few more indeed. What wonder that she suffered from palpitation of the heart, was reported abroad as being very ill ! They sent her, after Katharine's downfall, away from court to where her young stepbrother was lying ill with quartan fever. Twice had she seen a Queen of

England die upon the scaffold. Her own mother's broken heart and bitter end could never be forgotten, and Queen Jane even had not escaped, though hers was the natural tragedy of Eve.

Henry's grief was all the more overwhelming because, as they report, for once he seemed to have no new plan: —" Like the woman who cried more bitterly at the death of her tenth husband than all the rest put together, for tho' they had all been good men she had never buried one of them without being sure of the next."

They whispered that he might patch up things again with Anne of Cleves, but for this gossip there never was the smallest ground. That phlegmatic lady had played her part continuously. She had knelt in homage at the feet of Katharine, and proffered gifts at the New Year to her supplanter.

Henry had expended some of his rage and bitterness in punishing those who had been aiders and abettors, true or alleged, in Katharine's wanton doings. Half the Howard family stood in danger of their heads for this species of high treason.

The " old lady of Norfolk," the guardian of the young Queen's youth—she who knew, they said, that Katharine came no maiden to her sovereign, was in the Tower. Lord William Howard was under the same ban. Yet they were saved. Perhaps fact failed ; perhaps the gouty fury lessened—at all events in the year following (1542) they received their pardon.

Henry's recrimination spent itself in decrees against any who in future should conceal pre-nuptial misdeeds of any destined queen from him. Ribald jest spent itself upon the furious array of acts and penalties. The King could safely only take a widow !—and, in July,

1543, Henry did enter upon his sixth and last experiment in matrimony with Lady Latimer, who was a widow, and who became the third Queen Katharine of this King.

Katharine may have been submissive to the interests of the Parrs, her own relations, for she owned, in later years, that she already loved Admiral Lord Seymour and would have married him. The plastic Cranmer issued a licence to the King to marry where he would without the publication of banns, and two days later, on July 12th, Katharine became the wife of the King of England in a private oratory in the apartments of the Queen at Hampton Court, Gardiner, Bishop of Winchester, officiating. Katharine took her vows to be "bonayr and buxom," and, even though she did love Seymour rather than the King, she kept them honestly. The princesses were present, but the five-year-old heir seems not to have been of the royal party on that day.

The third Queen Katharine seems, on the whole, to have met with approbation : "A woman for virtue, wisdom, and gentleness most meet for his Highness."

Her previous wifehood had given her some training in the tactics of matrimony. Her position was sometimes perilous when the disorder of Henry's system churned him up to outbursts of splenetic frenzy. He had grown grey and stout after Katharine Howard's disgrace. When the "issue" in his leg was arrested—the "drainage tube" of those days blocked, it may be—the King and all around him were stirred with fear and fussiness. A course of guaiacum was discussed by his physicians, but they dared not propose the novelty for the sovereign's suspicious consideration.

The war in Flanders was not an unmixed evil. Henry had there some scope for his energies and his undoubted capabilities. Katharine was left as regent of the kingdom and as guardian of the King's children. In August, 1544, she wrote from Hampton Court to Henry at Boulogne:—

"My lord prince and the rest of your children are in good health."

The regent had anxieties, or oversights, in the financial line upon her shoulders. A creditor writes several times to an agent in England desiring him to remind the Queen of a debt of £360 owing by her to him and to his wife. He becomes more pressing on each occasion, and begs that the Queen's Chancellor and her secretary may be reminded of the matter.

Edward, now coming to years of perception, has attached himself to his stepmother, the first who can have had any significance for him. At the age of seven, he writes to her with early difficulties of penmanship and composition. He thanks her, prompted doubtless by his first tutor, for her kind acceptance of his "rude letters."

Elizabeth too, now in her early teens, sends as a New Year's gift a little book she has translated "out of French rhyme into English prose. It is named *The Mirrour or Glass of the Sinfull Soul.*" She hopes the file of the Queen's wit will polish it, and ends with good wishes to her stepmother for the New Year.

By this time young Edward's household was formally established. Cotton remains Comptroller, John Ritter is his Cofferer, or treasurer, (a William Ritter had served at court in the time of Edward IV).

George Tresham is one of the gentlemen-in-waiting and Cheke, a Cambridge graduate, is the head tutor.

Meanwhile he lives in various places, sometimes with the court, sometimes with his half-sisters, and sometimes, perhaps, alone with his entourage.

In 1540 his apartments at Enfield were undergoing repair, so that a coming period of residence may be inferred.   Next year he was at Hampton Court. His formal creation as Prince of Wales did not take place ; here and there is an informal allusion to him under that title, and the ambassadors of foreign Powers generally made use of the style in reference to him in their communications with their respective sovereigns. Let us turn to some of the small things which surrounded " my lord prince " in these his childish days.

CHAPTER XVIII

BY-WAYS OF THE COURT

THE infancy of Edward had felt the lack of blessed vanity of motherhood, of detail waited on by love. Red-taped formality besets the efforts of the well-intentioned *gouvernante*.

"The best coat my lord prince has," writes she to Cromwell, "is tinsel. He hath never a good jewel to set in his cap."

We know him, in a later day, in the cap, raised on one side, with its plumes and its gemmed badge, as Holbein painted him.

Mary it was, grim Mary, who gave the child, on his first New Year's Day, a cap which must have been of some elaborateness of material or workmanship, for it cost over £3 of current value.

Payments for his clothes are made among the royal disbursements when he was nearly two years old. Mary's gifts, as we have seen, sometimes took the form of rich apparel. Satin or velvet, with gold lace and bullion work or embroidery, these are the main materials. We know the form, the doublet with its padded shoulders, the trunks and the shoes with their exaggerated rosettes, the cap which Francis I

223

wore too, and which was going out with Henri de Navarre. Holbein tells us eternally of these.

The dresses of royal ladies of the day are familiar too to our eye.

Edward's mother would seem to have encouraged the styles of home rather than those of France. Her maid, Anne Basset, might crave for leave to wear her French hood, so much more becoming than the regulation bonnet, but she obtained but a short grace, for, though the ladies of the nobility followed French fashions, Jane Seymour objected to them for her ladies-in-waiting.

Anne of Cleves, however, arrived in our country in a French hood, and "then began all the gentlewomen of England to wear French hoods with bellements of gold." Katharine Howard, too, was a patroness of French fashions (her tailor made apparel for the aged Countess of Salisbury in the Tower), while Katharine Parr obtained inspiration, not only from Paris, but from Venice also, "a kirtle with French sleeves and Venetian stocks" being among her gowns, and Mary had a gown of carnation satin made in Venice style. The Queen's apparel has an air of regal matronhood. One dress is made of purple velvet with bodice of the same coloured satin, the velvet costing about six guineas a yard of our present value.

But what were all these gauds of royal ladies beside the bravery of Barbarossa, who landed at Marseilles dressed in a long robe of blue taffetas, brocaded with gold, with a large turban adorned with a black plume; a tunic of crimson satin over all. "Homme est il de petite stature bien gros et la barbe toute blanche." Barbaric Barbarossa!

To return to the English court. The kirtle, distended over buckram, or some still more rigid stiffening, had sometimes a front piece, a "panel," as we might describe it.

Yellow satin, at about £5 of our values per yard, is bought for another kirtle for this Queen. The hood is trimmed with an "'abiliment" of gems or goldsmith's work. Pearls, not always the real thing, adorn the hood, or English headgear, of the court-ladies. Gems and fine gold again compose the "border" which sometimes outlined the bodice, sometimes the frontlet of the hood. Mary's border, given by her father, requires some enlargement at the hands of the goldsmith.

Winter gowns were trimmed with fur. Ermine and miniver, the strictly regal, give place on lesser occasions to lucern. Budge still trimmed judicial robes or country gentlemen's attire. Choice black sables are also mentioned in the royal records, and leopard skins were becoming known and were very costly, being valued at perhaps £1,000 of present worth.

Queen Jane, we hear, would pay her maids-of-honour but £10 a year and they must have a waiting-woman. Their outfit, however, was not large. They were to have but two good dresses, one of satin, one of damask; on the other hand their underwear might be thought too coarse and must be replaced by new. The regulation headgear of velvet, with a border of pearls, was commanded by the Queen at the beginning of October, 1537, to be in readiness for her churching—which never took place.

Much contrivance was needed to provide "Mrs." Anne and "Mrs." Katharine (Basset) with the necessary outfit, modest as it was.

A great lady presented Anne with a new gown of woollen material, trimmed with black velvet. Her sister, not being in the royal service, had to be contented with an old black dress redipped, while skirts were made up for her out of other cast-off dresses. For her black satin dress a new bodice is necessary. Anne's benefactress comes to the rescue of Katharine with the gift of one of her own dresses of "tawny" taffeta trimmed with velvet of the same colour, and this is re-fitted to Katharine's form.

Goods must be obtained on credit : "the stuff . . . is nothing so good as what is obtained for ready money." Christopher Champion, the mercer, receives an acknowledgment from Lady Lisle, the mother of the girls, of satin, damask, velvet, and woollen materials to the value of over £5, for which payment is to be made in the coming March. Anne and Katharine again depend upon kind friends for their velvet bonnets with fronts, which are adapted for them from those of the elder ladies.

The mother of Mrs. Anne and Mrs. Katharine had given lavish orders only a month before for hats and furbelows from France. Three hats were to be trimmed with velvet, three with silk, and a seventh with gold.

"One dozen of cheap *crespins* for my daughters," she includes ; clearly Anne and Katharine must not outshine the mother-bird in plumage.

Great is the number of commissions entrusted either to Lord Lisle's agent in London or to a French lady at Dunkirk, who sends nightcaps on several occasions to Lady Lisle.

The London agent, Sir John Hussey, was a most versatile assistant. Nothing seems to have come amiss to him. He it is who gives orders to the mercers and other tradesmen. He arranges credit and forwards goods of every kind. Bruges velvet, Dutch linen, buckram and sarsnet for lining. Pins by the thousand are despatched to Lady Lisle at Calais. The good Hussey finds nothing too small for his talents. He arranges the dyeing of the ladies' gowns. One will not take tawny, but would succeed in black. On another occasion, scarlet dye cannot be obtained, nor would Baptist the dyer do it at the owner's price.

All the best silks are shipped from Antwerp to England, it was said a few years later. Embroidery silks could have been bought for less in Flanders than in London.

Then the agent explains how he has tried to find a carrier for Mrs. Katharine's kirtle. Katharine was living then with Lady Rutland, whose servant had declined to lade himself with Katharine's parcel. He may have had bigger game, for sometimes he carried gifts from Princess Mary to his mistress.

For young James Basset, a schoolboy in France, leather shoes and velvet caps must be supplied. A Book of Hours and his dancing-lessons figure in the school-bills.

The sympathetic Hussey wishes his lady health and comfort in a time of maternal anticipation.

Delay and disaster both would overtake these traffickings. Here is some taffeta, sent to be made up in London, wrecked off Margate. "I believe your taffeta is saved, but wet." The resourceful Hussey is not damped by these adversities. Within a fortnight of the day on which he imparts the distressful tidings the adventurous silk has been made up and is ready to return to Lady Lisle, with enough over to make two "placards."

Many letters are written upon some commission before it is finally performed. Delay occurred, letters would cross, and the negotiations seem interminable. At the house of the Governor of Calais, too, would occur irregularity. Mme. de Saveteuse writes to ask the viscountess to give her orders beforehand, for the Dunkirk carrier has been kept waiting an hour at the door of the *basse-cour* and he has goods to sell when he gets back from Calais.

Another English customer orders damask for table linen from Antwerp, and is told that it is not good, being not white, but "such slubberd colours as I would be ashamed to send you."

A compromise was effected with some other sort, for presently comes news that "the ship wherein I laded your diaper damask is departed hence, but the wind hath been so wavering that I know not where he is become." "He" may be the "old man"—the merchant skipper rather than the ship herself.

Antwerp was ousting Bruges from the premier position she held in the fourth Edward's day.

Lady Lisle's gifts were many and various. Hussey suggests that quails sent to Queen Jane should be fatter or are not worth thanks. A partridge pasty sent to her daughters, in Anne's early days at court, was as beset with adventure as the taffeta; for the vessel in which it travelled stuck in the mud in harbour and was beneath water for two tides, so we are not surprised that it came "not best fashioned" though "thankfully received."

Other pasties there were, of venison, or wild boar, or smaller game. "La pintade" visits England in this manner. Capons and rabbits flank the beef and boiled mutton, as in Plantagenet days. There are geese and sausages and brawn, and the "puddings" presented to the

Princess Mary may be inferred to be some preparation of the pig—black or white (hog's) puddings, which still survive in parts of England and of France, where they form a feature of the supper of *Reveillon*.

Essex and Suffolk cheeses are famous in the age; once, in a time of local insurrection, none of the former could be sent to London, which had to eat mouldy cheese in consequence. Cheeses of Llanthony, in Wales, had been a gift to Edward's grandmother, Queen Elizabeth.

The turkey is a novelty, and difficult to obtain. The "hen of Ind" is not lightly sold by its possessors in France, when sought by purchasers across the Channel.

Lent still calls for a fish-diet, for Henry's quarrel with the Pope has not undone the abstinence from flesh. Baskets of salted ling and "bacon" (the red) herring furnish coarser fare. Salmon and turbot, trout, eels, oysters, shrimps, and sprats and lampreys, fresh or pickled, are a more dainty provision, while carp pasties are a rarer delicacy still. Selsey cockles are a speciality.

Among the few menus of the time is that of a King's messenger, who dines substantially, upon his travels, on boiled mutton and roast beef, with capon for a second course. Boiled mutton and a rabbit form his simple supper. Ale is the main drink, and a "nightcap" of sweetened wine winds up the day.

The court drinks Orleans wine, both white and red, and "muscadel." Rhine wine is also there, as in the olden time. Sir Brian Tuke has a piece (cask) of very special wine from France for use on great occasions, and the Duke of Sussex "will drink none but mighty great wines."

For the troops are biscuit, cheese, and tub-butter, the

standard salted fish and "powdered" meat in casks, and "jambons" of bacon. The labourers at Calais or Boulogne have bread and cheese and onions. For the benefit of others elsewhere, 340 pounds of liquorice are ordered.

The crane is still a kingly dish, and there are smaller birds—larks, plovers, snipe, and teal. The latter, as well as puffins, may have been permissible as a Friday dish.

Beans and peas are among the commoner vegetables ; the "hartichoke"—which sometimes drops the aspirate— is a new-comer; the cucumber makes an occasional appearance.

Peascods (probably the edible-podded pea) were sent, a gift from France to Henry VIII, but a wily Frenchman had already raised some in his French garden at South-wark a few days earlier, and these had also been presented to the King.

A duchess writes, in 1550, to one of Edward VI's ministers, begging that litigation, in which her gardener is involved, may be hastened, as, until he returns, she can have neither salads nor sweet herbs.

Garlic-bulbs are sent from France to England, but sorrel plants [1] cannot be then obtained, explains a corre-spondent. Leek seed is also furnished for sowing.

The Yeomen of the Guard, founded by Mary's grand-father, Henry VII, used to present the princess with the emblematic leek upon St. David's Day. Their spangled uniform made a brave show. Are they not with us to this day ?

---

[1] The author thinks this may be the rendering of *ozeles = oseille*, which is left undetermined by the editors of the Henry VIII Letters and Papers, 29 Hen. VIII. Calendar, vol. 13, pt. 1, No. 10, R.O. *Osier* is a further rendering.

Strawberries and cream, cherries, and pippins are a native dessert. Does not Shakespeare, on the strength of an Elizabethan chronicle, immortalize for us the strawberries of the Bishop of Ely, growing in his Holborn garden in the fifteenth century? And on a July day in Edward's reign there sat in the pillory in Cheapside a guilty pair, a man and a woman who had sold pottles of strawberries, not full, but made up with fern. Damsons, quinces, barberries, and plums were among the fruits made into preserves or " pies."

Imported are oranges, pomegranates and chestnuts, also almonds and raisins, olives and capers. Mirabels are heard of, too, nor has green ginger failed since Yorkist days. March-pane or almond butter is eaten by princesses.

Lady Lisle had great repute in the matter of jam-making. We find her writing to a learned doctor for a reminder upon the proportion of fruit and sugar in the various kinds of jam. In Edward's babyhood, she sends a present of her jam to court, not, however, for the baby prince. It is Henry himself who commands young mistress Basset to write to her mother for a further supply of the damson conserve and for " cody-nack of the clearest making." Never had the King liked any better.

Lady Lisle is pictured clearly in the records and in her own correspondence as an energetic British matron, seeking her daughters' advantage, pushing their cause at court whenever a vacancy occurred, whether in the household of the Queen or in that of Princess Mary, or, again, in that of the little girl-princess, Elizabeth.

No place could be found for Mary Basset, for others had prior claim on vacancies in the princess's household, while as for the Lady Elizabeth, "the King will have none so young . . . but only ancient and sad persons."

Poor little girl Elizabeth, stifled among these solemn guardians.

Lord Lisle was for some years Governor of Calais, where his wife resided with him. Her son, James (Basset), was at school in France, and Mary Basset for some time was living in that country with a Madame de Bours, whose son she afterwards married clandestinely.

King Henry's approval of the jam did not prevent him from deposing Lord Lisle from his governorship of Calais. Like too many others, he was "clapped up" in the Tower. Suspicion, perhaps the mere outcome of Henry's goutiness, had arisen as to a possible intrigue between Lisle and the dangerous Reginald Pole, his relative, for the delivery of Calais into the hands of the latter.

"The Lord Lisle is in a very narrow place, from which no one escapes unless by a miracle."

After the disgrace of Katharine Howard, most ot her ladies had been sent home, but Henry, mindful of the unhappy circumstances of Anne Basset, had undertaken the charges of her board. It was, said the court chatterers, on account of his favour towards Anne that Lord Lisle was set at liberty from his imprisonment. The hapless man was doomed, however : dreadful foreboding, the trials of a prison, even the shock of joy at his release, told on his system ; he died within a short time of his release. Anne, his stepdaughter, continued in court service and was a maid to Katharine Parr.

Medicine and surgery were working out of the witch-dosing of earlier England. Drastic drugging might often induce maladies worse than those it sought to cure.

Here and there is some enlightenment, chiefly, it would appear, among French surgeons.

The young son of an English peer, a " noble impe " they would have called him then, is " sick of a great heat in the liver." Dosing with mustard is at the bottom of the trouble. " Belike somebody gave him mustard to drink, being young, for some disease [discomfort], but surely it was not well done."

Henry's physicians, as we have said before, would have liked to try a course of guaiacum for their patient's gouty troubles, but were afraid to suggest the experiment to the suspicious King. The Emperor Charles V, a less terrible patient, doubtless, experienced benefit from the use of the same drug, rather later on. " He took sixteen ounces of guaiacum in the bath."

Edward's unhealthy fatness as he left his babyhood was whispered of in secret by his physicians to confidential agents of the King of France.

Already, in these early years, there falls the first warning of ill-health. The waxen image might, in the superstitious view, be at the root of things ; the disadvantages of a neglected childhood are a far more likely cause. In the turmoil of events the child may well have suffered from the apathy or ignorance of his nurses and attendants.

Mary, as a young woman of twenty-four, was fresh-looking and given to healthy walking exercise. To please her father she swallowed the strong cathartics of the day. Her ill-health in later years arose from causes which motherhood and a happier existence might have averted. She, in accordance with the practice of the age, was bled at intervals, and it is curious to observe the casual manner in which the " barber-surgeon " receives notice. Mary's physicians are named in full, her apothecary, too, is surnamed, but when it comes to venesection, "one Harry" is sufficiently definitive ![1] Mary's dentist is also mentioned.

The ailments of a lesser world must not pass unnoticed. John, Earl of Oxford, has a "sciatica in his huckle-bone and a grudge of ague." The Governor of Calais has a pain beneath the ribs, and one physician sends him word that if he will say under which rib it is, he will find a remedy. Another glibly prescribes powdered ginger for wind under the left ribs. The pain, it would appear, visited the region beneath the right ribs, and for this, abstinence from fish and windy meats is enjoined and no late suppers. A French physician comes forward with treatment which bears the stamp of common sense. He reduces the number of meals to two and decrees a good space between dinner and supper. Pheasants are the only game permitted, mutton is to be eaten seldom, but stewed capon, with the broth, and pigeons are permissible. Raw fruit and vegetables must be eschewed, and even cooked, with the exception of certain savoury herbs. "All manner of pastry is contrary." Late eating is again condemned, and after supper nothing is allowed except a little "marmelade" or a roasted pear with sugar. The treatment is an advance upon the female sucking-pig nine days old prescribed by an English leech to one of Edward's ministers.

The amateur invades the field. A French lady sends *elixir vitæ* of her own concoction in a "quannequin." One great lady craves of another some walnut water for

---

[1] The "mystery" of the Barber-Surgeons had been the object of royal patronage in the reign of Edward IV.

her eyes.   Roche alum is another prescription, and among
the prizes in the French war of 1544 is a ship laden
with alum — "a sweet merchandise and will be ex-
ceedingly well sold, and that for ready money."

Good care and kitchen physic, too, receive their due.
Here is Bishop Latimer "faint all over, but chiefly in
the small of his back." His good nurse, Mrs. Statham,
has fetched him home to her own house "and doth
pymper me up with all diligence, for I fear a consumption."

Faith-healing must not be lost sight of.   The sovereign
sends forth cramp-rings by the dozen, gold and silver,
with the royal benison, and courtiers are found dis-
tributing these among their friends both far and near.
A piece of unicorn's horn is also credited with virtue.
It might, suggests the owner of the amulet, be set in
silver like a button, with a little chain attached.

They were more reticent about their digestions sometimes than some valetudinarians of to-day.   Says one
courtier, " I excused me of not coming to dinner because
I am of a precise diet, though I sent not him [the
Emperor's ambassador] that word."

The royal menagerie at the Tower had sunk into
obscurity by the time of Edward VI.   Bear-baiting,
however, had become a fashionable amusement and the
keeper of the King's bears is mentioned in the early years
of Prince Edward.   What "strange beast" it was that
Francis I sent as a gift to a great English noble we have
not found.   A collar was bought for it, at all events ;
perhaps it also needed a chain.   The crow-keeper and
mole-taker are still royal servants.   The Thames, whether
on account of storms or some larger foe of the deep
waters, teemed with strange inhabitants during this short

reign. For, if we believe the chroniclers, strange great fish were speared or netted as high as London Bridge, to the accompaniment of thunder, and dolphins too (porpoises perchance) were caught in the great loop round the Isle of Dogs. One of them was sent to the King, the others were sold.

A strange guest, too, was the seal sent as a present to the High Admiral, of which none of his servants would take charge. The excellent Hussey added to his many avocations the task of keeper. " I kept the seal here at Wapping five weeks or more. . . . She cost me some days 6d. in fish, and yet she had not dined " (!). After all this, the admiral declined the living animal but had her baked and sent to his wife.

Domestic pets were in favour at the palace in Edward's boyhood. His sister Mary had her greyhound ; it killed some sheep on one occasion and she compensated the owner. Mary had her cage-birds, too, a white lark which went about with her from one royal residence to another : canary birds were a new fancy, and there were parrots too, for which hempseed was bought. Katharine Parr had one and Lady Lisle two, one which talked, and one which promised well in that direction. Hempseed was bought for them, their broken perches were mended.

Among the great events of time there has come down to us the little story of a bird—its kind is not chronicled —which came from France as a gift to Lord Hertford, brother of Queen Jane, and which suffered shipwreck off Margate (in company with the taffeta of Lady Lisle). The little flutterer was saved from the deep and conveyed to London to meet with a sadly sordid end. For " the cat made her testament, which my lord of Hertford took right grievously." However, the donor, not to be beaten, sent her own bird to my lord ; the best in the town. "I would not do the same for any lord in England—except the King," declares she, with a reservation.

Jane the Fool figures in the court scene. Her head is shaved at intervals ; the clown of our own day preserves, by help of "make-up" at all events, this hallmark of the jester of old time. Her impish antics, her permitted licence, make sombre Mary smile. To clothe her, gowns and smocks are ordered and a pair of sheets provided. For Lucrece, too, there are garments. Is she another human toy ?

The amount of buying on behalf of others is very great in the sixth Edward's time. We found something of it in the Yorkist reigns. Oranges and dates and soft goods are procured in London for the womenkind at home. A Norfolk housewife does not hesitate to beg her husband, a county knight, to purchase for her small trifles that she needs.

In Edward VI's time quite an appreciable amount of diplomatic correspondence is taken up with ordering and despatching of goods from Flanders to England. Linen and velvet we have seen ; there were many minor objects. Noble ladies, by medium of their husbands, obtained rich stuffs, the murrey cloth, or velvet, for a gown and other adornments.

Simpler folks have their requirements too. Sabina Johnson and her husband, John, carry on a gay little correspondence when John is away. Their artless wants and sentiments live in the august fustiness of the State records. John writes from London, "Good wife (but sometimes shrew)," and Jane in good understanding, replies :—

"I have had an impediment this four days that many would have their wives to have it all the year. For four days I could not speak. It came with a cold."

Their baby, Charity, was weaned and had come home. They had apparently put her out to nurse.

"Forget not my sugar," writes Sabina, "or you are like to have sour sauce." A neighbour begs John to buy her half a pound of white thread.

John, gay dog, is next at Calais, on business of his own or of King Henry's. Thus writes he to Sabina at home in England :—

"If, according to your prayer, I were the one surviving man, you would lose your husband, for the women of this town would keep me perforce."

We need not run away with the idea that these shopping commissions of Tudor days became obsolete, for in the reign of George III we hear that the Countess of Hertford writes to the Duchess of Argyll asking her to send "two Scotch gauze gowns for my daughters for the King's birthday." [1]

There are still relics, from the earliest Edward's day, at court. The rush-strewn floors survive. The corridors at Edward's baptism were strewn with rushes, so was the floor of the Queen's closet or sitting-room at Greenwich.

There was still the juxtaposition of muddy reeds with sumptuous hangings and rich dress material.

The "tablets" of the royal persons, painted by the hand of Holbein, looked down from their background of solemn arras on the litter of this floor-covering, on which were pressed the footsteps of the greatest in the

[1] *Intimate Society Letters of the Eighteenth Century,* edited by the Duke of Argyll, K.T., vol. i. p. 209.

land. Conservatism showed in these same wall and floor coverings. Development displayed itself in the portraits by the painter whom to-day a world prizes as it scarcely then could prize him in the flesh.

Foreign wares included glass dishes for jam. Lady Lisle has to wait some time before some she wishes for can be obtained. The ones which she had coveted had been made at Bevois, between Paris and Abbeville.

Venetian glass-workers were in England for some part of the reign of Edward VI. Their absence from their own State was made illegal, and they received orders from home to return on the completion of their existing contract with the young King.

Was the " Jesrome" bracelet, of which we hear, named by any chance from the great Jesurum of the glass trade ?

Glass pots and flagons were Henry's New Year gift to Anne of Cleves, the discarded, in 1542.

There is a good show of plate at court. The "cup-board" (buffet) rises six tiers high with silver and four with gold plate. There are lesser objects too—a shaving-pot of white plate and silver snuffers. A case of gilt shears and knives is a present for a lady. There was pewter plate for the Queen's household. The Abbey of Westminster among its store has its silver-gilt spoons, each having "the apostle on the end."

Lord Cobham had candlesticks of a pattern "least cumbersome upon the table." A great contemporary has some copied from them for his own use. Arms were stamped upon articles of plate in some instances.

We hear a good deal about jewels, for Mary had a well-stored casket. A girdle set with pearls and rubies ; a carkenet or hair-net of gold, with gems ; necklaces, several brooches—one with a George of diamonds, another with the history of Moses. Mary gave to little Edward a gold brooch with an image of John the Baptist upon it. From her stepmother, Katharine Parr, she had a present of a pair of bracelets of gold set with diamonds, rubies, and emeralds. Less costly objects were cornelian bracelets and various rosaries in agate, coral, and garnet. Sycamore wood made other beads. Of the artistic value of her cameo brooch no record comes to us. Some of the ornamentation was in the form of grotesques, still lingering on from the days of the "babouines" on the cup of Isabel of Valois.

To Jane Gray she gives a gold and pearl necklace. Is this "Jana Regina," that most innocent of usurpers, whom she, reigning, was to kill?

Katharine Howard's diamond collar and rope of two hundred pearls are the most splendid of the jewels recorded.

Mary had "books" (either of the nature of lockets or boxes) containing portraits of her father and mother and a black enamelled picture of King Henry and Queen Jane. "Books of wax" are also mentioned, perhaps miniature figures or landscapes moulded in the substance.

The musk-ball of Lady Paston, of Yorkist days, had developed by this time into the "pomander," stored with musk or ambergris, civet or benzoin. Mary owned one in which was set a watch. Some were enriched with gems and enamel.

To scent the room the "fuming-box of silver" was an accessory. From the rose all kinds of fragrant products were derived, rose-water, rose-conserve, and honey being but a few upon the list.

The clock and watch, and their makers, are heard of several times. Edward, in his childhood, was given a clock made by Bastian; it was one of Mary's presents. The clockmaker comes to court to bring a new "pirling-wheel" for one of the princess's clocks. Also the repairers of musical instruments are kept busy. Mary's virginals and regals get out of order at intervals. It was as a teacher of the virginals that Monnocks first came to the notice of Katharine Howard. He and one Barnes were her instructors.

The regals are taking a place among the musical instruments of court and of the outside world.

It was a costly instrument in comparison with the "pair of organs" of the monasteries. One supplied to court cost £4 against the 6s. 8d. valuation of the other instrument at the time of the suppression of the monasteries. The organs may have been in an ineffective state; at the same time the figure is not discrepant with other contemporary estimates.

At Greenwich was "the King's great organ" in young Edward's princeling days.

The court band was in a developed state, including the "new sackbuts." Queen Jane and her son alike had their own "minstrels" and "players." Much foreign talent was engaged both for the royal service and for that of great nobles of the day. Paget's band, secured in Antwerp, consists of five musicians, each of whom can play upon five or six sorts of instruments.

There is, in spite of so much gloomy happening, a spirit of gaiety at court. Mary, in her girlhood, plays at cards, losing and winning shillings with the ladies of the court. She is fond of dancing and festivity, this gloomy persecutor of the 'fifties. Only seven years before her accession Edward in a priggish vein wrote to his stepmother (Katharine Parr) praying her "to beg his dear sister Mary to attend no longer to foreign dances and merriments, which do not become a most Christian princess." The shadow of the Puritan is cast before. In that very month of May Mary was in bad health, whether from the dancing or the sermonizing is not indicated.

In Edward's reign, Sternhold began his metric version of the Psalms, first for a private pleasure, but continued with the King's encouragement. Later, Hopkins joined him in the task.

Cranmer translated the Latin Church hymns into English and gave directions for accompanying music :— " The song added thereto should not be full of notes, but as near as may be for every syllable a note, so that it may be sung distinctly and devoutly."

Leland dedicated his *Itinerary* to the young King Edward, who also was a patron of Polydore Vergil, an Italian historian who lived and wrote in England. They wrote with quill and ink and had their box of sand for blotting script, their ball of sealing-thread to use with wax for fastening of a missive.

All these are little things, but we like to know of them, and to compare the ways of long ago with ours, to their disadvantage or our own.

CHAPTER XIX

THE KING

AS the days of Edward's boyhood are over-shadowed by the great events of the political and domestic affairs of his father's reign, so also are those of his kingship by that "multitude of councillors" provided by the late king's testament, and by the seething of the new religion. Now, on the one side, may the heretic Protestant make a definite advance into the land of England, travailing in disruption ; now, on the other hand, may Pole, writing to Paul III, express his hope that "an opportunity is afforded for regaining England." The co-operation of the Emperor is of paramount importance ; the influence of certain of the continental ambassadors is to be exerted "that England may resume obedience to the Apostolic See."

At Rome, it must have been difficult to master the idea of the confusion entailed by Henry's secession ; a confusion which indeed still presents itself to our own eyes in this twentieth century. For, where an honest desire for purification or a materialist or free-thinking spirit had pushed the Lutheran innovations, matters were fairly simple. In England, however, as we must remember, Henry's own libertinage, and not a brotherhood with Protestants, had made an artificial entry for the propagandists. Henry had quarrelled with the Pope, who would not sanction a wrong done to Katharine of Aragon, who would not annul the dispensation, given by a predecessor, for the marriage of Henry to the widow of Prince Arthur ; he had incurred excommunication for himself, and had cut his realm adrift from the Papal obedience ; all this and more had Henry done, but he had not cast off Catholic dogma and discipline ; the Reformers, eager to find in him a prime support in Europe, were brought up against an unexpected adherence to old systems and old ceremonies. Edward is still in his cradle when Philip Melancthon writes to Henry bewailing the persistence of superstitious ceremony. While relics are held up to obloquy and the monastic goods are being taken into the hands of the commissioners, Henry's candle burns still before the image of Our Lady of Walsingham. He is torn between the question of the requiem Mass and that of the suppression of the chantries, the properties of which have been taken into his own hands, an act explicable alone, if on any ground indeed, by the alleged evil and superstitious character of such Masses and the allied devotions.

The continental Reformers move for the abolition of the laws of abstinence from flesh-meat, but in Henry's realm one, at least, was hanged for breaking the King's command relating to the same, which tallied with that of the Catholic Church. In Edward's reign, the English have in view a compromise of almost childish character. They meditate changing the fish-days from the Friday and Saturday, then customary, to some other day, but not abandoning them entirely, in consideration of loss to the fishing industry around their coasts. Edward's father, however, sought out and punished the eater of flesh.

An Oxford bookseller confesses to having eaten with his household, in one Lent, twenty legs of mutton, five rounds of beef, and six capons—an orgy of meat. Greater than himself, certain clerics, including regulars, had feasted with him; the worthy townsman had even heard that pork had been eaten at Whitehall, under the royal roof itself. Not less than half a dozen Fellows of All Souls are likewise implicated. The " secular arm," in the persons of the Mayor and Aldermen of Oxford, conducts the bookseller's examination in company with university magnates, the Master of St. Edmund's Hall being one of them. Joan Butcher, the heretic and Anabaptist of Kent, had eaten calf's head on an Easter morning; perhaps before the hour of Mass released the faithful from the Lenten fasting. The Earl of Surrey, that poet of tragical remembrance, confesses to eating flesh, and, breaking windows with stone bows: owned that " he had done very ill." In Henry's mind confusion must have seethed. The country too must share the ferment. There was no simplicity of issue here. There were the purer-minded, ready to welcome a spiritual revival from within. There had been " Thomas More the Jester," Fisher of Rochester, the "glorious hypocrite," as the new party called the pair who had died for a great principle. There was Colet of the beautiful soul; Erasmus holding up the mirror to the viciousness of lazy friars, yet never achieving, with his finer handling within the river-bed, what Luther brought about by his grosser action in a diverging channel. There was Cranmer, the royal " handy-man," playing as Papal substitute self-constituted : there were the bishops waiting for the turn of events which should restore the King and England to submission. There were the heads of houses at

Oxford, who would not relinquish their emoluments. There were the people in the mass, driven like sheep, following authority where nearest ; there were those who were frankly ready to fall in with any views of Henry's if he would only impart to them his wishes. *They* were in most dubious case of all. The section which resented the interference of a foreign Power (for the Pope was unpopular with others besides the King) might have come to terms of a Cranmerian manufacture. An attempt to follow Henry's lead was, however, of all courses, the most difficult and hazardous. For what clearness could there be in Henry's outlook ? " You cannot eat your cake and have it too," declares the Duke of Norfolk. At that danger-point of life when the idealism of youth is waning, and when, unless intellectual vitality be great, sensualism is apt to involve the whole being, Henry had involved himself in a debauch of marriages. His act of revolution in the matter of his first divorce had involved his whole being in the whirlwind of confusion. He knew not what he wanted ; no sooner had he annexed one woman than his restless eye had lighted on another. He was torn with the irritant of his gouty sufferings and of complications he had himself induced. He had himself bastardized his surviving daughters and had compromised their futures, and created a potential foe to the kingdom in every suitor who might fail to accept that status in the English princesses, and who might lay claim to the crown of England in their right as heiress-apparent or presumptive.

And now Henry has gone to royal sepulture, while dark beholders see in the exudation from his corpse the blood licked by the dogs, prophesied before his end.

The boy Edward is now King on January 27, 1547.

THE STATE PROGRESS OF EDWARD VI

Melancthon, discreetly oblivious of the day when he had adjured the world of Protestantism to "cease to sing the praises of the English Nero," writes glowingly to Edward of his father's great qualities.

Edward, upon the news of his father's death, proceeded from Ware to London and took up a temporary residence at the Tower. Thence, five days after his father's burial, he made a state progress through London to Westminster.

The City was lavishly decorated for the occasion; sumptuous hangings of tapestry and cloth-of-gold hung upon the walls. Flags and pennants flew from the windows, on the ledges of which rested rich cushions.

The great officers of state and foreign ambassadors walked in pairs, and Cranmer with the envoy of the Emperor.

Garter was with the Mayor of London, who had been knighted a fortnight earlier.

The young King, preceded by the Protector Somerset, rode in advance of his canopy that all might clearly see him. Clad in garments of white velvet and cloth-of-silver, worked with true-love knots in pearls, and further adorned with rubies and diamonds, Edward sat upon his charger, with its caparison of crimson embroidered with pearls and gold Damascene work.

Behind the canopy the Master of the Horse led a second steed, a splendid mount with sumptuous trappings.

The French possessions of Normandy and Guienne were represented.

On either side of the vanguard of the procession marched the King's "poor men" and also men-at-arms with poleaxes.

The streets were strewn with gravel, and along one side ran a railing to keep the way and to ensure safety for the crowds who lined the route.

As the procession moved away there sounded "a very great peale of ordinance shote at the Tower."

At intervals upon the way the King halted to witness pageants and to hear loyal songs and declamations.

At the pump in Cornhill, and at the one in Cheapside, young children performed in allegorical episodes; and Valentine appeared, with Orson dressed in leaves.

At every halting-place red wine and clary ran from reservoirs through pipes into the streets, whence, when the procession had passed on, the populace were busy fetching it away for six hours following.

Eleanor's Cross in Cheap was newly gilt and painted. So it had been when Katharine Howard made her state progress as a bride. And here the Mayor received the King with an address read by the Recorder of London, and presented also a substantial offering of a purse containing a thousand marks in gold.

And in St. Paul's Churchyard, a Spanish acrobat shot down a cable, stretched from the steeple of the church to the ground, and, coming to the new King, kissed his feet and then swarmed up the rope again, and " played certain mysteries on the said rope, as tumbling and casting himself from one leg to another . . . which stayed the King's majesty, with all the train, a good space of time."

At Temple Bar, gaudy with paint and flags, were "viii French trumpetters, blowing their trumpets after the fashion of their country." And children sang to regals their homage to the King, himself a boy.

And so at length to Westminster and to his palace,

there to wait for the coronation of the coming day, on the last Sunday before Lent.

On Sunday, February 21st, Edward was crowned in the Abbey (called the Cathedral Church) of Westminster.

The breach with the head of the Catholic Church had necessitated a modification of the ceremonial, and also of the style of his Majesty of England. Yet, outwardly, many parts of the ritual remained as in the days of union. The garments of the coronation were devised with the necessary openings for anointing as for Catholic sovereigns elsewhere.[1]

Three crowns were placed successively upon King Edward's head, the ancient one of St. Edward, the imperial crown of England, and the third a very costly one made for the young sovereign. Cranmer and Somerset placed the crowns and the coronation ring, and the rest of the regalia was delivered by various peers of the realm.

The armlets, the sceptre, St. Edward's staff, the golden wand, the spurs and orb, were thus handed, some being at once withdrawn, as with the spurs.

The coronation took place before the high altar, where, earlier, the uncrowned King had lain prone while the *Veni Creator Spiritus* had been sung over him.

Then young Edward, wearing the imperial crown and bearing the sceptre in his right and the golden orb in his left hand, was carried, in his chair, as it appears, to the throne, and seated on St. Edward's chair. Homage was there separately done by the Protector and the Archbishop as the chief of the temporal and spiritual peers, and, to shorten the ceremony, the other peers together knelt and raised their hands as Somerset,

[1] See Appendix to chap. xx, *Court of Louis XIII*.

the Protector, voiced their homage. Then all cried together "God save King Edward!"

Then was said the Mass by the schismatic and heretic Archbishop of Canterbury, assisted by the Bishop of Winchester.

At the end, the King in a recess, screened off with hangings, changed the quasi-sacerdotal apparel of coronation for a purple robe with train and surcoat of the same, trimmed with miniver and ermine, and under a canopy, supported by the barons of the Cinque Ports, he returned to Westminster Hall for the coronation banquet. Here he dined alone with the swords of Mercy and of Justice upheld before him, and was served with the cup by the Chief Butler of England. Then, when he had been served, the rest of the company was waited on at different tables. In the middle of the Hall dined the orders of nobility, at tables to right and left were the barons of the Cinque Ports and other officers and the Lord Mayor and Corporation of the City.

And when the second course was finished, came Dymock, Challenger, in full armour on a splendid steed, gleaming with cloth-of-gold, and flung his gauntlet to any who should deny that Edward was truly King, "the which no man wolde take up."

Then Garter cried the styles of his Majesty in Latin, French, and English, and Edward VI was the first who bore alike, upon his coronation day, the Papal title of Defender of the Faith, and that of Supreme Head of the Church of England.

Then the officers of arms went to their dinner at a separate table, while the young King was served with hippocras and sweet wafers, as might be served liqueurs to-day.

The tables were cleared, and the King washed his hands and then stood " in the myddle of the hall place," surrounded by his lords, and was there served with a dessert of spices and confectionery.

Then the Lord Mayor presented a gold cup, from which the King drank and then handed it back as a memento.

Then followed a designation of Knights of the Bath, but the full ceremonial was not carried out on account of shortness of time, the Bath, in those days a real portion of the investiture, being omitted.

On Monday and Tuesday were knightly tournaments and " Carpet Knights " were dubbed. Lent brought a few days' interval, but on the Sunday following (Quadragesima) there was a further tournament, and the knights supped with " moste part of the court at the Goat in Cheap, where they had a right goodly and sumptuous supper."

Although, with Edward and his councillors, there strikes a more definite note of Protestantism, there is still a large remnant of the confusion existing in his father's reign.

Francis I had died almost at the same time as Henry, and one of the first events of young King Edward's reign was the singing at St. Paul's of a solemn dirge for the French King's soul, a stately catafalque having been erected in the church for the occasion. Yet soon there follows an iconoclasm. The altars are plucked down, the rood at Paul's is lowered. The Bishops of Winchester and London, who had temporized during Henry's reign, were now brought to bay. Refusing to accept the Edward VI Prayer Book and having both preached sermons of recalcitrance, they were deprived of their sees. The Bishop of Winchester, Gardiner, had weathered Henry's capricious vacillations; he was one favoured too, perhaps, on account of his reputed kinship with the royal blood. For, though the allegations are many and various, it would appear that he was an irregular descendant of one or other side of Edward's kindred.

One says that he was son of Richard Woodville the younger, who died with his father in the year of the "black star." Another, that he was the illicit offspring of Lionel Woodville, Bishop of Salisbury and brother to the queen of Edward IV. Yet a third, with which we are disposed to fall in, makes him descend, by an illegitimate grandmother, from Jasper Tudor,[1] brother (uterine) to Henry VI. For his favour with Henry VIII and Mary Tudor would be more clearly understood from such a private consideration than from his kinship with the Woodvilles, who, though Henry VII's consort was descended from them in the female line, had never been acceptable either to the loyal Yorkists and Lancastrians in general any more than to the courtiers or the masses.

Bonner, also deprived, was to occupy the metropolitan see again under Mary, when the fierce urgency of reaction was to brand his name, not altogether justly, with the tale of persecution.

Yes, we find young Edward writing little essays, with the faithful Cheke, or Cox, behind his pen: we read his half-priggish letters, his aphorisms upon the Bible.

It is not easy to glimpse any individuality in the boy

---

[1] Jasper Tudor, Earl of Pembroke, who married Katharine, a sister of Elizabeth Woodville, had an illegitimate daughter who is thought to be Gardiner's grandmother.

(one had almost said the *school*-boy) King. A few years
more and, with full executive, his being might have
declared itself. His father's undoubted capability,
joined to the gentle austerity of his mother, might
have given us a king who would have stamped his own
personality upon the new era. But the languor of his
fatal malady was stealing on him as the Regent's
dominance prevailed. They talk of his harshness to the
Dowager-Queen because he wrote in grievance at her
haste to wed with Seymour ; haste so unseemly that, as
the boy of ten reminds her, had she fallen at once with
child, it would have been a nice point whether paternity
lay with her husband or with the dead Henry (Henry,
who had fathered no son by any queen for a long ten
years !). Still, Katharine's action was a breach of good
form — to-day such hastiness would most seriously
perturb suburban etiquette — and might have given
colour to one more of the unending tales of royal complication. She had wrested Seymour from his philan-
derings with young Elizabeth. Poor Katharine, her day
was not for long. Mary writes to wish her good fortune
in her maternal anticipation, and, within a few months,
Katharine had died at the birth of a daughter.

"She made every day as Sunday," says one contemporary. Poor Katharine, there was a little too much of
her well-intentioned piety. Seymour jibbed ; he would
absent himself from the daily prayers ; a graceless being,
said the shocked beholders. Yet Edward's reprimand
was not a private condemnation after all : the boy wrote
as his councillors advised. He had perhaps little more
volition in state matters than Mary of Scotland when she
fulminated her decrees against Henry's ambassador,
charging the Earl of " Anguishe " to turn him out from

Tantallon Castle within forty-eight hours. Mary, in her cradle, with her fair baby limbs bared, but a little while before, to the same ambassador that he might bear witness to her goodly form and health. Mary, whose name stood on the deeds of Scotland while she sucked her thumb, cajoling mother Mary of Lorraine with infant witchery and standing in infant awe, perhaps, of nurse Janet Sinclair. In the first spring of her fateful life the baby Queen had been spoken of as a bride for the prince of England, Edward, then five years old. Growing apace, she bids fair to emulate tall Mary of Lorraine. At nine months of age she is crowned with Scotch austerity of ceremonial, " the solemnity used here," writes Henry's agent, " which is not very costly." Yet Scotland already is in fear that she may be swamped, by such a marriage, in England's greater powerfulness, and within a year from Mary's birth diplomatic relations are suddenly broken off, the marriage project is annulled, and there is talk of "spiriting" Mary away to France. Her young half-brother, the Duc de Longueville, sends his greetings to his little sister in a letter to his mother, wherein he encloses a piece of string that she may see his present height. But Mary did not go, as yet, to France, and the project of her marriage to England still kept alive until the first year of Edward's reign, when the influence of Mary of Lorraine, Queen-dowager, entailed the rupture with England which led to the battle of Pinkie and the removal of the four-year-old Queen of Scots to France.

In the third year of Edward VI matters were amended, and the triple alliance formed between England, France, and Scotland.

In 1551, a namesake of the girl-Queen, one Stewart, was plotting against her life, believing that he would, by

poisoning her, gain favour with the sister kingdom. In
that same year Mary, the Queen-mother, of Scotland,
visited London, and was received by Edward, with much
ceremony, on November 3rd. Then, on the next day, she
rode forth with her Scots lords and ladies, and, as the
cavalcade passed into Bishopsgate Without, there came
an unknown gallant and carried off the loveliest lady of
her train. So much is told us by a monkish chronicle.
The rest is silence. In years to come, in like manner
was James Hepburn to seize upon his Queen and ride
away with her before the eyes of her Scots lairds and
equerries—James the red-headed, the hot-blooded, who
was even now a figure at the court of Holyrood while
Mary was taking her youngest baby steps upon the *via
regia*. They must have talked of this before the little
Queen. Did the story lie within her mind and lead
eventually to that abduction of herself of which they say
she was the willing victim ?

Other marriage plans had come in the years between
Mary's babyhood and her departure for France. In
Edward's eighth year there was talk of a match between
him and Mary, daughter of the Emperor, and in the
same year another bride is suggested, a daughter of the
King of the Romans. Now with the weight of kingship
upon him, the boy himself begins to think of an alliance,
as it was fitting that he should ; so say the observers.
They say, too, that there was a visionary glimpse of Jane
Gray, daughter of the presumptive heirs to the crown, as
there had been before of Jane Seymour, another cousin.
But the Duke of Northumberland had more daring views
than this. He married one of his own sons, Guilford,
to the book-loving, gentle realist, Jane. Then Edward's
thoughts turned, or were turned, to Elizabeth of France,

daughter of Henri II and Catherine de Médicis, and sister of Margot, who became first queen to Henri de Navarre. But this, too, came to nothing; the affair was but a dazzlement devised by Northumberland, said rumour, to amuse the youthful King. It would have clashed too certainly with his own projects.

Elizabeth was to become third wife of Philip after the death of the English Queen Mary, of whom he was consort, while for Edward there was to sound the passing, not the wedding, bell. Death was to be the monitor.

"Who is this? behold thy bride!" [1]

The demands of the council with regard to the French princess's dower were substantial. One million and a half of *scudi* of France, "at which they make a mock." A further stipulation was that Elizabeth should be sent to England shortly before her twelfth birthday. But this Isabel de Valois did not cross the channel nor bring the dower at which France had pulled wry faces.

A friendly *entente* was maintained, however, between the Kings. In 1551 young Edward was a sponsor to a son of Henri II and Catherine de Médicis, who was christened Edouard Alexandre. Edward sent gold vases, flagons, and a bowl "wrought with divers devices of astronomy and Phismanyes" as christening gifts to his French godson. The Garter was conveyed to the French sovereign, and the order of St. Michael came to England. French envoys left no mark upon the days of Edward IV, in any matter of hospitality, beyond the charges out of the royal wardrobe for washing of their sheets, but for their entertainment in the reign of

[1] *Love and Duty.* A. Tennyson.

Edward VI there was much preparation. Plate from the King's storehouse was provided to furnish the galley on which the Lord Warden of the Cinque Ports was to meet the ambassadors on their journey up the Thames. Flagons, plates, and salt-cellars, three nests of bowls ; " a garnish and a half of vessell," which seems likely to be the implements of feeding, rather than *vaisselle* as that word meets us to-day across the Channel ; the *couvert* rather than the crockery. When they met, upon the river highway, the foreign guests were feasted by the Lord Warden and so brought up to London, where, at their lodging, all things for their comfort had been laid in from the " King's provision " ; from the hangings on the walls to the butcher's meat and poultry, fish, and wild-fowl. Nor was wax forgotten, whether for lighting them or for sealing their despatches. Then there were sports at Hampton Court, ·tilting in the ring, bear- and bull-baiting, and a great banquet at Sheen, after which the King and the court ladies watched from arbours round the course the running contests of gentlemen athletes. In Hyde Park, too, the ambassadors went a-hunting with King Edward.

The King is seen giving lustre to other social events. He was at the wedding of Robert Dudley with the ill-fated Amy Robsart. He witnessed the launch of the "Primrose" and the "Mary Willoughby" in those days of the young navy. Another time he was present at a sham fight—a brilliant spectacle as it reads to us. For on a Thames lighter was erected a sham fortress, and this was defended by a yellow pinnace. Against it came four pinnaces, and " men in wight ansomely dressed," and they put to flight the yellow pinnace, and then with rockets, squibs, and bombards assaulted the castle, the defenders of which finally jumped into the river. The admiral thereupon arrived and received surrender of the scenic stronghold and its captain.

In the City, too, were revels when the King's "lord of misrule" went down the river to Tower Wharf, and landing there, in bravery of purple velvet, ermine, and spangles, was met by the sheriff's lord of misrule, in whose company he rode through the City and back, and embarked at the Tower for his return, and the sheriff's lord "took leave of him and came merrily with his morris-dance dancing."

The jocund revellers did not always hit it off so well in the City, for in May, 1552, we find that a maypole, painted white and green, was set up in Fenchurch parish and the morris-dancers figured on the scene. Joy must have outrun discretion, for the Lord Mayor had the maypole seized and broken. Or did my Lord Mayor scent in the ancient English revels the survival of Catholic custom in England, "Mary's Dowry"?—of our Lady whose month is ever May.

"The Franciscan had laid stress on the humanity of Christ and had introduced the adoration of the Virgin. . . . The flowers became the flowers of Mary. . . . The cuckoo-flower was her mantle, the flowers of the purple digitalis were her gloves, the thrift was her cushion, the milk-thistle her comb, the calceolaria her shoe, the great mullein her taper, the galingale her garland. The butter-cup held her drops of sweat, and the cowslip her tears . . . fern and the sharp dock and the dwarf elder bore her name; the spikenard was her medicine, the meadow-sweet her favourite flower. But the human passion, strong and tumultuous, which throbbed in the poet's lay, frightened the friar into a condemnation of his own teaching." [1] We can give but these few words of the exquisite passage.

Now a more deadly foe than the frightened friar was to strike at the Mary homage.

For now was harsher action setting in than in the first year of the reign. The Virgin's feasts were kept by some, ignored by others. Then Corpus Christi was neglected. There was " much speaking against the Sacrament of the altar, that some called it Jack of the box, with divers other shameful names."

" And the Assumption of our Lady was such division through all London that some kept holy day and some none . . . and also the same division was at the feast of the Nativity of our Lady."

" Almyghty God help it whan Hys wylle ys ! "

Thus aspires the chronicler.

The bread for the Protestant communion was to be of circular form, but without the former emblem.

The new Bishop of London (Ridley) receives communion in Protestant manner, taking the (unconsecrated) wafer in his hands.[2] Bonner, the ex-bishop, was in the prison of the Marshalsea, lying upon straw because he had declined to bribe the King's gaoler to obtain a bed. Sir Anthony Browne was in the Fleet Prison for having attended Mass. Earlier still than this, in Edinburgh, was " neither Mass, nor matins, but people all running wild."

Nor was it only on religious grounds that Henry VIII's old servants were falling into disgrace. Lord Paget was degraded from the Garter as no gentleman,

[1] *Wales.* By Owen Edwards. " Story of the Nations " Series.
[2] The Catholic priest receiving Holy Communion, as one of the congregation and not as celebrant, would do so exactly as any layman.

" as though," cries an indignant recorder, " Henry VIII who gave it him had not known his origin."

A provision had been made in the previous reign that the book of the Garter should not be defaced by scoring through of names of such knights as had suffered attainder, or otherwise been removed from the honour, but that an explanatory entry should be made of the circumstance.

But let us turn again to the more intimate things of Edward's life.

CHAPTER XX

THE HOUSE DIVIDED

OF his half-sisters, now legitimated by Henry's ordinance, young Edward as a king saw less than in his earlier days. He had invited them to court for the first Christmas of his reign, but his relations with them had changed by virtue of his accession into those of authority. In regard to Mary, now a woman over thirty years of age, the position was one of peculiar complexity. Her seniority was, from the regal point of view, a matter to be neglected ; but she was his father's daughter, and, much more, she was his godmother. Yet by his own conviction probably, and certainly by the influence of his advisers, he now stood as regulator of her religious tenets, or, at all events, of the external manifestation of them.

This ill-fated life had now entered upon another phase. Marred and embittered by her own and by her mother's wrongs, crushed by brute force into acquiescence with some part of her father's unjust exactions as regards her status, she was now to suffer from Edward's attempts to deprive her of the practice of the old religion, as she had already suffered from his interference—an interference which tastes of Chadband and his kind—with her diversions. That dreary taint of self-righteousness, which it has become customary to call Puritanism, was already casting shadows upon Merry England. Already, his elbow jogged, no doubt, by heavy-minded teachers of his young idea, the boy-prince had sent, as we have seen, messages to her begging her "to attend no longer to foreign dances and merriments which do not become a most Christian princess." For Mary, in spite of all, had still her lighter moments. She could play quite notably on the spinet, and had taken lessons upon the lute and virginals. The mending of these instruments and strings for them were among the expenses of her privy purse. She still played her game of cards and lost or won the stakes with ladies of the court. She was a very decent scholar. Her Greek may have been less than that of her cousin, Jane Gray, but she had a knowledge of Latin, French, and Spanish.[1] With her needle, too, she was accomplished enough to embroider gifts for young Elizabeth.

We cannot deal at length with her nor with her story. "The Princess was destined," says Sir Frederick Madden, "almost from her birth to become an object of political intrigue with foreign courts," for, putting aside projects made in her infancy, and long before her brother Edward's birth, she was discussed as a bride for sovereigns and princes of every degree. The Emperor, his son Philip, the Dukes of Orleans and Vendôme, the Duke of Cleves, Reginald Pole, and, again, another of her cousins, the Marquis of Exeter, whose mother had been Mary's godmother. This last rumour held in it something of sinister, for the Courtenays, as descendants of Edward IV, were near to the succession after Henry's

[1] She translated a portion of Erasmus's paraphrase upon St. John's Gospel from Latin into English.

children. We hear that when the Master of the Horse brought the news of Edward's birth to the Marquis of Exeter, he " showed himself very melancholy." Yet the deponent considers that it was only from single-hearted love for the Princess Mary, whose prospects were so injuriously affected by this birth. " Willingly would he have shed his blood for her," had been his frequent protestation.

But there was another suitor round whom romance clings with the rosiest atmosphere. This was the young Duke Philip of Bavaria, who came to England in 1539. His is no dazzling figure in history ; " rather counted for a good gentleman than for a man of any compass " was Philip of Bavaria. But there was serious love-making between him and the English princess. They met secretly in a garden of Westminster Abbey, and kissed each other, and as lovers planning marriage. For swayed alike by her craving heart and her proud chastity, Mary would not have lightly held such converse in the secret garden of the Benedictines. The wanton blood of Anne Boleyn ran not in her veins. The Queen, her successor Elizabeth, who fondled Dudley or Essex and cast them off, was of another kind. Duke Philip gave Mary a cross of pearls and diamonds, a jewel which, later on, was taken from her by Henry's orders. In the last year of the reign there was again some talk on the Continent of this match, but in an early year of Edward's reign Philip of Bavaria had died. Perhaps the greater part of Mary's heart died with him.

Fresh persecution arose for the princess when the powers behind the throne moved Edward to insist upon her adoption of the new Book of Common Prayer (the First Prayer Book of Edward VI). For a time she had

had the royal licence for Mass in her own apartment, but now this was revoked, and Dr. Mallet, her chaplain, who had held office at the court of Henry VIII, was sent to the Tower. Her champion, Charles V, complains :—

"My cousin, the princess, is evil-handled among you, her servants filched from her, and she still cried upon to leave Mass, to forsake her religion in which her mother, her grandmother, and all our family have lived and died."

Mary was summoned to court, and at first she declined to come, but later she obeyed the King's command. This was perhaps the time when she and her retinue, to the number of eighty persons, carried each a black rosary to mark their Catholic fidelity. She stood before the King in the Palace of Westminster, and the boy laid on her his commands to renounce the Mass. And she stood before him, his godmother and his subject, and e'en a rebel, and answered that in her father's time her Mass had been secure. "Her soul," said she, "was God's, and her faith she would not change." She had already reproached the Council with action contrary to her father's will.

An understanding already existed between her adherents and the Emperor's emissaries, for next day there came a threat of war from Charles V if his cousin should be deprived of Mass. The ministers temporized. Edward's ambassador explained to the Emperor that Mary was a subject, not a sovereign. The war-cry seems to have been changed into an attempt to " spirit " Mary out of the realm, a renewal of the efforts that had been made in Henry's reign.

In the public sermon she was aimed at. At Paul's Cross the preacher " spake against the lady Mary as much as he might, but he named not her, but said there was a great woman within the realm that was a great supporter and maintainer of popery and superstition. . . . And also he said that King Henry the Eighth was a papist."

Marriage projects distracted the King's attention, but the way was being paved for the *coup* engineered by the Duke of Northumberland in the last days of the reign. His scheme involved the passing over of the claims, not of Mary only, but of the young Elizabeth, a task less plausible because she stood in—ostensibly—with the party of the new religion. Elizabeth, as Queen, betrayed that she, like her father, had no whole-souled partisanship with the Protestants. She, as the daughter of "the concubine," was compelled to give nominal adherence to the party which alone could justify her existence. Her "Stick to your text, Mr. Archdeacon," betrayed her hidden inconsistencies. The new régime of married clergy, which must be admitted with other subversions of the ancient discipline, did not please her inner judgment. Her *mot* on the wife of the Protestant Archbishop Parker, even if manufactured, had its generation in the attitude of her mind as appreciated by some observers.

"*Madam* I may not call you, and *Mistress* (Miss) I am loath to call you, nevertheless I thank you for your good cheer."

The Elizabeth of Edward's reign, however, was but a girl in her teens, and we have not the material out of which to evoke her personality that exists in the case of Mary. We see her, now and then, in the country residences where she dwelt in the young brother's reign. She evinces gleams of the intellectual vivacity which she would derive from Henry's mental equipment and of her mother's *galanterie*. Seymour, her stepmother's husband, had cast his eye upon her; there had been passages between them while Elizabeth dwelt in their household.

Katharine Parr had died at the birth of her daughter, Mary, the hapless child who had been, then, placed in the charge of the Duchess of Suffolk, who, from insufficient means, was obliged later to give up the care of the poor orphan, now deprived of her father, dead upon the scaffold.

From the royal wardrobe had been provided some necessaries for little Mary Seymour. Hangings "of the twelve months," a gilt bedstead, a tester of scarlet for the cradle with curtains of crimson taffeta, and four carpets, together with some plate, cups, a salt-cellar, and eleven spoons.

Seymour had passed out of Elizabeth's life, and then had come vague plans for her marriage with Philip, who afterwards became the consort of Mary, her half-sister; also with a son of Frederick, afterwards, as Frederick II, the King of Denmark. Meanwhile, Northumberland, a King-maker, like the earlier Earl of Warwick of Lancastrian days, was scheming for his own ends and for the virtual kingship of his son. The dangers of the succession of Mary he impressed on the young King; he spoke of the return of the country to Papal submission. This would snare young Edward and blind his eyes to the true outlook of the plotter. Yet it was not the inevitable horrors of the succession of Mary and of Elizabeth, as we understand them now, that troubled Northumberland. In an age which boiled alive a woman for a secular offence and in which the civil power, alike with the ecclesiastical, sought to save the souls of men by burning their bodies, these presenti-ments would not have told for much with the duke. Joan Butcher, the Anabaptist, had burned within the reign, indeed. The obloquy of persecution has fallen on Mary, who was sincere, and on Elizabeth, who had no substance of truth in her composition : they stand as name-marks in those fifty years of horror which were inevitable in a country upon which a new religion had been thrust at the will of a king who, driven, hither and thither, by forces he had himself evolved and by the necessity of accommodating his own course to the wider drift of the continental currents of reform, had been urged headlong into an *impasse* where the horrors of confusion and of cruelty must, of necessity, prevail.

The true horror lies not in the deeds wrought under Mary and Elizabeth, but in the system of which they, no less than the religious martyrs, were the victims. For the Marian persecution (carried out in chief by the Queen's advisers) was maintained in the name of Christ, who Himself prayed for His murderers—

> "Whose sad face on the Cross sees only this,
> After the Passion of a thousand years."

Elizabeth, too, could only justify her position as apparent head of Protestantism by the cruel penal laws of her reign.

It was inevitable that sovereigns representing the old and the new, and reigning by a cataclysm of coincidence just at so pregnant a point of time, should fill their reigns with blood and bondage. By a further extraordinary, well-nigh grotesque, deal of the hand of Fate these sovereigns were women.

Meanwhile, young Edward was hemmed in by the new family faction.

Somerset, his uncle, was gone, dying for treason on Tower Hill. His treason may be held an open question, his hatefulness to the Northumberland section is not in doubt.

His proud splendour had recalled those mediæval days when great prelates pulled down the mansions of antagonists to build their palaces. Both St. Mary-le-Strand and the cloister of St. Paul's had been razed to furnish stone for his Strand mansion, where in days to come Henrietta-Maria was to dwell, and where to-day the publican sits at receipt of custom.

Northumberland now had the young King in hand and worked upon him in furtherance of his purpose. He had persuaded Edward to imitate the methods of his father and to dispose of the succession by will. Against the plan rose protestation ; for what a precedent ! One more of Henry's baleful legacies to his dynasty.

With her fair young head, " Jana Regina," the ten days' Queen, was to pay the penalty of her father-in-law's bloated ambitions. She, buried harmlessly in the works of Greek writers, one of which had been a present from young Edward, was to play her part in a development as remorseless as Greek tragedy ; she, not poured by Nature into any heroic casting-mould, was to be human sacrifice. As has been said, incomparably, of another, " her fate was enormous." [1]

In the crevices of direful record crop up the little tales of marvel. At the Eagle Inn, eight miles from Oxford, Host Kenner's wife produced the infant prodigy, " a child

[1] See Preface to *Marie Antoinette* by H. Belloc. (Methuen & Co., Ltd.)

with two heads, four hands, four feet, and but one body, and the midwife christened them at home, and was allowed by the church ;[1] and lived fifteen days ; and while the other died, wake and looked with a merry cheer " (words are missing at intervals).

There is a confusion, not surprising, in regard to the singular or dual life of the phenomenon. The chronicler proceeds, " Item, also in that same cuntry was a henne hacchyd of a chekyn that had ii heddes and iiii fette." A calf, too, of like deformity had been produced at an earlier date and buried by order of the authorities.

There is a grim tale of a triple birth in Smithfield, when the wife of one Bodley produced and killed, with the alleged connivance of her servant and the midwife, twin children, and, after being taken to the police-court, or its equivalent, the " counter," she produced a third. All this took place upon the feast of St. Bartholomew. In the December following, the mother was hanged at Tyburn.

Also, upon one Easter Eve, " rydde a woman in a carte abowte London that dwelte in Aldersgate Strete that made aqwavyte for cardynge of hare mayde wyth a payer of carddes soche as doth carde wolle with-alle."

We are left in suspense with regard to the provocation received by the maker of *aqua vitæ* from the " carded " maidservant.

King Edward's Grammar Schools, though some were founded before his reign, have carried down his name with lustre to our day.

Christ's Hospital too, which has, in the reign of Edward VII only, migrated from its long-time home

---

[1] The Catholic Church sanctions lay-baptism, administered with pure form and intention, in cases of emergency. Presumably the Protestant authorities followed suit in the above instance.

in favour of his Majesty's mails, has preserved for us, in a royal foundation, the curiosity of a charity uniform of the sixteenth century.

And when John Heath of Fenchurch Street was buried in the last year of the reign, "there went before him one hundred children of Gray Friars, boy and girls, and he gave them shirts and smockes and girdles and moketors,[1] and after that they had wine and figs and good ale."

[1] As a dole.

CHAPTER XXI

THE LAST DAYS

EDWARD'S young life was growing dim. Never, except in his first infancy, had he been of true robustness. In his fourth year, his unhealthy fatness had been remarked by Marillac, the French ambassador, and he had suffered from quartan fever at Hampton Court, "unusual for a child of three to four, who is not of a melancholic complexion."

During the latter part of his illness, Mary had been with him, herself suffering alarmingly from palpitation of the heart, not wonderful after her own troubles and the agitating horrors of Katharine Howard's downfall.

The court was constantly on guard against the dangers of the "sweating sickness," an epidemic visitation so peculiar to England, considers one French authority, that he has classed it with the *plica polonica* as having a race restriction. Even in continental countries, the outbreaks were, it is alleged, confined to English immigrants. Katharine Parr, as regent, had sent messengers through the home counties to watch for outbreaks on behalf of the young prince.

Twice during Edward's reign reports had gathered of his death. He had shown himself publicly, walking in his gardens, to dispel these rumours.

Now, in April, 1552, he is attacked by measles and smallpox, a complication which must have had serious results on a frame of inferior vitality.

The cough, the "apostume," tell of the steps of his decline ; even those starry eyes of his the boy-King shared with other victims of tuberculosis. There was enough to bring him to an end in the course of nature, but the appositeness of his death to the plottings of Northumberland could scarcely suffer men to pass it over as the mortal tribute. They declined, as in so many other royal instances, upon the fell whisper of poison.

From his retreat on the Continent Pole was watching the passage of events in England, where his mother had died, at eighty years of age, within the Tower—an everlasting horror of the scaffold. England which, as yet, they hoped would turn again to the old faith and to the Papal obedience. England, where the men of the West Country had risen in revolt against the new decrees, resenting even the less vital matter of the vernacular in public worship.

This Pole, who, having so nearly been elected Pope in 1549—the second Englishman he would have been in fifteen centuries—had repelled the veneration offered in his chamber, saying that all must be carried out in Conclave, in the light of day, and who was to return to England and become Archbishop of Canterbury under the five years' restoration of Catholicism, and also was to die on the same day as his cousin Mary, this Pole watched and primed the powers with news and aspirations regarding the land which Gregory the Great had declared peopled, not with Angles, but with Angels.

Thus, 'midst the watching of the nations and the weaving of Northumberland's family intrigue, the young life passed into "the land where all things are forgotten."

The sister Mary whom, though without animus of personal ill-will, we may believe, he had persecuted, wrought her charity.

For her first act as Queen of England was the commanding of a Mass for the soul of her young brother and her godson, Edward VI.

EDWARD VII

EDWARD VII

CHAPTER XXII

"AVE, IMPERATOR!"

"YOUR Royal Highnesses, my Lords and Gentlemen, this is the most painful occasion on which I shall ever be called upon to address you."

When King Edward VII made, in these words, his first official regal utterance, he voiced the mourning of a world. For the influence and the fame of the Sovereign-Queen whom he succeeded had gone forth among all nations, even into the elemental hordes of savagery. The Queen, the Empress, the lady so little in stature, yet so impressive in dignity, seared with long years and sorrows, yet with so much of vigour in her outlook upon the land she ruled ; with an experience of sovereignty unparalleled in our history, both in duration of time and in eventfulness, she who had seemed undying, had, after four short days of helplessness, gone, almost suddenly, from among her people.

It is not wonderful that, for the moment, that death appeared as *Finis* to an era. For those who had been born at her accession were already elderly, while the few who could recall it were aged men. The peoples whom she ruled, whether as sovereign or as suzerain, comprising every division of the human race, could not, except among the most primitive, have held her as undying, and yet her death came almost as a wrong done to some ancient faith.

Some wondered that they could have outlived their royal mistress ; her monogram on drab official furniture became a cherished emblem ; and there were not wanting those who even declared that the affairs of the royal family of England could, from henceforward, be regarded by them with apathy alone.

In hearts of women struck a tender note of sorrow, for Queen Victoria, outside of queenship, had something of the tutelary power ; a goddess of the hearth she was in many unknown homes.

On Sunday, January 27th, the congregations at the services of the many sects of the United Kingdom, of the larger part, indeed, of the whole Empire, must hear the new names in the Liturgies ; the ministers of religion must suppress her name, which, with the rarest exception, had been in their mouths throughout their career. In the Catholic churches, the Latin chant must be adjusted to another name, and the *post-missal* prayer for the English sovereign must, for the first time since the re-establishment of the hierarchy in these islands, include a petition *pro regina consorte*.

Then, on Candlemas Day, the dead Queen had been carried in honour and great state *per mare, per terram*, and laid in her Taj Mahal beside the husband of her youth, and then, as days passed on, in black-swathed England men began to wonder how the King could make a mark after so great a reign. And some, not in the outer circle only, questioned in the solemn way of England whether one who had shown ever so full a faculty of the *joie-de-vivre* could in truth now bind himself to the arduous and unremitting task of ruling.

And it was in a very little time that his people saw that, from their new ruler, the Empire was to receive a stimulus to fuller life, and that a cordon of goodwill was to be formed around the " splendid isolation " of the mother-country ; by a thousand evidences, they quickly apprehended that all their honours and their interests were in the high keeping of a great man of affairs.

CHAPTER XXIII

THE PRINCE OF WALES

WHEN, on Lord Mayor's Day, 1841, shortly before 11 a.m., Queen Victoria gave birth to her eldest son, it was eighty years since an English prince had been born as Duke of Cornwall. The nation, not waiting for the sovereign's will, nor for the exercise of letters-patent, acclaimed, with loyal fervour and joyous heedlessness of accuracy, a Prince of Wales.

At the civic banquet on that same evening was blazoned the device of the three feathers, with the legend "God bless the Prince of Wales" along the gallery ; the *Times*, with academic scrupulosity, might indeed lay down the rightful law of things, but the *vox populi* hailed, upon his birth, the infant heir-apparent by the ancient title, annexed from the Principality by those early Edwards, his forefathers.

When that child, whom the Duke of Wellington described to Lord Hill as " a fine boy, very fine boy, almost as red as you, Hill," was carried by his nurse, Mrs. Driscoll, into the room where the Ministers of State were waiting to testify to the birth of the heir-apparent, he came before them not alone as son and first subject of the sovereign and future wearer of the crown, but as a royal and human entity in whom were associated strains almost uncountable. "Saxon and Norman and Dane are we" was true of none more certainly than of Queen Victoria's firstborn son.   In him was blood of the Bruce and Stewarts, and of Capetian kings imported by Isabel de Valois, and by the *mésalliance* of Katharine de Valois with Owen Tudor.   In him was combined the blood of great English nobles and of the House of Guise.   Four of the six preceding sovereign Edwards were his direct ancestors.

Of later date was the importation of the blood of Hanoverian *Kurfürsten* and of the princes of Saxe-Coburg, of whom came his grandmother and his father, thus a first-cousin once removed to his first son.

He was also the first heir-apparent born to a reigning sovereign-queen of England.

He was a month and one day old when he was created, by his girl-mother, Prince of Wales.

"We do invest him," ran the ancient formula, "by girting him with a sword, by putting a coronet on his head, and a gold ring on his finger, and also by delivering a gold rod into his hand that he may preside there and may direct and defend those parts."

The Queen commanded that his name should be placed in the public prayers after that of Prince Albert.

The christening of the prince, unlike that of Edward VI, did not take place till he was ten weeks old.

Great preparations had to be made both for the ceremony and for the reception and entertainment of a crowd of foreign guests who came to Windsor.   From the royal stores at the castle were selected seventy or eighty bedsteads, more than the Wardrobe of the Beds could have furnished under Edward IV or VI; and historic chambers in the ancient towers were made ready for a host of royal and noble personages such as had not enjoyed the hospitality of Plantagenet, York, or Tudor king.

For St. George's Hall a special carpet was provided, patterned with heraldic emblems and having St. George and the Dragon in the centre.

The indigenous rushes of earlier days were replaced by cocoanut matting (the raw material of which had grown in lands unknown to the sixth Edward) and by crimson drugget.

The heating of St. George's Chapel was carried out in a manner almost as primitive as in its earlier history.

Stoves were kept burning day and night, not without protest from alarmists, who feared for the safety of the historic fane. By slow degrees, after several weeks, the temperature was raised to a point of comfort.

London, Windsor, the whole country shared in the rejoicings on January 25th.

In glittering procession, the royal family and their friends and kinsmen entered the chapel. Here the golden font stood upon a plinth draped with purple velvet.

The christening was performed with water from the Jordan, presented by a clergyman, the officiant being the Archbishop of Canterbury.

A splendid banquet followed, and the townspeople and the poor of Windsor also feasted in the royal borough.

The duties of her sovereignty called the Queen away, at intervals, from the baby heir. She tells us in her own Journal how she started with Prince Albert and their eldest child, the Princess Royal, on their first visit to Scotland, the Prince of Wales being brought to her to say good-bye before she started.

We have heard of the pains bestowed upon his education; of the unduly pedagogic flavouring of it indeed; of his visits in boyhood to the City, or elsewhere, upon some state occasion, in his parents' or in his father's company, and of the somewhat dull and isolated residence at Oxford.

The restraints which must always penalize royal status seem to have been imposed in somewhat rigid fashion. Yet we must remember that the 'fifties were, in general, a more punctilious decade than our own.

Here, in Oxford, the prince could see before his eyes foundations of those earlier Edwards, his ancestors. On that "parcel of land called *la Oriole*," once held by Eleanor of Castile, had been founded by her son, the second Edward, the House of St. Mary, later called Oriel College. In the High Street, Queen's College recalls the memory of Philippa, consort of Edward III, and of her chaplain, who founded it under her patronage, and in whose honour is yearly handed to the Christmas guests a threaded needle, as *rebus* of his name.

Still, in the prince's time, did Town and Gown meet in occasional combat. Did they not do the same in the reigns of the first Edwards? Here, in 1295, we have them quarrelling over some trifle, "so that learned and lewd all ran to the fight, and the townsmen carried away many kinds of stuff from the lodgings of the clerks." Several were killed on this occasion. In an earlier uproar, "the scholars of Oxford broke up the gate that leadeth towards Beaumont."

Of old, the university authorities were given to harassing the monastic orders established in Oxford, and the King would at times intervene on their behalf. Edward II gave orders to the Chancellor and Fellows concerning the Whitefriars, whom " they presume to molest, to the King's astonishment." A little later, the Chancellor and Fellows are still " grieving the Friars Preachers." To the Carmelites the same King gave a manor-house by the North Gate, in fulfilment of a vow made by him in some moment of danger.

Sometimes the university and the civic authorities would be associated in measures decreed by the sovereign. Thus, in the reign of Edward III, the Chancellor and the Mayor were to keep the assize of weights and measures in the town and suburbs.

Presently, the town is under censure, for there is a " grievous complaint of the Chancellor and scholars to the King and Council of the number of malefactors who continually come to the town and suburbs of Oxford to commit trespasses, which go unpunished because malefactors are harboured in the town and suburbs. The Mayor and bailiffs are to see that there be no occasion further for like complaint."

Oxford Castle, once occupied by kings, has, in modern times, become a gaol and court-house.

At Cambridge, too, where another period of somewhat dreary residence was the lot of the latest Edward, had been stirring times in the days of the Plantagenets. While Edward I was still a youth the younger university had, on account of contentions between the scholars and the townsmen, obtained royal permission to migrate to Northampton. The exile was not a long one ; the Cantabs were soon back in their old habitation. In the reign of Edward VI, the Cambridge students were so poor that a penny piece of beef was shared by four, and broth, thickened with oatmeal, was their main diet.

Cheke, Edward VI's tutor, had retired to Cambridge to engage in literary work in 1549.

The universities had shared in the convulsion of the forced Reformation.

Colet and Erasmus, those gentler souls who had understood the evil of degenerate monasticism, but who would have swept the house, not razed it to the ground, had failed where greed and iconoclasm were to prevail.

Now, a memorial of noble kind, the Edward VII Chair of English Literature, has, in October, 1910, been founded and endowed at Cambridge by Sir Harold Harmsworth.

In some of the college chapels at Oxford may be seen to-day vestiges of the ritual objects of the old religion. In an age more tolerant, an age, indeed, which has not the necessary intensity which infuses the bigot ; though the new religion has prevailed, yet the monastic orders are not only in existence within the universities, but are suffered to set up licensed halls of residence for Catholic undergraduates.

The Protestant bishopric of Oxford, founded on the spoils of the Abbey of Osney in the childhood of Edward VI, remains. Its cathedral is Christchurch, its canons are of Christchurch—the college which, as Cardinal College, Wolsey founded.

Hard upon the prince's university life, followed the loss, so sorrowful to himself, so terrible a calamity to his mother, of his father, who for twenty-one years had been not only Queen Victoria's well-loved husband, but in countless ways her right-hand man.

England, suspicious of "the German," began only after his death to realize how honourable had been the aims, how devoted the labours of this good man.

Before his death, the Princess Royal of Great Britain had married with a Hohenzollern, of the royal house of Prussia, now rising up among the Great Powers, with whom in the reigns of the past Edwards alliances so great had not been made.

The cloud which had fallen upon his young life was soon to lift, for plans for his marriage were being carried out. The eldest daughter of Denmark was to cross the seas as Anne had done, the bride of James I, the Prince of Wales's ancestor.

In the quiet sea-kingdom Princess Alexandra had grown up a beautiful girl, in the refined simplicity that has no dependence on wealth or extensive luxury. She and her sisters, from their happy home, were to come forth to make three of the greatest royal matches of their day.

She had been the prince's choice among the brides of Europe.

Our fathers have told us of her as she came, a girl-bride, to her new country. Our own eyes have seen her; we who have begun to think of Time and of his searing hand—and yet she is still young.

"Of the princess's personal charm it is not permitted to us to speak," says a contemporary witness. We, in a less reticent age, might take example from this restraint, and yet our warmth of admiration will not admit of bonds. Perhaps—for the "delicate bloom of colour" could pale before emotion on her wedding-day or could be chased by grief—it may be that her Majesty's defiance of the years is really due in chief to the beautiful oval outline of the face which has outworn her years among us.

She came that day in early March and made her progress through the City, amidst the delighted welcome of the people. The accessories had greatly changed since the days when Eleanor of Castile and the brides of Edward II and III passed on their way. There were no men in armour, no pageants at street-corners, and the streaming flags and banners lacked artistic effectiveness ; but the eager faces, the cries of joy and welcome, can never have been more fervent, more intense, for any of old time.

"Since she has been seen in the streets of London, a fresh reality has been given to the popular feeling that the Prince of Wales is the most fortunate of men."

On March 10th was the wedding, so brilliant on the one hand, so tinged with melancholy on the other.

There was the bride in her dress of white and silver, embroidered with the flowers of the three kingdoms ; the bridegroom in the flowing mantle of the Garter ; and the bridesmaids [1] in white silk and tulle, with wreaths in which the more poetic heather replaced the prickly Scottish thistle ; and round them the shimmering throng of family and state. Princess Mary of Cambridge, always so popular with the English people, was there with her cousins, the Queen's young children ; and there, hanging on his mother's hand, and scarcely able to mount the steps of the chancel, was Wilhelm of Prussia, then four years old, and, even then, of great activities.

There were the heralds, "a gorgeous group, walking stiffly in their magnificent but most uncomfortable tabards," and more discreet than those boisterous gentlemen of Tudor times of whom we heard in Edward VI's babyhood.

All these flashed and shone and glittered. And, on

---

[1] One of them replaced a daughter of the Duke of Abercorn, who was prevented by an attack of measles from attending.

the other hand, the women of the brilliant court were clad in tints of half-mourning for him who was not there to see his son a bridegroom, and in the royal closet, "the pew in the wall," the Queen in her widow's garb looked down upon it all, weeping, too, sometimes, out of sight, before too piercing memories.

And London wrote herself in fire upon the night, and for the first time was used the arc light to illuminate St. Paul's Cathedral and the Monument.

Although nearly six centuries had passed since the title of Prince of Wales was adopted by the English sovereign for his heir-apparent, yet, according to the *Times*, only four Princes of Wales have been married in this country. Of these, the Black Prince was the first. None of these marriages had been of happy auspice. The interest and rejoicing in the marriage of Albert Edward and Alexandra, which, in happy allusion to the motto of the Danish family order, was styled "la parfaite alliance," were but the beginning of the story of national enthusiasm for the royal pair who entered on their wedding-day into a State alliance and also into the closest of human ties.

Of those nearly forty years in which, as Prince and Princess of Wales, they entered in so many ways into the English national life it would be superfluous to speak. The story has been told, and will be told again, with the authority of official utterance.

They were the parents of six children. Their youngest and their eldest son died. They knew the Egyptian night which surrounds the death of the firstborn. Their remaining son was married, to the heartfelt satisfaction of the nation, to a princess brought up in standard English way. One of their daughters married, as princesses of old time had done, into the ranks of the peerage ; another, by a historical development as romantic as any fairy-tale, has become a Queen of Norway "o'er the faëm."

The Prince of Wales lived to the full his life of strong and mixed experience.

He drank the "wine of life" and walked in sunshine, drawing round him, too, men of all variety in a manner which sometimes exercised the well-starched decades in which he lived his earlier manhood.

The royal habit of to-day is to ignore all tale of calumny. Reports and rumours do find currency, some so obviously baseless that it is a perpetual astonishment that they can ever have been uttered or believed. Some, hatched, it may be, in the superheated imagination of second-rate journalists with the drink-habit, enjoy a little spell of life in certain strata of society. Others persist because their baselessness is not perceived by honest persons unaware of the circumscriptions to which royal persons are committed.

With the accession of Victoria, the girl-Queen, English court life had assumed a condition alike more healthy and more clean in tone than that which had obtained under most of the preceding Hanoverian sovereigns. To her mother's influence may justly be ascribed the beginnings of this rehabilitation. Victoria of Coburg had regarded with disfavour the down-at-heel condition of court morals under her brother-in-law's régime. She had held aloof from court and had kept her young daughter apart in a way that was not without elements of overstrain. To the unpopularity of the reformer she had added the aggravation of her alien and subordinate status. Even her daughter was sensible, to some extent, of the gall of discipline entailed by her mother's purism. Yet, granting some errors of method, it is to the Duchess of Kent that we must ascribe the initiation of the high tone maintained for over seventy years at the Court of St. James.

Royal admirations, royal favours, royal amours have provided an endless resource for the gymnastics of the pen and of the tongue. Reticence, indeed, to some extent has veiled the situation in English court life; there is not the ormolu mounting of similar French court episodes.

A haze of glamour invests these situations, where the atmosphere is regal. Yet hard, cold research returns us little but the sordid. In no vein of delicate romance was the court Laïs sought or found. Against one gentle, broken heart we have a vast assemblage of greed.

One La Vallière dims her sight with weeping, against a multitude whose glittering eyes keep watch upon their own venal aims. Nor is the bargain unfair to the royal purchaser. Henri IV and his grandsons, Le Roi Soleil and Charles II of England, sought no complement of their higher aspirations in the ladies of the Louvre, of Whitehall, or of Versailles.

From the English court these scenes have dissolved, probably for ever. Social ordinances are always a monitor more potent than the clauses of a Decalogue. The argument as to good form or bad prevails where pulpit diatribes fall blunted on the indifference of the hearers.

In curious days gone by a gentleman displayed his mettle by getting through his three bottles, and village congregations would assume the omission of a sermon on the ground that " passon he had doined wuth squoire o' Sarturday."

To-day it is bad form to exceed in wine, and gentlemen therefore avoid drunkenness. Laxity of other kinds is not accorded the same tenure of tolerance it once received in court affairs.

But if there has been essential change in the status of such matters there has been, in direct proportion, a tendency to exaggeration in regard to such episodes as have occurred. The item of fact has involved the travail of whole mountains of legend. One royal indiscretion may be matched with twenty in some smug suburb, yet it overtops them all in its alleged atrocity. One pebble sets an ocean in commotion. A jovial "splicing of the main-brace" and behold! the cry of intemperance!

A single entanglement, and erotic headlines span every column of social intercourse.

The most cruel retribution which falls on royal heads is the knowledge that, from the date of one fallibility onwards, a sinister reading will be made of the most stainless intention. An interview in the presence of a score of witnesses will be whispered of by the uninformed as an illicit assignation.

The seventh Edward did not escape from some fault and from a vast amount of rumour. His strong vitality, his very genial instincts, led the way. Yet who, remembering Agincourt, troubles over the roystering princedom of Harry of Monmouth? Who would have listened to Richard Plantagenet's crazed outcry if Edward IV had redeemed, by a great kingship, the debt of his libertinism?

Into his kingship, Edward VII obtruded no unseemly thing. In the hours of his youth he may have known less worthy moments; as sovereign, he ever burned his light before the shrine of Duty.

In the veins of princes is the blood of men ; for all alike, in the last hour, is assigned the *Ne Domine reminiscaris :* " Let the ignorances and offences of his youth be unremembered."

Reluctantly, has one trenched upon the shading, in deference to such critics as fear too strong a touching-in of the high-lights. It is a great remembrance that throughout the lifetime of the seventh Edward none found him guilty of an act of meanness.

CHAPTER XXIV

THE INITIATION

WHEN the seventh Edward came to the throne of England, his realm was that on which the sun never sets.

True that the French possessions had gone, Boulogne and Calais last. True, also, that the earlier American colonies, planted since the days of Edward VI, had been lost "on account of a chest of tea." But regions unknown to the England of Edward VI are now her "dominions beyond the seas."

Of India, whence in Edward Tudor's time came spices, Edward VII was the first Emperor, the second English sovereign to hold imperial power over her "many peoples, nations, and languages."

Under the English régime in Egypt, the Nile has been constrained to yield the utmost of her fertilizing power, while English judicial methods have imparted stability to Oriental forensics.

King Edward himself travelled to lands more distant than had been visited by any of his predecessors. His sons, and especially his successor, made a great portion of the world their own.

Australia, Africa, and America have seen the English heir, now sovereign, in a royal progress through the

Dominions of those Continents. India and the Mediterranean have their experience too, and even the most southerly of the Crown Colonies, the Falkland Islands, was visited, in far-off days, by one who had then no dream of kingship.

The face of Europe too has changed politically in a great degree since Edward VI reigned. The Emperor of Almain's dominions are divided and subdivided since the days when Hartmann Hapsburg was the betrothed of a daughter of the first Edward ; or, again, since Charles V threatened hostilities if Edward VI coerced his step-sister into use of the new Prayer Book and the Declaration of Faith. Yet a Hapsburg reigns, a venerable sovereign bound with ourselves in a political alliance.

Between the reigns of Edward VI and Edward VII had been two revolutions and the dreadful deed of 1649, when a sovereign, not ill-meaning, paid the debts of faulty predecessors to brutal soldiery and politicians.

The union of England and Scotland, and of England and Ireland had taken place.

Through the centuries, by action and reaction, the evolution of the Constitution of England and of the form of royal sway had worked itself into its modern being.

Into the hands of each successive sovereign of England this Constitution comes, a mighty Trust, to be maintained and guarded for the nation.

How Edward VII acquitted him of this great charge we all know well ; in what spirit he entered on his office, how he toiled, how, without assertion of prerogative, he by his own personal prestige balanced affairs in several acrid crises—these things are on the open page in writing not yet dry.

In the issue of the *Times* which announced his birth, a leader-writer says :—

" Never perhaps was the British, or any other crown, worn by a succession of sovereigns who 'bore their faculties so meek,' or were 'so clear in their great office' as the Princes of the House of Brunswick.

" It has been from first to last (whatever imperfections might be pointed out in the personal history of some of them) their characteristic praise to have endeavoured to understand and act according to the spirit of the Constitution under which they reign."

Of none of the sovereigns of the dynasty could this have been asserted with more justice than of Queen Victoria and of her son, Edward VII.

In the Accession Declaration, which to-day we may regard as the most individual expression of the sovereign during his reign, King Edward uttered his resolves and gave his undertaking " to follow in her [his mother's] footsteps, and to labour while there is breath in my body."

With a splendid fidelity he carried out his undertaking: with, indeed, a literal accuracy which made of his death-chamber a scene of far more lustre than the field of battle.

CHAPTER XXV

THE CROWNING AND THE CLOUD

THE year of mourning was at an end. Accession Day, now always rather an anniversary of the dead than of the reigning sovereign of England, had come, and in the second year of the King's reign the nation was looking forward to the revival in court life and to the coronation, after sixty-four years' interval, of their King and Queen.

There had been all the preparation, all the considering of precedent and ceremonial, all the provision for the entertainment of representatives of foreign Powers entailed by the great event.

The Earl Marshal had found the weight of duty in his ancient office. The various holders of long-descended posts at court, or in the State, had advanced their claims to assist on the great day. Some, as had been the case in former reigns, had been allowed and dispensed from their attendance.

There is no coronation banquet now; no Chief Butler hands the cup from the "cupboard" to the newly crowned King; no Dymock, Challenger, rides his charger into Westminster Palace and hurls his glove as attestation of the sovereign's rights.

But the great officers, as of old, bear sword, or spurs,

or cap of maintenance and the other paraphernalia of coronation.

The Primate of All England now is established as of right to crown the sovereign, while "Dr. Maclagan successfully claimed at the last coronation the right of the Archbishops of York to crown the Queen Consort." [1]

Some of these offices were claimed by more than one. In one case, that of the Hereditary Standard-bearer of Scotland, the claim of one *prétendant* was allowed, but, subsequent to the coronation, this decision was quashed in favour of the other claimant.

In a ceremony based, as it is, upon the Mass of the Catholic and Roman Church, but now dissociated from that root significance, it is not surprising that there is some want of clearness in the minds of those who are concerned with the modern adaptation of it to Anglican requirements. Queen Victoria, said a Lord Chamberlain of her reign, was one of the few who understood points of state etiquette and ceremonial. She had herself been witness, even victim, of the ill-informed assistants at her own crowning in 1838. The prelate who hurried in, and hurried out, knowing little and helping less, she had taken note of. The swelling of her finger, the incorrect one, on to which the celebrant had squeezed the ring intended for the smaller one, the wine and sandwiches on a side altar, an incongruity which struck hard upon her girlish perception—these were among the details which would not occur again while the Queen could be consulted.

But those who had been at her coronation and in a position to recall it or describe any of it were, of course, exceeding few.

[1] *Daily Mail*, 20 September, 1910.

Slowly and carefully the committee worked out the plan.

As has been of later years the custom, rehearsals took place of all possible portions of the ceremony and its contingent incidents.

The royal team of Flemish creams was exercised and inured to every kind of noise and manifestation. The most ample regulations for the traffic and for the public seating arrangements were devised and issued. London was faced with pine planking at every point; along every thoroughfare which was to be traversed by the King and Queen, or which gave a view, even remote, of their passage.

The crown had been taken in a bag from Windsor to the court jewellers in London by a Scotland Yard detective, guarded by two subordinates, to be altered suitably for King Edward's use.

New robes had been ordered by peer and peeress, with the suitable embellishments of ermine, and the velvet for the King's mantle had been woven in the manner of old time.

Throughout the country schemes of every magnitude had been worked out so that all England should make of June 26th a day unforgettable.

The King and Queen, with their descendants, had made state entry into London, and of reverse few dreamed.

Then, out of all this blue, the bolt fell in a moment.

We need not speak of what all can remember.

Of the shocked apprehension, of the overthrow of so great preparation, of the loss and disappointment, even of the abandonment of the smaller social events planned on the background of so great a day in history; or of the enormous weight of wasted food. All this was known, was suffered, throughout the land. Of the difficulties, the inconveniences, the disappointments, none could hope to reckon.

Coronations had been put off before. We know that that of the first Edward was changed in date more than once, and such alterations had occurred in later times. But never was there a disaster like this one.

The royal guests landing at the moment, or journeying to England, some already here; envoys from the four winds, from every quarter of the globe—all these must share in the swift blow.

In the days of Plantagenet Edwards, envoys had come from the sovereign of Armenia. Edward II and Edward III had had relations with the King of Georgia and the Emperor of Trebizonde. The ruler of the Medes and Persians, the Emperor of Cathay, the sovereign of the Tartars, live again in the ambassadors and missions of potentates, greatly more numerous, coming to do honour or homage to a great ruler of the twentieth century.

They turn and leave the country to which they came in such high spirit.

Now, we cannot pen nor paint the confusion and distress which then occurred. We felt and can recall them.

But all the inconvenience, all the turmoil, were as nothing to us in comparison with the trouble of our souls at this fell happening.

The hushed and grieving crowd peering through the railings of the palace where the King lay, watching the windows of his room, were, with all England, sorrowing with a depth, which they had not awaited in themselves, for the trouble which had fallen on the King, upon his family, and upon them all.

The swift dealing of the surgeons, the fear of the
result of such an operation on a patient whose youth
had passed ; those moments, prior to it, in which the
Clerk of the Closet (the Bishop of Winchester) had been
with his Majesty, all these things mounted up into a pile
of gloom before us.

Then how swiftly hope returned as daily the King
grew better. With the consideration which marks
the dealing of our royal family with the nation, it
was announced that their desire was that, as far as could
be, festivities in the provinces should take place as
arranged. Thus the children's joy was not too much
impaired by all that had happened in that anxious week.
In some parts of the Empire, where cable communica-
tion does not exist, the arranged celebrations were carried
out to the full in complete ignorance of the overthrow
of the main ceremony which had prompted all these
rejoicings.

The deferred event took place on August 9th, in
shortened form, the aged Archbishop carrying out his
office with trembling hands. Some of those who would
have been present on the original date did not return
for the finally accomplished coronation.

It could not be so grand, so joyous as a spectacle, or
as a public holiday again, but the strengthening of their
affection for their King, by the calamity which had
befallen himself and them, made a depth in the devotion
of his subjects which could scarcely have been reached
save through their hour of darkness.

And from his bed of pain King Edward rose resolved,
as it would seem, to labour, as none had ever done
before, in the years for which the dial had gone back-
wards.

CHAPTER XXVI

PEACE WITH HONOUR

IF, in a retrospect thrust too suddenly upon us, we ask ourselves what was the root-idea of King Edward VII in his ruling of our land during those nine years, so thick with event and with initiative, it comes upon us that while, in the *manner* of performance, he brought his individuality into full play, his real claim to be considered as great among sovereigns lies in his having laid hold upon what he found before him and dealing with it with a master-hand.

It was along the line of her own inherent potentialities that he aided England.

A "nation of shopkeepers" we are—however much we may resent that bald pronouncement of Napoleon or of Taine, or some one else, some older and obscurer *dictor*. It was to aid her commerce and to ensure her craftsmen's undisturbance, no less than to work for a great ethic scheme, that the King threw himself, with all his energy and all his suavity, into the work of making friends with Europe.

"Edward and Co.," as some, affectionately jesting, have described it, was the premier firm in the trading circles of a world.

For the cause of peace, as we well know, he did work

which the *Huis ten Bosch* and all its assemblies have never even distantly approached.

When, at a desperate moment, the blood of slain fishermen cried from the foam for vengeance, it was the King who with saner apprehension of the situation, staved off a crisis.

When friction made the wheels drive heavily, his was the hand to pour oil upon the overheated bearings.

In the days of the fourth Edward there were those within the realm to whom "the French nation was more odious than a toad" and who detested the French peace. Indeed, it was in far more recent days than those of any of the six earlier Edwards that Jean Crapaud did not hit it off with John Bull's thicknecked insularity.

"Nous avons changé tout cela," for "le Roi charmeur" (as the Earl of Rosebery has named him) made of his personal credit and long friendship a factor in the happier understanding which, for the time, prevails.

In the face of a stern *impasse*, which for the moment threatened, he won his way in his own genial fashion.

The earlier Edwards claimed sovereignty, claimed it too with sword and spear and arrow, in the land of France, but the seventh Edward held a sway there of greater power and worth by virtue of his personal impressiveness.

France has certainly suffered no loss of prestige by the friendly hand. It is but with amusement that one reads the crusty comment of the *Tägliche Rundschau* that "France has sunk to the level of a vassal of England."[1]

In Edward Tudor's reign, an English statesman lays it down that, though "Germany cannot match England

[1] So reported in the *Daily Mail* of 26 September, 1910, in connection with the Turkish Loan.

in sweet herbs, it can in nettles and such as have skill in stinging."

The Germany of to-day is not the same entirely as the power which called forth this utterance. A Hohenzollern, not a Hapsburg, rules the vigorous young Empire which is coming up alongside with such a vital stride, with such a head of steam, with such a bravery of horse-power.

On his "shining mail" her ruler suffers no rust to gather.

He, and they, do well, and might in several points be desirably imitated by the jelly-backs of other nations.[1]

It is not less our duty to keep a cautious eye, without hysteria, upon that militant strong sister across the Northern Sea and upon that growing water-brood which owes its being to her ruler. It may be an exaggeration to see in every German royalty a scout, marking out the land, but when a member of the House of Commons cries that, if his faction had sway, " would there be 'Dreadnoughts' built?" we must ask whether it may not be under the lee of the "Dreadnought" that he will ply his awl and plough his field in peace. Who shall live will see, as Gallic proverb has it.

War wears a hideous face, more hideous than ever in these days of the refinements of science, and we may feel as though the world should be weary of her. Yet there is turbulent young blood in healthy youthful veins, and to some a world where wars should cease might seem, as did a jubilee of matrimony without a difference, to one commentator, "aye peacefool but varra monortonous."

King Edward was no sentimentalist, nor of those egoists who deem that their finger shall beckon on mil-

---

[1] Miss Wyllie in *My German Year* puts well the admirable side of German habit for the general reader.

lennium, but he created everywhere he went an atmosphere wherein the germ of peace might flourish, with, and between, the nations.   For there was in this King of ours nothing of the schoolboy who with his cake woos allies in a corner of the play-yard.

No! we feel in all his efforts, and in all his completions, a genial wish that all might be the better friends.

We felt as well that what he had in hand might be left there, for it would go safely.

The ground of all our confidence in him was not as a founder of new systems of ethics or of intellect, it lay in the feeling of security he inspired by his absolutely clear and honest handling of affairs.

So great was this conviction that, at a time when the tactics of certain place-seekers had caused obstruction, a voice cried that if King Edward could have been invested for ten years with absolute sovereignty, England would emerge in safety from her internal discords.

Again, there was that truest dignity of simplicity which he applied to his undertakings which gave such weight to all.   There was no arrogance, no fussiness about this King of England.   In a word not academic, yet very forceful, King Edward had no " side " about him.

Within a year of accession, the new coinage, bearing the sovereign's head, is now customarily issued by the Mint. The standard of our English gold is so high that the sovereign, the pound piece, is acceptable in any part of the civilized world.   Even in the seventeenth century the English were able to compare, rather ungraciously, their currency with that of France, in the matter of Henrietta Maria's dower, to the disparagement of the latter country.

No longer does the King of England exercise the power

of depreciation, or of appreciation, of the currency to suit his aims of the moment. Edward VI could do so to the injury of his subjects, but such royal interference vanished long before the day of Edward VII.

Farthings, first coined in the reign of Edward I, are still with us. We may recall the major hindrance to the decimal schemes of Anthony Trollope's *Prime Minister*, that of the impossibility of naming their substitutes as "quinths." The "angel," the "noble," and other coins have disappeared. They warn us of the suppression of the "crown," which, for general circulation at all events, was last minted in the reign of Edward VII.

The square coin with its indented lines, which facilitated fracture into four parts (farthings), the penny of the earliest Edward, was succeeded by the round coin, roundness having become compulsory; and round our coins still remain.

No longer are Jews and others hanged for clipping coin, as they were under the Plantagenet rulers, though the making of counterfeit coin is still a grave offence. The debased and spurious pieces coming from abroad added to the difficulties of the Plantagenet statesman who sought to rectify the vicious state of the Edwardian coinage in the thirteenth century. Walter de Langeton did in one short year clear out the "pollards, crockards, slepings," and the rest. It was a giant feat. "Sterling" still lives among us, derived they say from some of those piratical peoples, the Esterlings, who gave their name to coin of the realm made by their hands, and whom we last saw chasing our fourth Edward into the shallows of the Flemish coast.

The Maundy money is still coined, and is given to poor recipients by the King's Almoner. The "little

bag" or purse of Edward Tudor's time remains ; but
a money gift replaces the "robe" or "kirtle" and the
shoes which that predecessor of Edward VII added to
the Maundy.

The operation of coining has become extended to
an immense degree, yet its *venue* is restricted to "the
Mint."

York and Canterbury were not the only cities possess-
ing a local mint in the times of other Edwards. The
great Church statesmen of their days had sometimes
their own mints. The Bishop of Durham in Plantagenet
times was granted royal licence for his, and received
a set of dies and punches for coining there.

The Great Seal, the impress of which was handed to
Queen Victoria with the patent of her heir's creation as
Prince of Wales, has to-day a tale of less vicissitude than
its predecessors under the early Edwards. For we see
the record of its handling, its journeys, its exit from the
sealed bag in which the Chancellor held it, its restoration to that retirement. Now it is carried to Edward I
on the cock-boat "St. Edward" ; again it is "eloigned"
from Edward II, or even for a time mislaid altogether.
For cleaning it, sponge is bought under those early
kings. In times, with which we are not dealing, it
has been sunk beneath the Thames.

Treason, though it remain upon the Statute Book,
seems almost a dead-letter in our day. It has become
a thing of innate impossibility with almost any Englishman, and isolated instances of disloyal or disrespectful
public utterance strike upon us as tinged with the
obscene, no less. Upstart ignorance, hampering the
painful toil of experts, may indeed arouse sedition in
our Empire—"woe to the man by whom the offence

cometh " : it is a lesion of the interests of Greater
Britain, and as such it claimed condemnation of a constitutional monarch. One of the few occasions on which
King Edward VII vented sternness was in such association, and not for any personal *lèse majesté*.

The custom of royal silence under personal attack
or calumny is certainly one of dignity.

Things were different under earlier kings : in the
reign of Edward IV, for instance; when the King
caused to be put to death a London citizen who, playing upon words (as he protested), had declared that his
son was heir to the " Crown," which was his tavern-
sign. The head of " Walker, London," paid for the
gymnastics of his tongue.

Or, in young Edward Tudor's childhood, when a
searching judicial spirit and Henry's gouty suspicious-
ness combined to invest the most mild gossip of the
ale-house with sinister significance. Here is a little
picture of the day. We have the village housewife
in some Kentish country-side. The time is Advent,
and fish she needs on that account. To her door
comes selling, just as he might to-day, one Grant,
a fisherman, with the spoils of the sea—Dover plaice
or codling from Whitstable, or what it may have
been. While the housewife chooses and haggles over
the slippery wares, the fisherman tells her of the gossip
he has also caught by the way. On this day of Advent
it is something really big that he has to tell. For they
say that the King is dead. At the news of this report
the law is set in motion. An inquiry is instituted and
many witnesses examined on the story told by this
Kentish village matron. The tale is traced to the
Chequers Inn at Canterbury, thence it descends into

a stable at "St. Martin's beside Canterbury"; it harks back to the Chequers: "Be not too hasty to pay your money!" one Higgins said to Held, "for the King is dead."

Now we are taken into the dwelling of the parish priest of yet another Kentish hamlet, where he and a *confrère* talk together, shortly after Prince Edward's birth, and wag their heads, saying that the Queen, his mother, was not crowned, and that something evil will befall in consequence. One of the clerics confirms the story, but his guest offers the first denial and says that he neither heard nor mentioned name of Queen or Prince. So much for all the sifting of the judges!

Here again, a little later, is the same process at Salisbury. A cleric, a butcher, a tailor and a "singing man" are the chief *dramatis personæ*, and their tale was this. The widow Deland had heard that Jane, the uncrowned queen of Henry VIII, had appeared to the royal widower at Portsmouth, and adjured him to go on pilgrimage to St. Michael's Mount. The widow was quite sure that she had heard a round half-dozen of male beings gossiping over the report, but these, upon examination, retreated altogether from the field, by denying that they had heard any word about the King.

However, another party did admit telling his landlady of the alleged apparition, though with the substitution of an angel for Queen Jane. The husband of the landlady, however, disclaimed all knowledge of his lodger's story. Enter, another widow confessing to a spreading of the tale, and implicating a married neighbour who had added to the original vision the material detail that Henry had vowed a noble as an offering at St. Michael's Mount.

Four years later, we come upon a similar inquisition in Henry's French possessions. English Tom and French Pierrot taking their glass together. To them enter one Anthony "very drunk" (Anthony was not French), and desired to take a glass with them. Anthony, not cheered by previous cups, was full of grievance. His way to his home had been stopped, he grumbled ; whether the right of way had been interdicted, or whether some officer of public discipline had barred the way, or whether Anthony's vision had played him false ; all this is silence. Tom, at any rate, was a good outspoken character. He had answered the fool according to his folly, by promising that next time he had audience of the King he'd see to it that a new road was made for the obstructed Tony. But he, now rudely vinous, blurted his retort, and "Hang the King," he hiccupped, "and them that made the way." Tom speaks his righteous horror at such speech—Tony it is that should be hanged for such words.

"Wa wors?" then questions Tony, oblivious of his surroundings and his speech. "He then fell down and went to sleep."

What a comedy ! We can see it going forward at the Savoy Theatre, perhaps, in the reign of Edward VII, but not before H.M.'s judges. Yes, we live amid more dignified conditions.

It is a paradox, one more among other perplexing facts, that, under more liberal conditions, the proportion of attacks upon the life of sovereigns has gone up. For the wrongdoing of others the innocent must suffer in all estates of men. A Louis XVI, a Charles Stewart, are doomed, while predecessors who piled up the evil and the error died in their beds. The decadent vanity which forms so large a factor in the impulse of the modern regicide feeds just as well on innocent blood. The reformer among rulers is indeed in danger of suffering from the first rebound. Why died Alexander II and Carnot, or sad Elizabeth of Austria, while others had escaped? The utter uselessness of the crime even to achieve some disordered scheme of wiping kings from the face of the earth has not deterred the assassin.

Our country has, happily, not known the horror in full extent, for, although so many attacks were made on Queen Victoria, they were without result, and on King Edward one only, as far as is generally known, was made, and that before his reign ·began. The miserable degenerate who fired his revolver into the railway coach at Brussels was but the catspaw of a faction. Again, woe to the man who shall cause one of these little ones to offend.

Britain's rulers may enjoy upon the whole a sense of security. There is a very real personal as well as official devotion among the guards of our kings. We see Inspector —— running, upon his own initiative, beside the royal carriage to keep an eye on things.

To one's ears has come a rumour, possibly quite baseless, that Queen Victoria, in some strange house, required the presence of a trusted retainer in her ante-chamber during the night, but so actual a bodyguard is doubtless rare. King Edward would have, we hear, dog Cæsar in his bedroom, but the canine attachment probably counted here, and not a sense of caution. And, for his ordinary moving about, King Edward had no escort nor even stopping of the traffic. There might one see the royal foreman of the realm on his way to some race-meeting, or family visit, jostling the traffic in King's

Road, the chauffeur warily alert to clear the omnibus on the off-side or the costermonger's ass ahead.

The sovereign no longer signs death-warrants, though respite and detention of murderers are still within the prerogative of his clemency or his pleasure, exercised, however, only upon the recommendation of the Home Secretary.

Nor does a queen now kneel before her lord in such grim instance as did Philippa of Hainault, whose intercession for the Calais burghers is said to have been chosen as the subject of a personal Christmas card by Queen Alexandra.

The first Edward " loved the Mass, though caring not for sermons," and the seventh Edward made it known that he desired the omission of the sermon at the services he attended as sovereign. He was always exact in such attendance, whether at the private chapels of the palace or at the parish churches of Sandringham and Crathie, or again at the English chapel at continental resorts visited by him. England now enjoys a freedom unexampled alike in her past history and among the nations of the world. Creed and ritual of the most divergent character find State toleration among us. It is fortunately now regarded as not good form to offer adverse comment on the religious practices of fellow-subjects. Perhaps, too, a certain amount of apathy, born of a tired generation, combines in securing peace among the better-bred of the community. We have now in our country the State Church, whose doctrine is admittedly still somewhat vague, having, even after three hundred and fifty years, still some of the incertitude which was born from the confusion arising out of Henry's breach with Rome and of the more thorough methods of dogmatic alienation which the advisers of Edward VI had set before the boy-King's vision. The old religion of the kingdom has never regained its national sway, yet it flourishes to-day side by side with its supplanter. The suppression of the monasteries has not prevented religious orders of every kind from being here in England in the reign of Edward VII. Religious of both sexes chant their office and carry on the labours of their rule in an essential continuity with their forerunners under mediæval Edwards. Lamenting such errors and indiscipline of the past, as may claim the censure of conscience, the members of the Catholic Church are free to practise their religion in a security greater even than they could ever have enjoyed under the often turbulent Catholic sovereigns of old time ; infinitely greater, too, than that prevailing in the Catholic countries of Europe at the present day. Like those of his mother, King Edward's relations with the Sovereign Pontiff were always marked by delicate and genial courtesy.

He visited three successive Popes at the Vatican, making his visits as sovereign with those precautions which should satisfy alike the requisitions of the Holy Father and of the British and Italian nations. Yet Rome has no nuncio at St. James's. Queen Victoria, staunchly Protestant as she was and observant of her oaths, never failed to show consideration for her Catholic subjects. At her coronation one of the young girls chosen by her Majesty to bear her train was the daughter of a Catholic peer.[1] In the last days of her reign the Queen of England commanded that her carriage should draw up by the wayside near Cimiez while a religious procession of some obscure village passed by. The customary

[1] *Queen Victoria's Letters* (John Murray), i. 145.

oath, devised to voice the alarms of an Orange faction more than two centuries ago, has, it is true, been grievous to Catholics, as being, from their point of view, a blasphemous utterance. With the wording of it, however, King Edward VII was not in any way concerned. We now see measures in progress which shall annul the sacrilege, while leaving clear the Protestant obligations of the English monarch. Looking upon Edward VII, we are conscious of good fortune (nor do we overlook his successor), and if King Edward could not be *Fidei Defensor* in the same sense as that in which the title was granted to his predecessor, Henry VIII, he yet might truly wear the name of Defender of the Faithful. And, were every other instance suppressed, his Catholic subjects can never forget how their King permitted access to documents which established the marriage of the Prince, afterwards George IV, with Mrs. Fitzherbert, as valid from the Catholic standpoint. This was a great act of chivalry and should establish King Edward as rightfully a "first gentleman in Europe."

Another large body of his subjects lived in the days of Edward VII under widely differing auspices from those existing in the earlier Edwardian reigns. When King Edward died, the Jews in every synagogue poured out in vivid Oriental imagery their sense of bereavement in the removal of the "light of their eyes." The tale of their sorrows in our land is a familiar one. From the barbarous activities of persecution, which were in keeping with the spirit of the days of the Plantagenets, on through the tale of political and civic disabilities, their story goes. Their racial faults, intensified by their surroundings, their estimable qualities of sobriety and domestic worth ignored, they were too often in mediæval times, and even later, as the dog to whom the village persecutors tie the tin pot of torment. Under Edward I, all of them in England were cast into prison *en masse*, were banished, were deprived of their synagogue, on the site of which, in Lothbury, stood later the tavern of the windmill. Did one succeed in gaining a position of confidence, straightway the " unco' guid" would put forth question of his fitness. Aaron the Jew, or Bonenfant, was one who held a key of the City chest. Could such be trusted ?

The conversion of the race to Christianity was a matter of earnest effort among the Plantagenet Edwards. Privileges were granted to the converts, who, from what we know of their present-day representatives, were not the most desirable specimens of their nation. The newly founded Order of Preachers was enlisted in the work. Pressure was put upon the Jews in the London and other Jewries of the kingdom, to persuade them to hear the preaching of the Order.

The dark story of persecution is bound up in the archives. The crucified child, at Norwich, or at Lincoln or at Nottingham, perhaps a myth entirely, certainly falsely multiplied, is terribly alleged against them.

Their nefarious dealings with the coinage of the land we may be less unready to accept. Here, for example, must have been "hard swearing" somewhere. Manasseh tells his tale of malice, and how clipped coin, with the forceps employed in clipping it, tied up together in a cloth, was thrown on the top of his house in the City of London and there found, by reason of which he was imprisoned on suspicion.

Or, Hannah, wife of Solomon, is found falling foul of a Christian neighbour, and uttering " contumelious

blasphemies " against her faith.   Hannah, too, declines
to eat her words ; she is ready to take her trial before
King Edward I himself, or his justices assigned for
dealing with the Jews.

And here in twentieth-century England, under King
Edward VII, is the inextinguishable race in both
Houses of the Legislature, in the highest of *la haute
finance*, and in the chair of my Lord Mayor.

The genial cordiality prevailing between the sovereign
and the City in the reign of our seventh Edward
calls for no comment, nor do we need to linger with
the tale of very different affairs which sometimes filled
the relations of the court and of the chief magistracy with
turmoil in olden days.

The first Edward swooped down upon the City in
1285 and deprived it of its charter because the Mayor
had suffered himself to be bribed by the bakers.   The
bakers had been the cause of earlier disturbances as well.
However, a judicious gift from the dischartered citizens
led to the restoration of their privileges.

Edward III took a mayor to task for leaving the
streets in a disgracefully insanitary state, and peremptorily
ordered him to return to the better methods of his
predecessors.

To-day the City honours and is honoured by foreign
rulers, guests of the nation and of the sovereign.
Hospitalities, which bear a flavour of old England, are
splendidly dispensed, and the picturesque figments of
the crimson rope and proffered sword alone recall the
ancient claims, the now long-buried hatchet.   To the
Lord Mayor is sent the first message of the new sovereign announcing the melancholy fact of the " demise
of the crown " and he, among the earliest, congratulates

the English ruler, or condoles with him, upon events of national or of family import. A baronetcy, an honour new since the days of Edward VI, is commonly bestowed upon the Lord Mayor in whose term of office occurs a royal event of special significance. There was a rare occasion on Lord Mayor's Day, 1841, when King Edward VII entered the world within a short time of the swearing in of the Chief Magistrate. Except for private celebration, the King's birthday was always kept upon another date in the United Kingdom, in order not to interfere with the ancient anniversary of the civic custom.

There are no longer scenes such as occurred in the reign of Edward VI, when the London Mayor left the banquet in a rage because of some slight in the matter of precedence.

Such are a few comparisons, lightly made, between the days of Edward VII and earlier Edwards in the larger order of things.

Smaller subjects, too, are not without their worth. To them we will now turn.

CHAPTER XXVII

THE OLD AND NEW IN LESSER THINGS

NO longer are the chronicles of the kitchen and the wardrobe to be sought among the antiquarian things of England, as we sought for them under the story of the six preceding Edwards.

Our interest in them is now involved with our present-day curiosity and attachment in and for the royal personages who live lives, not unlike our own in many points, yet still including custom and tradition which stretch away beyond the first Edward into unarchived centuries.

In this place, and by our hand, it is fitting only to adduce a few examples illustrative of contrast or development, of change or conservation.

In the midst of echoes from the past and of ancient offices preserved unto our time, are found the more strenuous working methods of to-day. With King Edward's accession, much was remodelled which it would have been almost impious to change while the aged Queen Victoria was alive. Ponderous and somewhat tasteless decoration, which had been in keeping with prevailing taste in the early years of her reign, now made way for something more satisfactory to modern views of art as well as of hygiene. There was not, it is true, disorder of the kind in which Queen Victoria and her consort wrought reform in their young married life in the royal palaces. The plaintive remark of George III, on beholding the accumulations in the cellars of Windsor Castle, "I should have thought something might be done with all these cinders!" would not have been called for under his successors. Still a good deal might be needed in the way of bringing working methods up to the latest standard of efficiency, for, with the quite moderate Civil List of our English King of the twentieth century, costly or wasteful methods of working could not be entertained. Some few offices, effete with time, have been suppressed; picturesque pages-of-the-back-stairs may have given way to efficient individuals of the domestic servant kind.

The court gentlemen and grooms of the Bedchamber have less literal functions to perform than their predecessors under Edward VI, but work of the bureau has enormously increased within the palace walls, as in all departments of the State.

Often enough, in the reigns of the earlier Edwards, we see the long dragging out of negotiations, the cumbersome exchange of correspondence, when horse-power only was available.

King's messengers still travel with despatches, but their path is on the iron way, their journey furthered by the energies of steam-hustled crank or turbine. One of the messengers met his death on duty in King Edward's reign, for the powers of ocean still contend with human artifice for lives.

The electric wire in its several developments, ay, the very ether, has been called into the service of the Empire and of the royal household.

Edward IV had his secretaries, English and French ; his queen, too, had her own ; but their work, even though done by script alone, must have been a small affair in comparison with that of King Edward's private secretaries.

Formal petitions are no longer presented, save through the Secretaries of State, but an immense number of informal requests, inquiries, and representations are made, and are dealt with by the private staff in methods of business and of patience.

The centenarian and the mother of triplets are assured of gracious wishes or of royal bounty ; the latter, of whom, in the time of Edward VI, we told so sore a tale, now receives £3 from the sovereign to assist her in this emergency of Nature's prodigality.

" As always happens, none sought out the sorrowing," said Mlle. d'Orléans in the seventeenth century. None could say this of our King Edward VII nor of his queen. Nor is there any longer a trace of the *insouciance*, which seemed cruelty and yet was but economic ignorance, of that Dauphine who inquired, " If the people have not bread, why do they not eat cake ?" For the King carried on, into minutest detail, the knowledge of and interest in industrial affairs which owed so largely its initiation to his father's efforts ; and where, with his incomparable tactfulness, the sovereign refrained from a command in the inception of a public fund for charity, there the King's wife came forward potently, initiating, with ever living sympathy, some great endeavour for the submerged tenth. What a variety of personal touches came from this Queen ! No longer does a King of England, or his consort, wash the feet of God's poor at the Maundy, but in service more true and more intimate Queen Alexandra has never failed. She rises, a radiant apparition, beside the docker in the wine-vaults of the London Docks ; she, in the interests of working wives, desires to find some cupboards in industrial dwellings. In some corner of pain, she bends over the incurable girl who had longed to see her Queen before she died, and her own sorrows have but opened her heart still wider. Nor must it be forgotten that King Edward, loving youth and jollity around him as he might, did not forget to seek out ladies whose riper years made illness and financial distress the sorer burden.

With the help of her camera, her Majesty gave us not long ago a picture-book of snap-shot insights into more familiar moments of her own and the King's existence. We saw her with her nearest kin and saw our King, in some informal moment, sitting by the wayside in the Highlands and laughing, with his daughter-in-law, over some jesting of the suite. It seemed as though her Majesty had said to us, "Come and share my little joke with me." And who could fear for the naval supremacy of England who beheld the broad shoulders of an Admiral of the Fleet who was indeed King Edward ! And has she not—an honour infinitely greater—admitted us into the holy places of her grief ?

Of Queen Alexandra's interests in some social and political affairs we have not been made aware. We do not even know whether she would second that rigid dictum of her mother-in-law, Queen Victoria, regarding female suffrage, that " Lady —— ought to be whipped." Certain it is that this Queen has never forgotten those acts of warm-hearted kindness which do much to alleviate the disadvantageous position of the English-woman of the middle or of the working classes. Her pitying heart, they tell us, led to those gifts of woollen garments which were bestowed upon the poor derelicts of the Embankment ; wreckage lying beneath the winter stars in a way which publicists declare to have no parallel in the great cities of the world. If it were but an imperfect salve upon so sore a wound, yet may her act, by the very personal touch of it, have given an impulse in some battered heart to a fresh struggle against innate viciousness or cruel exterior odds.

With music, Queen Alexandra has associated herself more intimately than with literature or economics. She herself is a Doctor of Music *honoris causâ*, and a patroness of the home, now called Queen Alexandra's House, at South Kensington, for music and art students. She has always been a faithful attendant at the Royal Opera House. Herr Direktor Neumann tells us how, as Prince and Princess of Wales, King Edward and his wife gave themselves a great amount of trouble in order to be present at the first performance of the " Ring Cycle " in London.[1]

King Edward again, within the last year of his life, came forward most generously as patron of a woman's effort, by commanding a performance of " The Wreckers," the opera of Miss Ethel Smyth.

This was but one of the immense variety of this King's solicitudes for the personal interests of his subjects. Amidst the crowding happenings of foreign diplomacy or of colonial developments or domestic polity, were interspersed touches, almost innumerable, upon the little lives of England. One lady receives a visit to celebrate her century of life ; the valiant explorer, who on his own initiative sets forth to

[1] *Recollections of Wagner.* Angelo Neumann.

capture the Heart of the Antarctic, is sent on his way with his sovereign's encouragement and a flag from the Queen ; the Japanese artist, who has shown us all the beauties of London in the rain, and who was one of the sufferers from the postponed coronation, is not forgotten ; and even the talented schoolmaster of an Oxfordshire country town is commanded to Sandringham to exhibit an educational accessory of his own invention.

It was in the reign of the seventh Edward that the Blue Coat School, founded, or at all events confirmed, by Edward VI, has at length been pushed into green fields away from its classic lodging, now absorbed by the Postmaster-General. Penny postage was seventy years old at King Edward's death, and the general mail carried some part of royal correspondence. The work of the King's messenger has narrowed yearly.

The interest of the King's son (H.M. George V) in matters of philately is known too universally to need a comment.

Although those having authority may be able to correct the common impression in some detail, it will be held by the general public that there was a most marked resemblance in King Edward to his mother.

The eyes, blue and prominent, the fullness of the face and the finely-cut nose were those of Queen Victoria, the last-named feature having been, it is true, common in resemblance to both parents.

The form and general outline of the King became, as years advanced, strikingly like that of Queen Victoria.

"I wonder whom our little boy will be like?" queries the girl-Queen Victoria, in the manner of all mothers.

It was considered, by some who had the opportunity of conversing with King Edward, that he retained, in certain points of utterance, traces of his more immediate German ancestry.

As with Queen Victoria, his delivery of public speeches was clear and of good diction.

Of the felicity of his minor speaking, his after-dinner speeches, in pre-eminence, the fame has lived through many years and no one needs reminding of it.

The sovereign to-day dresses in general like anybody else. King Edward was always regarded as a monitor in correct masculine attire. The hand-loom velvet made by an aged weaver for the coronation robes is one of the remaining links with earlier Edwards. The cost, too, of the exquisite fabric was nearer to the values of Edward VI than that of most textiles of to-day.

Since sumptuary difference is scarcely found, royalty comes now before the public eye without the trappings which by right of faëry should belong to it.

Once upon a time, a prince, since sadly dead, went to pay a call upon a lady in an English military station.

The door was opened by an Irish servant, who announced that her mistress was not at home. Would the gentleman leave his name?

The caller said it did not matter.

"But shure, sir," responded the Irishwoman, "the misthress will be after asking who called."

"Very well; please say Prince Edward of Wales."

"So thin," related the heroine of the tale, "I down wid me curtsey."

"Well, and what did you think of our future king?" inquired the hostess when the experience was detailed to her.

" Why, shure an' isn't he just the seme as any other jintelman ! "

This observation was afterwards repeated to the Prince, who answered, laughing :

" Why ! did she think I would look like an Indian chief ? "

An excellent simplicity is marked in English royalty in general.

We find it constantly in Queen Victoria. In her religious outlook ; in her gratitude to those who had the honour of offering her hospitality or service ; in her regrets that cares of Empire should make her seem unduly silent in the company of her ladies ; in the womanly *naïveté* with which she looked aghast upon the evil of this world.

King Edward displayed, in other aspects, this same quality.

Ready to be pleased, interested, and interesting others, even amid the wearisome restraints inseparable from royal existence, this King could seldom have been bored.

Little stories reach us, too, of younger generations, brought up to make their courteous request to their grandmother's subjects for hospitality when Windsor Castle was overfilled with foreign guests. " I am desired by my Papa to ask you," in a schoolboy hand, prefaces the request, to a lady associated with the court, for sleeping accommodation for himself and his elder brother.

To write of dress in connection with Queen Alexandra is to write of a rare combination of fashion and fitness. This Queen has seen more change in styles of dress than was known to all the queens of earlier Edwards in the passage of centuries.

From the day when she was first seen on the deck of the yacht which brought her to us for her marriage, dressed in white, " with a few coloured flowers in her bonnet," or in the grey silk dress, with purple velvet mantle trimmed with sable, and the white bonnet in which she made her first triumphal progress through London, she has stood for an authority among us. As Princess of Wales and Queen of England, alike, she has been noted as a leader of fashion within refined prescription.

Upon state occasion, Queen Alexandra might appear in stately vesture, in coils of pearls and sparkling gems. As a Lady of the Garter, too, she wore its broad blue ribbon across her corsage. We heard of her robe of fairy tissue worn at the coronation, embroidered by the women of her husband's Indian Empire, under the superintendence of a viceroy's wife,[1] but we know her much better in her yachting dress or in the morning gown in which, as lady of the manor, she goes out to feed her pet animals at Sandringham House.

To-day we must look on her, with sorrowful homage, in her garb of widowhood.

Some fabrics known of old have survived to the day of the seventh Edward ; the names even of some varieties are the same.

Velvet and taffeta and *gros grain* come from centuries ago. Even the Ryselles worsted may have its modern counterpart in the "Russell cord" of the nineteenth century. Calico is the "callicut cloth" of Edward VI.

Frieze is a revival both of craft and name. The Duchess of Sutherland has been a great promoter of its manufacture among cottage industries, and at the

[1] The late Mary, Viscountess Curzon.

sale held on behalf of her *protégés* at Stafford House, King Edward more than once became a purchaser.

England need no longer send to the Low Countries for her table-linen, for sister Ireland can furnish the finest, and the royal family are patrons of her output.

Lace, however, still comes to us from Brussels, Bruges, and Malines, or named after those ancient Flemish cities, and to it we can provide no compeer.

Queen Victoria was a staunch supporter of home-work in lace-craft, her wedding-dress being veiled with Honiton point; and other royal ladies have encouraged the revival of point and pillow lace in Ireland and in the counties of Buckingham and Bedford.

Royal patronage, indeed, is never lacking for home manufactures.

Queen Victoria, whose Indian tribute included Cashmere shawls, aided the distressed producers of the Paisley imitation; she and the Duchess of Kent both wearing shawls of the kind at the christening of the Prince of Wales in 1842, and modern instance is unfailing.

"Mrs." Basset and her companion maids of Edward VI's boyhood have their counterparts, whose emoluments are certainly an advance upon the £10 paid by Queen Jane (Seymour). The maids-of-honour to Queen Alexandra have had, however, a very different experience as regards the dress question. The "two good gowns" of Anne Basset mean an extensive wardrobe to her compeers of to-day. Though here again no example of senseless profusion, or of outlay, has ever been given by Queen Alexandra or by any of Queen Victoria's daughters to the lesser ranks of society.

In the regalia are some survivals from the earliest Edwards. *La cerise* of the days of Edward I, which was at one time in the ward of Eleanor, his queen, is it conceivably the ruby which, in the nineteenth century, was set in the crown of England, and was associated with the time of Edward III ; and which, indeed, is probably in the crown as used for crowning Edward VII ?

A diamond crown, made to the special design of her Majesty, was the one placed on her head by the Primate of England on August 9, 1902.

We have told of the crowns of Edward III and Philippa, pawned for cash in their financial straitness, and of the "fetterlok" and the ornament on which John Fastolf lent money to the father of Edward IV.

There was, again, that pendant of a pear-shaped pearl lost by Edward VI on a ride to Southampton in 1552, but recovered later.

What, however, were these or any other royal gems beside the great gleaming of the jewels of India and Africa, the Kohinoor and the Cullinan, which now are among the crown-jewels—the latter, the largest diamond in the world, having been presented to King Edward, and some of its lesser portions, after cleavage, to Queen Mary.

The lesser of the two principal fractions has been worn occasionally by Queen Alexandra. Thus have King Edward's subjects been able to see the African gem, of which the largest portion can only figure in some rare event of coronation or great pageant (see p. 342).

These crown jewels are occasional and important inmates of the Tower of London.

Of the royal dwellings, Windsor remains the only one

inhabited alike by Edward VI and Edward VII. The Palace of Westminster is no longer even a *Palais de Justice*, except on rare occasion. Hampton Court is a present to the people. Buckingham Palace, the London residence of our sovereigns, is at length under consideration with a view of dignifying the smugness of its grimy stucco front. In the ancient masonry of Windsor Castle bathrooms have been pierced, where, in the days of Edward IV, an honoured guest took his bath in his chamber beneath a canopy, and dried himself with towels of the Queen's "ordonnance," perhaps woven under the supervision of Elizabeth, Queen Consort. To-day, gifts of worn linen from the royal palaces are made to London hospitals, to which is also sent game from the royal coverts.

Many great officers of the royal household have ceased to deal with the intimate matters of the palace which were their care under the previous Edwards. The Lord Chamberlain is associated in our minds far more with the licensing of plays and playhouses than with his ancient duties. No longer, at any rate, does he attend guests of his king in their chamber and even in their bath, as did his predecessor in the time of Edward IV. The Mistress of the Robes has her place in pageantry, but her duties end outside the door of the Queen's bedroom, the aid she gave to earlier consorts being now relegated to the hands of "dressers," by whom queens and opera stars alike are tended.

An ancient office is that of Coroner of the Verge, whose predecessors bore the wand before our earliest Edward of England's day.

His functions are but rarely exercised, and, as far as memory serves, the sudden death of a servant in the royal mews at Buckingham Palace gave the only occasion for them during the reign of Edward VII.[1]

The Board, for which Green Cloth was furnished in the reign of Edward VI, survives in office, though perhaps without its exact condition of old time.

Horticulture has become, since the days of Edward VI, a matter of keen science. Royal gardens call now for the ministrations of a staff of experts. Adam and John, who cared for the garden at Windsor at 2d. *per diem* under the earlier Edwards, would be as ignorant as the merest amateur, of the nature as well as of the names of most of the specimens cultivated by their successors. The six women-weeders who worked in the King's garden in Prince Edward's boyhood, in the sixteenth century, might perhaps find their labours lessened by modern knowledge. Even the "keeper of the King's arbours and grafts" would find much to surprise him.

The vineyard at Windsor, which Edward IV displayed so proudly to a foreign guest, is replaced by vineries under glass. We hear of the Black Hamburg grapes, and other varieties, which supply the King's table.

At Sandringham, reclaimed from poverty of soil, are the expressions of individual taste on the part of King Edward VII; still more of that of Queen Alexandra, whose artistic powers have found a principal channel in this direction.

Hyde Park, where Edward VI went a-hunting with his guests from France, is now a "lung of London." The royal buckhounds have been suppressed, tame stag-hunting, an ignoble form of sport, having for some time before the reign of Edward VII been falling into dis-

[1] In the case of one of his Majesty's guests who died suddenly at Sandringham, on the King's birthday, an inquest was not necessary.

repute. Armed with other weapons than the cross-bow of their Plantagenet ancestors, King Edward and his sons have been keen sportsmen in other directions.

"The little new gardens by Thames side, at Hampton Court," which Edmund the gardener tended in Edward Tudor's boyhood, are now, by royal gift, a joy to the nation. Here may one watch the water-wagtail skimming across great lily-leaves and see, through beautiful iron gates, the adjacent park, also a place of public resort, and wonder indeed why one ever troubled to go to Versailles.

Pet animals have become to-day a feature of royal, as well as of private existence ; King Edward's terrier, which went everywhere with him during the last years of his life, and which, in his funeral train, struck a note unparalleled in the sympathetic hearts of thousands, has the greatest public reputation ; Queen Alexandra and most of the King's family have favourites of different kinds. A princess of the blood breeds a choice variety of cats.

The King had no private menagerie of wild beasts either at the Tower of London or elsewhere, the gifts of Indian or African rulers being generally handed over to the gardens of the Zoological Society.

Following the example of his parents, King Edward, both as Prince of Wales and sovereign, was much concerned with farm-stock and owned some of the finest in the world.

For Queen Alexandra's fancy poultry at Sandringham the accommodation must be much greater than that required at Southwark when Edward Tudor was a child and the King's carpenter put up houses for the King's fowls in the royal gardens there.

In spite of his having won the Derby on three occasions, King Edward's racing stud was not considered, on the whole, to have been a successful one.

The previous Edwards knew not of national horse-racing, their steeds displaying their form in the tourney and the joust.

Edward III had his stud in the park of Windsor, and there were royal mews at Charing. Prior to this, irregularities had occurred in connection with stud affairs, for there is a complaint that worthless sires are being pastured on the King's lands with "his great plough-mares," resulting in a debased progeny. Some ten years later, the Master of the Horse (not that he bore that title) is commanded to take charge of the King's palfrey, "Grisel Pomele" (dapple grey).

Under Edward VI they sent abroad for fresh blood to improve the royal stock at home.

On the buffet at the christening of Albert Edward in 1842 were displayed racing trophies won by preceding Princes of Wales.

King Edward failed perhaps in a good many racing events, but took reverses like a true sportsman. Edward VI had been unlucky too, for when he and his courtiers played against others at tilting at the ring at Greenwich they lost the prize. "They took never, which seemed very straunge," ponders the boy-King.

Yet, on the last Derby day of his reign, the seventh Edward triumphed, for did he not win, with Minoru, the classic stakes and lead the winner through the living lane of his delighted subjects, proud of such a king—the first sovereign to run a Derby winner?

With regard to the royal commissariat, the fusion of ancient custom with the new is full of interest. The boar's head, the game pasty, the baron of beef still make an appearance, chiefly ornamental, at Christmas-time, when royal cygnets also find a place upon the list of provender. The sovereign has still prerogative claim over the sturgeon cast upon our island shores, a claim not pressed beyond the formal surrender and the royal waiving of the right to a receipt of the fish. "Peppercorn" rents may still survive, but modern tenants probably do not pay that rent of five herring pasties by which Robert Curzon held of the Plantagenets. The "subtleties" set upon the royal buffet no longer bear the name they did under Edward of York, but they have advanced immensely in intrinsic refinement.

France still provides our kings with cooks. M. Ménage has held sway where Pierrot the Frenchman did in the young days of Edward VI. We must not look, however, in royal circles for the exuberance nor for the exotic intensity in raw material which marks the effort of the plutocrat.

Charles VII of France regaled his officers on a *gigot* and some fowls, and from a *ci-devant* ambassadress we learn of the mutton and boiled chicken, followed by an apple tart, which she shared, in Queen Victoria's reign, with the ladies and gentlemen of the household.[1]

It was always understood that at Sandringham and Marlborough House some advance, due to a larger cosmopolitan spirit, was made on this wholly simple English bill-of-fare. The thin bread-and-butter offered at Windsor would in the other royal establishments be diversified by the sandwich and hot cakes which were also familiar in ordinary English households.

There is a notable simplicity in the menu of the state-

[1] *Letters of a Diplomat's Wife.* By Mary King Waddington.

banquets during King Edward's reign, and nothing to surprise the ordinary person.

We may take for granted that within its limits every dish displays perfection, but anything *extravagant* (in the Gallic sense) or related to the "freak" monstrosities of entertainment is entirely absent.   Modern appliances would, in King Edward's reign, doubtless mitigate some of the difficulties of service in the great spaciousness of Windsor Castle.   Queen Victoria's remark that " food always tasted better in small houses " suggests that to serve a meal "piping hot" may be easier, after all, even in the despised " semi-detached" than in the vastness of royal dwellings.   The splendid gold plate, used upon state occasions, obtrudes still further the difficulty of imparting to such material, or to finest porcelain, the temperature requisite for keeping sauce or gravy in eatable condition.   Upon the royal sideboard (the " cupboard" of Edward IV and of Edward VI), is massed this splendid service of gold when sovereign guests are entertained, or at the courts held by King Edward and his queen, and at which were practised those innovations which have added so greatly to the comfort and convenience of subjects " paying their respects to their Majesties."

Venetian glass, which was blown in England by immigrants in the reign of Edward VI, is still prized among us, but England too can produce table-glass of lovely quality and form in the great factories of the glass-blowers of Stourbridge and elsewhere.

English porcelain, too, has risen into being since the reign of Edward VI.

We hear of the Rockingham china service made to the command of William IV, King Edward's great-uncle, and used, for the first time out of London, at the royal christening banquet of 1842.

There, too, did Mr. Mauduit, Yeoman of the Confectionery, deck the christening cake with rose, shamrock, thistle, harp, and leek in sugar replica, and also imitate, in coloured sugar-work, fruit of all kinds, to the great admiration of the guests.

Of special tastes on King Edward's part the general public has heard but little.

The hare cooked in the manner of Poitou has been, however, mentioned as a favourite dish.[1] This was the *plat* said to have been personally prepared by its author, a French statesman.

"One can hardly fancy," observes Mr. R. H. Sherard, in *My Friends the French*, "the same sort of thing in England—Lord Avebury, for instance, jugging a hare in Lloyd George's back-kitchen. Every restaurant within three hundred yards . . . received callers who, smelling the fragrance in the air, wanted particularly to know what was being cooked, as they would like some."

Of course, any tale of commendation on the part of royal guests is liable to discount in the light of the anecdote told of H.R.H. the late Duke of Cambridge, who, having spoken kindly of a dish of pork at a mess luncheon, was for a long time pursued by similar fare at every mess which he honoured, until, in a moment of exasperation, the Duke exclaimed : "I wonder why they always give me these pork chops !"

The less robust health entailed on King Edward by his serious ailment in 1902 made careful diet a necessity. The Marienbad régime in a modified form was found suitable.

[1] *French Household Cookery.* By Mrs. de Keyser.

Noticeable was the simplicity of a *déjeuner* served to the King on one of his visits to Paris. The simple cutlet, the buttered eggs with asparagus points, prepared, of course, with true Parisian distinction, yet innocuous to the impaired digestive faculty.

In the royal cellars may be found the wines of which we heard in earlier times. Wines of Bordeaux are there, St. Emilion still among the list. Rhine wine, too, and Madeira, the "malvoisie" of those earlier reigns, or rather its modern counterpart. Wines too there are less known to previous Edwards, though Chaucer tells of them :—

> "Whyte wyn of Lepe,
> That is to sell in Fish-strete or in Chepe.
> This wyn of Spayne crepeth subtilly
> In othere wynes, growing faste by,
> Of which ther ryseth swich fumositee,
> That when a man hath dronken draughtes three,
> And weneth that he be at hoom in Chepe,
> He is in Spayne, right at the toune of Lepe."

After King Edward's accession large stocks of sherry were disposed of, but the subsequent gift of a relative must have filled some portion of the vacancy.

To-day these wines do not deteriorate, by reason of their poverty, as they did in earlier times, nor do the products of the great brewers of Burton degenerate so direfully as the home-brewed of the Plantagenets, nor even as the ale which in the days of Edward VI "became as vinegar."

We have no knowledge of a "yeoman of the bottles," such as he who held a post in Edward Tudor's time and furnished to the King's stepmother (Katharine Parr) ten bottles at one time, most probably empty ones for containing those various home-made cosmetics or simples, compounded of the rose—rose-water, julep, honey or conserve—which now would be supplied by royal warrant-holders, rather than by the palace still-room.

The enormous provision of wax made for earlier Edwardian kings has been supplanted by petroleum products and by forms of lighting which to the Middle Ages, and even to Tudor England, would have stood for something necromantic. The arc light, used on the occasion of King Edward's marriage, has been supplemented by the incandescent wire which is the application of electricity now in use for interior and domestic purposes.

The gases of coal and of acetylene, these are there to take the place of the wax light and of the tallow-dip of old, yet from the wax-candle is still derived the most beautiful, if the most costly, form of interior illumination.

In the domestic servant staff, radical changes have taken place.

The simple John and Edmund, who were the castle janitors in Plantagenet days, are replaced by sterner sentinels, who add to their other duties the task of dealing with the deluded persons who, not infrequently, approach royal residences with some imaginary mission to the sovereign or grievance for his rectification.

We hear no longer of intruders, such as the London *gamin* of the 'forties who hid under a sofa in Queen Victoria's dressing-room.

It was understood that King Edward, when dining out, was attended by his own servant, an arrangement which perhaps was useful in precluding such an accident as the Duke of Cambridge had to deplore on one occasion when Queen Victoria dined with him and some fish-sauce was spilled upon her Majesty's dress.[1]

Perhaps the most revolutionary event upon King Edward's accession was the arrangement by which royal servants receive third-class fares in travelling allowances.

The royal liveries bear some likeness to those of Tudor times, when the Queen's footmen wore their scarlet and their crimson velvet, having also two yards allowed for their running coats, which to-day they do not need.

A permanent Court Band was not maintained in King Edward's reign, though the King's " Master of the Musick " still preserves his office.

The Children of the Chapels Royal sing as they sang in Edward Tudor's day, though regals and the "pair of organs" have given place to nobler instruments of music.

Sir Walter Parratt and other musicians compose Church music for great occasions, as did John Marbeck his anthems for St. George's Chapel in the day of Edward VI.

" My place is with the King," said Queen Alexandra, as she climbed, amid the protestations of the suite, into the invalid carriage in which King Edward left the palace after the operation of 1902.

Always, in time of sickness, has this Queen's place been by her suffering family.

To modern skill in healing, Edward VII was a great debtor. The operation performed upon the King in 1902 was one which could not have occurred at the time of Edward VI. The nurses, whatever their personal

[1] *Life of H.R.H. Duke of Cambridge.* By Rev. Canon Edgar Sheppard, D.D.

devotion, under Plantagenet and Tudor sovereigns, were incapable of practising the methods with which the knowledge and discipline of to-day equipped those nursing experts who were auxiliaries to the great surgeon and the other medical attendants of a twentieth-century King.

English were they all, and sufficient for their purpose. The Earl of Warwick, in Edward Tudor's reign, craves the services of a French or Flemish surgeon, in place of the English one, whose attentions have given birth to fear and suffering in Lady Warwick, " who looketh hourly to have her leg sawed off."

The perityphlitic affection by which King Edward was attacked would, in an earlier Edward, have spelt an almost certain death, with rumour whispering blackly of " Poison ! " over the tortured frame. " Poison " was indeed the frequent glib alternative to incapacity of diagnosis in days much later than those of our earlier Edwardian kings.

With the nursing of the sick poor King Edward VII and his queen were most closely associated.

King Edward's Hospital Fund and the Queen's Nurses, both dating from their days as prince and princess, are a great monument, and there are other royal institutions, such as the Osborne Convalescent Home for military officers, which are scarcely secondary.

The Finsen light owed its initiation in this country to Queen Alexandra's gift of a lamp to the London Hospital.

Another " Lady of the Lamp," whom we are mourning as these words are written, was the first among women to receive the Order of Merit at the hands of King Edward.

The Baths of Buxton, closed by Thomas Cromwell, lest superstition should involve itself in their therapeutic powers, are still in use by English sufferers to-day, though King Edward's own treatment was that of Marienbad.

King Edward had a remarkable experience of fires during his lifetime. There was nothing, it is true, to compare with that which destroyed so much of the Palace of Westminster in the reign of Edward I, nor with the lesser one which damaged royal plate and kitchen-gear in the time of Edward VI, when also a great fire occurred at the Tower of London. Still, there was a fire at Marlborough House, and two at Sandringham, besides a slight outbreak at Buckingham Palace.

King Edward shared to some extent in his mother's interest in the Stewart ancestors of their House. He lent personal belongings, relics of the royal Stewarts, to the exhibitions held in the previous reign. Noting an error in the description of an exhibit, the prince pointed it out as not his property; but, shortly after, coming upon another object wrongly ascribed, he remarked in a bantering tone, "Now, that is too bad, for that really *was* my own."

Royal personages do not to-day accept gifts in the indiscriminate manner of their predecessors. We know that Mary Tudor accepted articles of almost every kind, fruit, cage-birds, cheese, and sausages, for all of which the donors were over-richly paid. Still, in times of Jubilee, this rule has been relaxed, and Queen Victoria was pleased to accept small personal gifts, such as a work-bag, made and embroidered by an aged subject in her own eightieth year of life and in the fiftieth of the sovereign's reign.

They live before us at the present day, these

descendants of Edward. I, and we know them as good friends. Their children grow up before our eyes, prepared, as far as may be, for the peculiar duties of their state.

We see experiments in democratic education. The royal cadets live, to a large degree, the lives of their fellow-subjects.

It may be said that "Fellows are not allowed to hit the prince," but it is easily inferred that this rule is applied, as far as the authorities are able, to every individual.

Recently—a still more advanced communism—a prince of England enters a private school open to various conditions of English youth.

With a republican form of government, England has not shown herself accordant. The changing rulers, the stranger personalities who, at short intervals of years, might preside over our destinies, under an elective form of government, would bring some features of uncertainty absent from our hereditary monarchy.

These we have watched ; we know the general trend of court and family affairs. They are ready to hear and to consider even tiresome trivialities. They regard public wishes and complaint with almost too great forbearance.

A murmur arises because the royal car is closed, and an explanation is returned that neuralgia compelled an occupant to this course.

When the programme of music for the Prince of Wales's (Edward VII) christening was under consideration, some protest was made because a march from Handel's "Hercules" was included, the ground of grievance being that the subject was a non-sacred one. To-day, when "Handel's Largo" is performed in churches, no one walks out because the opera, of which it forms a number, is labelled "Xerxes." Yet Queen Victoria showed such gracious deference in the matter that a march from " Joseph " was substituted for the one originally chosen.

We like to have our opportunity of seeing them among us, passing through our midst with some of the lustre of old English pageantry.

King Edward understood this very real satisfaction to his people, and in every scene Queen Alexandra was associated.

If there were no other feature repellent to us in another form of government there would remain that entailed by the loss of such a beautiful and kindly personality as hers : "Such," said M. Constant, the painter, " as I imagine the great Queens of France of past times to have possessed."

Of royal portraits we have to-day a store of varying merit. From the first drawing in water-colour by Mr. Ross of the infant Prince of Wales, down to those which at King Edward's death may have remained un-finished, there are " command" and "permit" represen-tations of persons and events. Frith, lately dead, painted the King's wedding, and representative men, or ones chosen by the sovereign on private grounds, have handed down their impressions, extending to the last sad pencil sketch of the dead King by Sir Luke Fildes. " Command" work, on some state occasion, is less often a success than more informal performance, but the value of the sovereign's patronage is, in such matters, a consideration probably weighing more with the sitter than the standard of the result.

'A few there are which stand out among their fellows,

and names, of which none needs reminding, have added one more to their laurels by a presentment of a king or queen.

These things and many more will find their place in the great records of a nine-years' reign.

Note, p. 327. The Cullinan Diamond. Since the paragraph relating to this gem was written, the " Star of Africa " and its lesser mate have been introduced into the sceptre and crown of England.

CHAPTER XXVIII

"VALE, IMPERATOR!"

"THE King has no politics!"

Such was the answer returned, by command of Edward VII, to an inquirer. Such was the truth, a principle from which King Edward never swerved.

Predecessors had fallen in with one side or the other. Queen Victoria, ardent as she was for duty, had, especially in the days of her youth, felt and expressed strong bias.

Edward VII stood clear of the swing of the pendulum—

> "Holding no form of creed,
> But contemplating all."

We too, here, have no claim to deal with political questions.

The reign of Edward VII saw that split of parties, the most rending which had occurred since the Home Rule issue, upon the Free Trade and Tariff Reform contentions.

It was a contention apposite to the genius of our commercial being. Free Trade had been tried and had, said some, Mr. Joseph Chamberlain being a leader, been found wanting.

Political Economy establishes Free Trade as an unshakeable, an axiomatic verity, says one side.

Political Economy, being an applied science, must swing with the movements of social economics, replies the other. About these there is no rigidity.

In the days, three and a half centuries ago, of Edward VI there had been a leaning towards the idea of a free market :—

"It was agreed that it was most necessary to have a mart in England for the enriching of the same, to make it the more famouse, and to be lesse in other men's daunger, and to make all things better cheap and more plentiful.

"The time was thought good to have it now because of the warre between the French King and th'Emperour. The places were thought metest, Hull for th'East partes, Southampton for the South partes of Englaunde, as appereth by tow bils in my study. London also was thought non ill place ; but it was appointed to begime with the other tow."

In the bills, to which the King alludes, are given several reasons for establishing the mart in England, among them being that—

"Southampton is a better port than Antwerp.

"The Flemings have allured men to make a mart there with their privileges, having but little commodities ; much easlier shal we do it having clothe, tinne, seacole, lead, belmetal and such other commodities, as few realmes christian have the like nor they when they began had no soche opportunite."

England has been doing lately a good deal of thinking over her "free markets."

The Parliament of 1906 contained for the first time a substantial proportion of "Labour" members.

"Labour" has talked itself hoarse in capital letters, almost to the detriment of honest English toil sometimes, it may be feared.

Labour howls at Capital and Capital occasionally retorts with a "lock-out," and what is one to the other? Only—as ever—in the inevitable interdependence of limbs and organs which was told in fable more than two thousand years ago in the days of Roman kings.

> "'Tis the Leviathan Labour watching there in the darkness,
> Watching and waiting the hour to spring with a roar from his
> dockyards."
>
> RICHARD LE GALLIENNE: *The Thames.*

Except the dockyards were there—and Capital was there first to install them—where were Labour? The two are like dogs in leash, and we know that these must pull together.

And then in the last year came the Veto question and the threat to draw the Crown into the fray.

This would have been the vision which would have rendered the first Edward breathless.

If vituperation could hoist its storm-cone with even the same reliability as the Meteorological Office, strawberry leaves should tremble—dukes, that "poor but honest class" (Lord Rosebery has said it—*finita causa*), will doubtless survive, as Apsley House survived a little stone-throwing some eighty years ago.

It was sad to all of us that the last days of a great reign should have been filled with such interior discord.

"Nothing," said Lord Curzon on the day before the end of the reign, "has so shocked the country as the way in which the Crown has been brought into the present political controversy. . . . The sovereign of this country may be trusted to exercise his prerogative with due regard to constitutional precedent and with that perfect sense of propriety which has always distinguished his Majesty's conduct."

And while cheers were greeting this utterance, the King, although we knew it not, lay dying.

One had sometimes questioned how long a sovereign advancing to ripe age could maintain the unremitting and strenuous activities which our King brought to all his undertakings. Sometimes, too, a wave of ill rumour would pass and would subside. But there was at no time a thought of such a sudden ending of the reign.

The King was ill; on that May morning we knew that much, and were aware that bronchial affections were serious at the extremes of life.

But the King was sitting up; he had received in fare-well audience one leaving to take up the government of an over-seas Dominion (that peer has a great reminis-cence); the country caught at comforting reflection.

Then came that last short rush of so few hours when England hardly knew of her great visitation; the cautious bulletin, shorn by the King's own hand; the gathering fear; the check to life which the overworked nerves gave from the switch-board of the brain; the stagnation of the congested pulmonary vessels; the restricted possibilities of stimulation involved by limits of arterial resistance.

The final regal acts, accomplished with eyes open to the ultimate inertia, while the blue, fateful haze crept upwards—the Queen, the wife, racing Death in the storm

—the oath made nine years earlier "to work while there is breath in my body," kept with an exactitude so tragically faithful until the last few hours of coma. And then the end. It came not in the heat of battle, as it might have come to earlier Edwards, but it came no less gloriously in the ardent toil of sovereign endeavour. And it was "dying game."

If one was grieved at having understood so little of the serious nature of the King's illness, it must yet be remembered that consideration for the convenience of his subjects was always a ruling idea of our late King's. The markets of the world may sustain depreciation from the rumour of a royal illness : "The papers, which don't know what to invent to lower the Funds, said that you had been unwell on the 10th," wrote Leopold I to Queen Victoria (*Letters*, i. 288), and, with modifications, this depression occurs to-day. Edward VII would struggle on, in suffering, to avert inconvenience from his subjects. It was not till he lay helpless in 1902 that we learned that on his entry into London the King had felt so ill that he could scarcely lift his hat to his people.

He worked up to the end, as many young and vigorous men do not—and would not—work ; though his stamina had been impaired by the shock of operation and by mechanical disabilities which were unguessed. He steered our ship with an unflinching watchfulness, for, without belittling, for one moment, the labours of the staff, which must be arduous, the thousand personal touches of the King were the *vis viva* of the imperial manœuvres. They were the indispensable. And at our pleasures, too, he sat among us, often in those hot and crowded scenes which were so undesirable for a catarrhal subject. With the zest of the good workman, too, must have mingled often the sense of immensity rising ever up ahead.

Then he lay still, this seventh Edward who had gathered up the threads of a long line and made of them fair weaving.

There, where are scenes from the Wars of the Roses which embroiled his ancestors, those of his household bade their last farewell. There, in the Palace of Westminster where six earlier Edwards kept their court, he lay coffined in oak from Windsor Forest, whence of old were beams and shingles furnished for the building of royal dwellings. Under that pall which had, some years earlier, veiled his mother's coffin, and in which the ladies of a school, founded under his sister's patronage, had set stitches, copied from the ancient broidery of England, he lay in state while England paid her homage.

Thence, with mourning and affection, they bore him to royal Windsor, where other Edwards sleep ; the first Edward to travel to the grave upon the iron way.

With magnificent solemnity going before and after, the dead King passed along, and in his funeral train nine sovereigns.

It was a Pageant of the Powers.

Yet such was their mourning that this splendour fell but as a second thought upon the crowd beside the way. Even the glow of the spring-day, said one, seemed a wrong thing.

There passed along the potentates who represent to-day the Powers who were contemporaries of earlier Edwards.

The King of Georgia, the ruler of the Persians, the sovereign of the Tartars, live again in modern developments, *mutatis mutandis.*

A Hapsburg comes to represent the venerable sovereign who is no longer Emperor of Almain. Haakon is there, though of another dynasty to that of him who was contemporary with Edward I, and from whose land the Maid of Norway came.

A king comes from the country of the Flemings, ruled by Charles le Téméraire when our fourth Edward reigned.

France has no king to send, yet sends us friends, and a prince has journeyed from the East to be the representative of all the Russias and their autocrat.

Sovereigns and princes from the Vikings' lands and from the new régime of Greece are there.

It is a King of Italy and not a Pope of Rome who sends his envoy for to-day's sad pomp. And young Braganza and young Bourbon mourn in one a kinsman and a king.

And one there is of whom the other Edwards have not known, a Hohenzollern with the wingèd helm, a German Emperor. Twice has he been with us in our national woe, and the workman in the street, with "Thank you, Kaiser!" has voiced our gratitude, and on such a day as this we turn away from every other aspect of our relativity.

Has not indeed a hopeful flower of fellowship sprung from King Edward's coffin![1]

The King passes, and it is no looking on at the grief of strangers that stirs the crowds who line the way.

With them, the widowed Queen, her children and her kinsmen, we are, in this, as one.

For it is as one great family that the children of the Empire mourn their chief to-day.

[1] The Anglo-German memorial of Sir Ernest Cassel.

And so in the Chapel of Our Lady, St. George, and St. Edward, which his Plantagenet ancestors founded and in which his christening, his marriage, and his burial took place, he rests at last among his forefathers.

There, where, among his styles, is cried by King-at-Arms that he was Sovereign of the Garter—now in the sixth century of its existence—Edward VII rests and his works do follow him.

" We may still hope," said the Duke of Cornwall (H.M. George V) to some of the far-distant tribes who mourned the loss of the great Queen, on his Empire tour of 1901.

So may we also hope. For in those who, by their loss and ours, have come into their sovereignty, there may be strong the call of blue water and of the country-side.

Yet is their call to Duty even stronger.

" God of Hys mercy sende hym goode locke and longe lyffe, with prosperite !"

Such loyal cry out of old Tudor time may be our own.

INDEX

NOTE.—Sovereigns and principal royal persons are, in general, indexed under their Christian names.

Prelates are indexed under their respective Sees.

The sub-headings under the Seven Edwards are arranged in logical, and not alphabetical, order.

Under the heading "Royal" is indexed a large amount of miscellaneous matter.

351